Seventh Edition

Keys to Effective Learning

Habits for College and Career Success

Carol Carter

Sarah Lyman Kravits

Boston   Columbus   Indianapolis   New York   San Francisco   Hoboken
Amsterdam   Cape Town   Dubai   London   Madrid   Milan   Munich   Paris   Montreal   Toronto
Delhi   Mexico City   Sao Paulo   Sydney   Hong Kong   Seoul   Singapore   Taipei   Tokyo

Editor-in-Chief: Jodi McPherson
Acquisitions Editor: Paul Smith
Editorial Assistant: Kathryn Hueber
Development Editor: Claire Hunter
Executive Marketing Manager:
    Amy Judd
Vice President, Marketing, Workforce Readiness
    Learning Services: Margaret Waples
Director of Field Marketing, Professional &
    Career: Leigh Ann Schmitz

Marketing Assistant: Kelli Fisher
Director of Strategic Marketing, Workforce
Readiness: Derril Trakalo
Program Manager: Joe Sweeney
Project Manager: Janet Domingo
Art Director: Diane Lorenzo
Senior Procurement Specialist: Roy Pickering
Text Design: Cenveo® Publisher Services
Publishing Services and Composition:
    Cenveo® Publisher Services

Credits and acknowledgments for material borrowed from other sources and reproduced, with permission, in this textbook appear on the appropriate page within text or on p. 329, which constitutes an extension of the copyright page.

Many of the designations by manufacturers and sellers to distinguish their products are claimed as trademarks. Where those designations appear in this book, and the publisher was aware of a trademark claim, the designations have been printed in initial caps or all caps.

Copyright © 2017, 2011 by Pearson Education, Inc.

All rights reserved. No part of this publication may be reproduced, stored in a retrieval system, or transmitted, in any form or by any means, electronic, mechanical, photocopying, recording, or otherwise, without the prior written permission of the publisher. Printed in the United States of America. For information on obtaining permission for use of material in this work, please submit a written request to Pearson Education, Inc., Rights and Contracts Department, 501 Boylston Street, Suite 900, Boston, MA 02116, fax your request to 617-671-3447, or e-mail at http://www.pearsoned.com/legal/permissions.htm.

Library of Congress Cataloging-in-Publication Data is on file at the Library of Congress.

1 2 3 4 5 6 7 8 9 10

Bound Book
ISBN 10: 0-13-440551-X
ISBN 13: 978-0-13-440551-3
Student Value Edition
ISBN 10: 0-13-447311-6
ISBN 13: 978-0-13-447311-6

AUSTIN COMMUNITY COLLEGE
LIBRARY SERVICES

This edition is dedicated to today's courageous students as they navigate a world of rapid technological change, high costs in education, and workplace instability.

Students everywhere: You have the heart and the potential to persist and to make the world a better place in ways that are significant no matter their scope. Our mission is to help you build habits that give you the ability and drive to take action. The world needs your talents, and we all eagerly anticipate the time when we will benefit from what you have to offer.

About the Authors

Carol Carter has spent her entire career in the business world, where she has a track record of success in corporate America, entrepreneurship, and nonprofits. Her student success work is driven by firsthand knowledge of what employers expect and demand from today's graduates. As president of LifeBound (www.lifebound.com), an academic and career coaching company, she drives the company's goal to help middle school and high school students become competitive in today's world, and she teaches study, interpersonal, and career skills to students as well as training and certifying adults in academic coaching skills. As cofounder of GlobalMindED (www.globalminded.org), the standard-setting conference of leaders committed to Access, Equity, and Opportunity in education, she brings education, business, and policy leaders together to improve outcomes for students, especially those who are first generation to college.

Carol speaks on educational topics nationally and internationally and is an expert blogger for the *Huffington Post* under "Impact," "College," and "Business." Carol is a co-author of many books for Pearson, including the *Keys to Success* series as well as *Keys to Business Communication* and the *Career Tool Kit*. She has also published a series of books for K–12 students through LifeBound, including *Dollars and Sense: How To Be Smart about Money* and *Majoring in the Rest of Your Life: Career Secrets for College Students.*

Sarah Kravits teaches student success at Montclair State University and has been researching and writing about student success for 20 years. As a parent of three children (ages 16, 14, and 10), a collaborator, a co-author, and an instructor, she lives the strategies for success she writes about, striving daily for goal achievement, productive teamwork, and integrity. Sarah is a co-author of the *Keys to Success* series, including *Keys to College Success*, *Keys to Community College Success*, *Keys to College Success Compact*, *Keys to Effective Learning*, *Keys to Online Learning*, and *Keys to Success Quick*.

Sarah presents workshops and training on student success topics such as critical thinking, risk and reward, and time management at schools all over the country, including an annual success workshop for the entering class of Jefferson Scholars at the University of Virginia. Having attended UVA as a Jefferson Scholar herself, she continues to manifest the Jefferson Scholars Program goals of leadership, scholarship, and citizenship with her efforts to empower college students to succeed in school and in all aspects of their lives.

brief contents

Contents

Chapter 3

Time and Money: Managing Important Resources   52

Contents

Chapter 6

Chapter 7

Reading and Information Literacy: Targeted and Critical Strategies 168

Chapter 8

Listening and Note Taking: Taking in and Recording Information 194

Contents

Chapter **9**

Memory and Studying: Retaining What You Learn 220

Contents

Chapter 12

In this road-tested student favorite text, the **Habits for Success** framework helps students develop persistence, planning, questioning, connecting, coaching skills, and more. These self-directed learning skills give readers tools to build a bright future personally and professionally, and are exceptionally helpful to underprepared students. This seventh edition features strong study skills coverage, accessibility for a wide range of students, and diverse role models who inspire students of all ages, stages, ethnicities, and life circumstances.

What's New, What's Better

Personalized Learning with MyStudentSuccessLab™

MyStudentSuccessLab is an online homework, tutorial, and assessment program designed to engage students and improve results. Within its structured environment, students practice what they learn, test their understanding, and pursue a plan that helps them better absorb course material and understand difficult concepts. It fosters the skills students need to succeed for *ongoing personal and professional development*. Whether face to face or online, MyStudentSuccessLab personalizes learning to help students build the skills they need through peer-led video interviews, interactive practice exercises, and activities that provide academic, life, and professionalism skills.

This learning outcomes-based technology promotes student engagement through:

- **The Conley Readiness Index (CRI)**—a research-based behavioral diagnostic, developed by Dr. David T. Conley, that measures readiness around a skill set and builds ownership of learning.

- **A Full Course Pre- and Post-Diagnostic** test, based on Bloom's Taxonomy and linked to key learning objectives in each topic.

- **A Pre- and Post-Test** for each individual topic in the Learning Path; an **Overview** of objectives to build vocabulary and repetition; access to **Video interviews** to learn about key issues "by students, for students"; **Practice** exercises to improve class prep and learning; and **Graded Activities** to build critical thinking skills and develop problem-solving abilities.

- **Student resources**, including Finish Strong 24/7 YouTube videos, Calculators, and Professionalism/Research & Writing/Student Success tools.

- **A title-specific version available** as an option for those who teach closely to their text. This course would include the national eText, chapter-specific quizzing, an extended Feature set, and Learning Path modules that align with the chapter-naming conventions of the book.

Increased Focus on How College Efforts Promote Career and Life Success

Revised! **In-chapter coaching strategies.** Research shows that students who have been coached or have a coaching framework do better in college and career, experience less stress, and make more effective choices than those who do not. Coaching within each chapter promotes self-directed learning, love of challenge, absolute accountability, and the capacity to achieve goals and outcomes both in class and out.

- **Inside Tips** provide advice from one of the two co-authors. Carol gives **career-focused** advice, and Sarah provides **academic advice.** Each author's questions promote increased self-knowledge, agency, and accountability.
- Powerful Questions ask students chapter-specific coaching questions, with the element of **peer coaching**, asking pairs of students to work together. Students build self-efficacy and develop coaching skills, learning how to be both **mentor** and **mentee.**

Revised! **Habits for success theme.** The Habits listed below are the foundations of academic, professional, and life success. The coaching framework builds the accountability, teamwork skills, and problem solving that modern employers expect and require.

Persist ⟶ Finish strong

Learn ⟶ Self-direct

Anticipate ⟶ Plan

Communicate ⟶ Connect with purpose

Imagine ⟶ Expand

Perceive ⟶ Build awareness

Inquire ⟶ Excavate

Contribute ⟶ Add value

Listen ⟶ Understand

Risk ⟶ Extend

Adjust ⟶ Optimize

New! **Engaging, motivating role models.** Readers will be inspired by chapter-opening case studies featuring the personal stories of students and graduates who have worked for cutting-edge companies (Google, GlobalMindED), started their own successful ventures (MindFULL Learning Institute, Roots Java Coffee, Sunesis Nexus), and created organizations that bring transformative change to their colleges and communities. Each story demonstrates the role of that chapter's Habit in facing a challenge and making a difference, so that students can see how it's done.

New! **Habit in Action wrap-ups,** new to this edition, precede the end-of-chapter exercises. Each wrap-up continues the chapter-opener case story, describing how the person met a challenge and continues to make a difference, and gives readers an opportunity to connect the story to their own lives.

Improved Thinking and Study Skills Coverage

Revised! **Updated study skills material textwide.** Study skills materials feature strategies that reflect the wide range in how students learn today (in person, online, using technological tools, in teams, etc.). Coverage of study skills remains extensive, with two chapters on reading and two chapters on test taking as in the 6th edition. Specific updates include the following:

- Memory and studying coverage are paired in Chapter 9, with the comprehensive "journalists' questions" structure of study strategies (When to study, Where to study, Who to study with, What to study, Why to study, How to study). This chapter is moved from its previous location to a more logical spot following the chapter on listening and note taking.
- The second reading chapter (Chapter 7), which still contains material on reading different subjects, now focuses more extensively on Critical Reading and Information Literacy, incorporating the information on literacy material previously found in an appendix.
- Chapter 8 presents strategies for electronic note taking.
- Chapter 9 provides expanded material on test anxiety.

Revised! **Updated life skills material textwide.** Life skills strategies honor the modern student and reflect the latest science and trends. Specific updates include:

- Increased focus on coaching strategies and powerful questions in Chapter 1 and throughout.
- Revised material on time management, with details about the myth of multitasking and expanded material on procrastination.
- Updated money management and financial aid material in Chapter 3.
- Physical and mental wellness material in Chapter 4 that reflects the most current statistics and science.

- Multiple intelligence grids, which have been retained in Chapters 3 through 11. Each grid presents learning preferences strategies linked to a chapter topic, poses a related problem, and asks students to generate MI-based strategies that will work best for them.
- Early learning preferences coverage with integrated applications. An early chapter remains on learning how we learn and showcases several learning styles/preferences and personality inventories.

New! **Brain-based learning and metacognition.** Thinking materials are updated with the latest in brain science—building intelligence, how memory works, the cost of switch-tasking, and more. This information builds student metacognition in an approachable and interesting way. Examples can be found in Chapter 1 (introduction), Chapter 5 (thinking), and Chapter 9 (memory).

Revised Exercises Increase Relevancy and Application

Revised! **In-chapter self-assessments.** Newly titled "All About You," the in-text self-assessments (which appear at least once per chapter) provide readers with the opportunity to reflect on chapter material in the context of their own lives.

Revised! **Take Action in-chapter exercises.** These exercises, in many cases updated and streamlined, provide a midchapter chance to apply chapter material to personal situations and needs.

Revised! **Note the Important Points.** Previously, a mix of subjective and objective questions, the end-of-chapter summary exercise has been revised to feature exclusively objective questions for a more straightforward look at retention of chapter material.

Revised! **End-of-chapter (EOC) exercises.** The tried-and-true set of exercises has been retained and revised. Each chapter's EOC set builds essential skills for college and life:

- Critical thinking (Critical Thinking: Applying Learning to Life)
- Teamwork and interpersonal skills (Team Building: Collaborative Solutions)
- Test preparation and test-taking skills (Test Prep: Start It Now)

One last note: Many of our best suggestions come from you. Instructors and students, please send your questions, comments, and ideas about *Keys to Effective Learning* to Carol Carter at caroljcarter@lifebound.com or Sarah Kravits at kravitss@mail.montclair.edu. We look forward to hearing from you, and we are grateful for the opportunity to work with you.

Instructor Resources

Online Instructor's Manual (www.pearsonhighered.com/irc)

This online manual provides a framework of ideas and suggestions for activities, journal writing, thought-provoking situations, and online implementation, including MyStudentSuccessLab recommendations.

Online PowerPoint Presentation (www.pearsonhighered.com/irc)

This comprehensive set of online PowerPoint slides can be used by instructors for class presentations and also by students for lecture preview or review. The PowerPoint presentation includes summary slides with overview information for each chapter to help students understand and review concepts within each chapter. These downloadable sets of slides are fully customizable by individual instructors.

MyStudentSuccessLab (www.mystudentsuccesslab.com)

This title is also available with MyStudentSuccessLab—an online homework, tutorial, and assessment program designed to engage students and improve results. It includes the Conley Readiness Index (CRI). Within its structured environment, students practice what they learn, test their understanding, and pursue a plan that helps them better absorb course material and understand difficult concepts. It fosters the skills students need to succeed for *ongoing personal and professional development*. Whether face to face or online, MyStudentSuccessLab personalizes learning to help students build the skills they need through peer-led video interviews, interactive practice exercises, and activities that provide academic, life, and professionalism skills. Beyond the Full Course Pre- and Post-Diagnostic assessments, and the Pre- and Post-tests within each module, additional learning outcomes-based tests can be created/selected using a secure testing engine and may be printed or delivered online. If you are interested in adopting this title with MyStudentSuccessLab, ask your Pearson representative for the correct package ISBN and course to download.

Course Redesign (www.pearsoncourseredesign.com)

Collect, measure, and interpret data to support efficacy. Our resources can help you rethink how you deliver instruction, measure the results of your course redesign, and get support for data collection and interpretation.

Implementation and Training

(http://www.pearsonmylabandmastering.com/northamerica
/mystudentsuccesslab/educators/support/training-options/index.html)

Access MyStudentSuccessLab training resources such as the Planning Tool Kit, Implementation guide, How Do I videos, Self-paced training modules, and Live Online Training sessions with a Faculty Advisor.

CourseConnect (www.pearsonlearningsolutions.com/courseconnect)

This title is also available with CourseConnect-designed by subject matter experts and credentialed instructional designers; it offers customizable online courses with a consistent learning path, available in a variety of learning management systems as self-paced study.

eTextbooks Online (such as www.vitalsource.com)

As an alternative to purchasing the print textbook, students can *subscribe* to the same content online and save up to 50% off the suggested list price of the print text. With an e-textbook, students can search the text, make notes online, print out reading assignments that incorporate lecture notes, and bookmark important passages for review.

Custom Services (www.pearsonlearningsolutions.com)

With this title, we offer flexible and creative choices for course materials that will maximize learning and student engagement. Options include custom library, publications, technology solutions, and online education.

Professional Development for Instructors
(www.pearsonhighered.com/studentsuccess)

Augment your teaching with engaging resources. Visit our online catalog for our Ownership series, Engaging Activities series, and Audience booklets.

Resources for Your Students (www.pearsonhighered.com /studentsuccess)

Help students save and succeed throughout their college experience. Visit our online catalog for options such as loose leaf editions, eTextbooks, Pearson Students program, IDentity Series, Success Tips, and more.

A terrific team has made this revision happen through persistence, dedication, and many months of hard work. Many thanks to:

- Our reviewers who helped us improve both this new edition and the accompanying MyStudentSuccessLab:

Germaine Albuquerque, Essex County College

Crystal Allen, Lone Star College System

Harriett Allison, University of North Georgia, Dahlonega

Oluwunmi Ariyo, Vance–Granville Community College

Kristi Barker, South Plains College

Marie Basche, Capital Community College

Darin Baskin, Houston Community College

Jon Beard, Midlands Technical College

Mary Bendickson, Hillsborough Community College, Dale Mabry Campus

Deborah Blanchard, Montana State University

Kay Bone, Kirkwood Community College

Lawrence Brown, Florida Agricultural and Mechanical University

Merissa Brown, University of Hawaii

Brett Bruner, Fort Hayes State University

Deborah Burris, Pfeiffer University

Elaine Bush, Darton College

Todd Campbell, University of North Georgia, Dahlonega

Matthew Carlson, Minnesota State University, Mankato

Diane Cimorelli, SUNY Ulster

Kathy Clark, Florida SouthWestern State College, Lee Campus

Jody Conway, University of South Florida

Sylvia Cox, Southeastern Community College

Kimberly Crockett, West Georgia Technical College

Christine Damrose-Mahlmann, Tidewater Community College

Chip Dennis, Pfeiffer University

April Dill, Western Oklahoma State College

Trakenya Dobbins, University of Arkansas, Little Rock

Briland Driver, Texas Tech University

Maryann Errico, Georgia Perimeter College

Ann Fellinger, Pulaski Technical College

Italia Folleco, Broward College, South Campus

Dwight Fontenot, University of Michigan

Dava Foster, Troy University

Wanda Fulbright Dennis, Mt. San Antonio College

Maria Galyon, Jefferson Community and Technical College, Downtown

Karen George, Ashland Community & Technical College

Megan Glenn, Florida State College at Jacksonville, Deerwood Center

Tonya Greene, Wake Technical Community College

Laurie Grimes, Somerset Community College

Kerry Hammock, Brigham Young University

Jeff Hardesty, Owens Community College

Amy Hathcock, University of North Carolina, Wilmington

Derrick Haynes, Community College of Aurora

Ericka Haynes, University of Louisiana, Lafayette

Bryan Herek, Chowan University

Paul Hibbitts, Central Georgia Technical College

Sarah Howard, Ohio State University, Newark

Sarah Hughes, Ohio State University, Newark

Liese Hull, University of Michigan

Ramona Hurston, Auburn University at Montgomery

Amy Ingram, Auburn University at Montgomery

Courtney Jauregui, Collin College

Terri Jedlicka, Kirkwood Community College

Jamil Johnson, University of Central Florida

Ray Keith, Community College of Aurora

Wendy Kennedy, Darton College

Sheree King, Oral Roberts University

Chris Knierim, College of Central Florida

Dana Kuehn, Florida State College at Jacksonville, Downtown

Deonne Kunkel, Chabot College

Mark Kwoka, Sierra College

Jim Lanfrey, Blinn College, Bryan

Judith Lanfrey, Blinn College, Bryan

Dawn Lee, Charleston Southern University

Gail Malone, South Plains College

Heidi Marshall, Florida State College at Jacksonville, South

Louise Mathews, Technical College of the Lowcountry

Sam Mayhew, Bainbridge State College

Judy McCray, Florida State College at Jacksonville, South

Rita McReynolds, Mississippi State University

Bobbi Miller, Kirkwood Community College

Carey Miller, University of Baltimore

Al Mitchell, Meridian Community College

Laura Mullins, University of North Georgia, Dahlonega

Darryl Myles, Hillsborough Community College, Dale Mabry

Kris Nerem-Lowery, Iowa Central Community College

Mary Newburn, University of Georgia, Dahlonega

Kathryn Overstreet, Kaskaskia College

Latonya Parker, Moreno Valley College

Laura Pate, Mississippi State University

Medea Rambish, Waubonsee Community College

Mark Rembacz, Western Wyoming Community College

Jacqueline Robinson, Milwaukee Area Technical College

Vlad Sabou, North Greenville University

Becky Samberg, Housatonic Community College

Maggie Seymour, South Plains College

Karen Smith, East Carolina University

Cheryl Spector, California State University, Northridge

Katelin St. Clair, Texas Tech University

Jaqueline Starren, Valencia College

Ayanna Stevens, Virginia College, Jacksonville

Nicole Stock, Minnesota State University, Mankato

Rebecca Stultz, University of North Carolina, Wilmington

Suzanne Tapp, Texas Tech University

Jennifer Taylor, Francis Marion University

Kim Tran, University of Arkansas, Little Rock

Chip Turner, Valencia College

Rich Underwood, Kirkwood Community College

Chelsey Vincent, Mississippi State University

Andy Wallace, Angelo State University

Kristina Walters, University of Louisiana, Lafayette

Summer Washington, West Georgia Technical College

Harold Waters, University of Michigan

Margit Watts, University of Hawaii

Chad Wiginton, Western Oklahoma State College

Vicki Williams, Georgia Perimeter College

Ginger Young, Freed-Hardeman University

- **Previous edition reviewers:**

Andrew T. Alexson, Tennessee Temple University

Arne J. Anderson, College of DuPage

Erskine P. Ausbrooks III, Dyersburg State Community College

Glenda Belote, Florida International University

John Bennett, Jr., University of Connecticut

Ann Bingham-Newman, California State University–LA

Mary Bixby, University of Missouri–Columbia

Linda Blair, Pellissippi State Technical Community College

Barbara Blandford, Education Enhancement Center at Lawrenceville, NJ

Jerry Bouchie, St. Cloud State University

Tracy Cantelmo, Youngstown State University

Rhonda Carroll, Pulaski Technical College

Mona Casady, SW Missouri State University

Janet Cutshall, Sussex County Community College

Marie Davis-Heim, Mississippi Gulf Coast Community College

Valerie DeAngelis, Miami-Dade Community College

Dede deLaughter, Gainsville State College

Rita Delude, NH Community Technical College

Judy Elsley, Weber State University in Utah

Katherine Erdman, South Dakota State University

Jo Ella Fields, Oklahoma State University, Oklahoma City

Carlesa Ramere Finney, Anne Arundel Community College

Shirley Flor, San Diego Mesa College

Pat Grissom, San Juacinto College South

Sue Halter, Delgado Community College in Louisiana

Vesna Hampel, University of Minnesota, Twin Cities

Suzy Hampton, University of Montana

Dr. Jennifer Hodges, University of Akron

Maureen Hurley, University of Missouri–Kansas City

Karen Iversen, Heald Colleges

Gary G. John, Richland College

Jeremy Jones, Lee College

Ken Jones, Metro Community College, Omaha

Kathryn K. Kelly, St. Cloud State University

Deborah Kimbrough-Lowe, Nassau Community College

Heidi Koring, Lynchburg College

Nancy Kosmicke, Mesa State College in Colorado

Christine Laursen, Westwood College

Polly Livingston, Portland State University

Jeanine Long, Southwest Georgia Tech

Frank T. Lyman, Jr., University of Maryland

Deborah Maness, Wake Tech

Jo McEwan, Fayetteville Technical Community College

Barnette Miller Moore, Indian River Community College in Florida

Kathie Morris, Edison Community College

Rebecca Munro, Gonzaga University in Washington

Melissa O'Connor, Minneapolis Com & Tech College

Dr. Rhonella Owens, City College of San Francisco

Maria Parnell, Brevard County Community College

Virginia Phares, DeVry of Atlanta

Robert Pontious, Brunswick Community College

Brenda Prinzavalli, Beloit College in Wisconsin

Dr. Terri Provost, Utica College

Linda Qualia, Colin County Community College

Laura Reynolds, Fayetteville Technical Community College

Mary Rider, Grossmont College

Tina Royal, Fayetteville Technical Community College

Maria D. Salinas, Del Mar College

Jacqueline Simon, Education Enhancement Center at Lawrenceville, NJ

Dr. Paige Sindt, Arizona State University

Carolyn Smith, University of Southern Indiana

Leigh Smith, Lamar Institute of Technology

Joan Stottlemyer, Carroll College in Montana

Fatina Taylor, Prince George's Community College

Karla Thompson, New Mexico State University, Carlsbad

Thomas Tyson, SUNY Stony Brook

Lisa Taylor-Galizia, Carteret Community College

Karen N. Valencia, South Texas Community College

Mary Walkz-Chojnacki, University of Wisconsin at Milwaukee

Peggy Walton, Howard Community College

Mary Walz-Chojnacki, University of Wisconsin-Milwaukee

Rose Wassman, DeAnza College in California

Michelle G. Wolf, Florida Southern College

Helen Woodman, Ferris State University in Michigan

Patricia Wright, Lenoir Community College

Leesa Young, Asheville Buncombe Technical Community College

Michael Young, Valdosta Tech College.

- The extraordinary people who volunteered their case studies in an effort to inspire and motivate students: Jairo Alcantara, Albert Gonzales, Misa Gonzales, Chanda Hinton, Garrett Mintz, Michele Weslander Quaid, Clifton Taulbert, Elise Tran, Johancharles Van Boers, Donique Wray, and Austin Yellen.

- Art Costa and Bena Kallick, for their work that led to the development of the Habits of Mind, their generosity in permitting us to use the Habits as a framework for this text, and their valuable insights about our evolving approach to the Habits.

- Our editor Paul Smith, developmental editor Claire Hunter, and editorial assistant Kathryn Hueber for their insight, hard work, and dedication.

- Our production team for their patience, flexibility, and attention to detail, especially Susan McNally and the staff at Cenveo; Diane Lorenzo, Cover Director; Joe Sweeney, Program Manager; and Janet Domingo, Project Manager.

- Our marketing gurus, especially Amy Judd, Executive Marketing Manager; Margaret Waples, Vice President, Marketing, Workforce Readiness Learning Services; Leigh Ann Schmitz, Director of Field Marketing, Professional & Career; Kelli Fisher, Marketing Assistant; and Derril Trakalo, Director of Strategic Marketing, Workforce Readiness.

- Vice President for Student Success and Career Development Jodi McPherson and Senior Development Editor Charlotte Morrissey for their vision, effort, and continued commitment to the *Keys* series.

- The Pearson representatives and the management team led by Eric Severson, Executive Vice President, Higher Education Sales.

- The staff at LifeBound for their support, especially Maureen Breeze, Mary Haynes, Suzanne Stromberg, Angelica Jestrovich, Valerie Menard, Saule Aliyeva, Ryan Shanahan, Anu Reddy, and Robbie Fikes who manages the website at www.keystosuccessu.com.

- Garth Kravits and Cut and Dry Films for developing creative new companion videos that bring humor to some of the text's most important topics.

- Our families and friends, who have encouraged us and put up with our commitments.

- Judy Block, whose research, writing, and editing work was invaluable, and who supports us and our goals to help students in myriad ways.
- Joyce Bishop, who created the learning preference assessments, contributed to the success of this book over the past fifteen years, and continues to support college students with her wisdom and insights.

Finally, for their ideas, opinions, and stories, we would like to thank all of the students and instructors with whom we work. Sarah would like to thank her students at Montclair State University who have granted her the privilege of sharing part of their journey through college, as well as the insightful instructors and advisors affiliated with the Center for Advising and Student Transitions at MSU. Carol would like to thank the team at GlobalMindED, as well as the people who have gone through her coaching training and who continue to strive to improve students' ability to succeed, including Donna Bontatibus, Barbara Gadis, Dana Calland, Jennifer Gomez-Mejia, Vanessa Harris, Deb Holst, Nancy Hunter, Lynn Troyka, Melissa Vito, Kathy York, and Katrina Rogers.

Students and instructors, through this book you give us the opportunity to learn and discover with you—in your classroom, at home, on a bus or train, and wherever else learning takes place. More than ever, we are committed to bringing together the various gifts, talents, and abilities of people from every background, especially first generation to college student leaders. We believe that education has the power to alleviate the discord and bridge the divides among diverse populations, through collaborative endeavors and meaningful work that can both power our economic future and heal the world.

Pearson Course Redesign

Collect, measure, and interpret data to support efficacy.

Rethink the way you deliver instruction.

Pearson has successfully partnered with colleges and universities engaged in course redesign for over 10 years through workshops, Faculty Advisor programs, and online conferences. Here's how to get started!

- Visit our course redesign site at www.pearsoncourseredesign.com for information on getting started, a list of Pearson-sponsored course redesign events, and recordings of past course redesign events.

- Request to connect with a Faculty Advisor, a fellow instructor who is an expert in course redesign, by visiting www.mystudentsuccesslab.com/community.

- Join our Course Redesign Community at www.community.pearson.com/courseredesign and connect with colleagues around the country who are participating in course redesign projects.

Don't forget to measure the results of your course redesign!

Examples of data you may want to collect include:

- Improvement of homework grades, test averages, and pass rates over past semesters

- Correlation between time spent in an online product and final average in the course

- Success rate in the next level of the course

- Retention rate (i.e., percentage of students who drop, fail, or withdraw)

Need support for data collection and interpretation?

Ask your local Pearson representative how to connect with a member of Pearson's Efficacy Team.

MyStudentSuccessLab

Help students start strong and finish stronger.

MyStudentSuccessLab™

MyLab from Pearson has been designed and refined with a single purpose in mind—to help educators break through to improving results for their students.

MyStudentSuccessLab™ (MSSL) is a learning outcomes-based technology that advances students' knowledge and builds critical skills, offering ongoing personal and professional development through peer-led video interviews, interactive practice exercises, and activities that focus on academic, life, and professional preparation.

The **Conley Readiness Index (CRI), developed by Dr. David Conley, is now embedded in MyStudentSuccessLab.** This research-based, self-diagnostic online tool measures college and career readiness; it is personalized, research-based, and provides actionable data. Dr. David Conley is a nationally recognized leader in research, policy, and solution development with a sincere passion for improving college and career readiness.

Developed exclusively for Pearson by Dr. Conley, the Conley Readiness Index assesses mastery in each of the "Four Keys" that are critical to college and career readiness:

Topics include:

Student Success Learning Path

- Conley Readiness Index
- College Transition
- Communication
- Creating an Academic Plan
- Critical Thinking
- Financial Literacy
- Goal Setting
- Information Literacy
- Learning Preferences
- Listening and Note Taking
- Majors and Careers Exploration
- Memory and Studying
- Online Learning
- Problem Solving
- Reading and Annotating
- Stress Management
- Test Taking
- Time Management
- Wellness

Career Success Learning Path

- Career Exploration: Know Yourself
- Career Portfolio
- Customer Service
- Interviewing
- Networking/Job Search Strategies
- Personal Brand
- Self-Management Skills at Work
- Teamwork
- Workplace Communication
- Workplace Etiquette

Assessment

Beyond the Pre- and Post-Full Course Diagnostic Assessments and Pre- and Post-Tests within each module, additional learning-outcome-based tests can be created using a secure testing engine, and may be printed or delivered online. These tests can be customized by editing individual questions or entire tests.

Reporting

Measurement matters—and is ongoing in nature. MyStudentSuccessLab lets you determine what data you need, set up your course accordingly, and collect data via reports. The high quality and volume of test questions allows for data comparison and measurement.

Content and Functionality Training

The Instructor Implementation Guide provides grading rubrics, suggestions for video use, and more to save time on course prep. Our Best Practices Guide and "How do I…" YouTube videos indicate how to use MyStudentSuccessLab, from getting started to utilizing the Gradebook.

Peer Support

The Student Success Community site is a place for you to connect with other educators to exchange ideas and advice on courses, content, and MyStudentSuccessLab. The site is filled with timely articles, discussions, video posts, and more. Join, share, and be inspired!
www.mystudentsuccesscommunity.com

The Faculty Advisor Network is Pearson's peer-to-peer mentoring program in which experienced MyStudentSuccessLab users share best practices and expertise. Our Faculty Advisors are experienced in one-on-one phone and email coaching, presentations, and live training sessions.

Integration and Compliance

You can integrate our digital solutions with your learning management system in a variety of ways. For more information, or if documentation is needed for ADA compliance, contact your local Pearson representative.

MyStudentSuccessLab users have access to:

- Full course Pre- and Post-Diagnostic Assessments linked to learning outcomes

- Pre- and Post-tests dedicated to individual topics

- Overviews that summarize objectives and skills

- Videos on key issues "by students, for students"

- Practice exercises that instill student confidence

- Graded activities to build critical-thinking and problem-solving skills

- Journal writing assignments with online rubrics for consistent, simpler grading

- Resources like Finish Strong 24/7 YouTube videos, calculators, professionalism/research & writing/ student success tools

- **Conley Readiness Index student inventory to measure college and career readiness skill set**

Students utilizing MyStudentSuccessLab may purchase Pearson texts in a number of cost-saving formats— including eTexts, loose-leaf **Student Value** editions, and more.

CourseConnect™

Trust that your online course is the best in its class.

Designed by subject matter experts and credentialed instructional designers, CourseConnect offers award-winning customizable online courses that help students build skills for ongoing personal and professional development.

CourseConnect uses topic-based, interactive modules that follow a consistent learning path—from introduction, to presentation, to activity, to review. Its built-in tools—including user-specific pacing charts, personalized study guides, and interactive exercises—provide a student-centric learning experience that minimizes distractions and helps students stay on track and complete the course successfully. Features such as relevant video, audio, and activities, personalized (or editable) syllabi, discussion forum topics and questions, assignments, and quizzes are all easily accessible. CourseConnect is available in a variety of learning management systems and accommodates various term lengths as well as self-paced study. And, our compact textbook editions align to CourseConnect course outcomes.

Choose from the following three course outlines ("Lesson Plans")

Student Success

- Goal Setting, Values, and Motivation
- Time Management
- Financial Literacy
- Creative Thinking, Critical Thinking, and Problem Solving
- Learning Preferences
- Listening and Note-Taking in Class
- Reading and Annotating
- Studying, Memory, and Test-Taking
- Communicating and Teamwork
- Information Literacy
- Staying Balanced: Stress Management
- Career Exploration

Career Success

- Planning Your Career Search
- Knowing Yourself: Explore the Right Career Path
- Knowing the Market: Find Your Career Match
- Preparing Yourself: Gain Skills and Experience Now
- Networking
- Targeting Your Search: Locate Positions, Ready Yourself
- Building a Portfolio: Your Resume and Beyond
- Preparing for Your Interview
- Giving a Great Interview
- Negotiating Job Offers, Ensuring Future Success

Professional Success

- Introducing Professionalism
- Workplace Goal Setting
- Workplace Ethics and Your Career
- Workplace Time Management
- Interpersonal Skills at Work
- Workplace Conflict Management
- Workplace Communications: Email and Presentations
- Effective Workplace Meetings
- Workplace Teams
- Customer Focus and You
- Understanding Human Resources
- Managing Career Growth and Change

Custom Services
Personalize instruction to best facilitate learning.

As the industry leader in custom publishing, we are committed to meeting your instructional needs by offering flexible and creative choices for course materials that will maximize learning and student engagement.

Pearson Custom Library

Using our online book-building system, create a custom book by selecting content from our course-specific collections that consist of chapters from Pearson Student Success and Career Development titles and carefully selected, copyright-cleared, third-party content and pedagogy.
www.pearsoncustomlibrary.com

Custom Publications

In partnership with your Pearson representative, modify, adapt, and combine existing Pearson books by choosing content from across the curriculum and organizing it around your learning outcomes. As an alternative, you can work with your Editor to develop your original material and create a textbook that meets your course goals.

Custom Technology Solutions

Work with Pearson's trained professionals, in a truly consultative process, to create engaging learning solutions. From interactive learning tools, to eTexts, to custom websites and portals, we'll help you simplify your life as an instructor.

Online Education

Pearson offers online course content for online classes and hybrid courses. This online content can also be used to enhance traditional classroom courses. Our award-winning CourseConnect includes a fully developed syllabus, media-rich lecture presentations, audio lectures, a wide variety of assessments, discussion board questions, and a strong instructor resource package.

For more information on custom Student Success services, please visit www.pearsonlearningsolutions.com.

1

habits for success in college, career, and life

DONIQUE WRAY, *student,*
University of North Florida

Growing up in the Jacksonville Housing Authority in Florida, Donique Wray faced challenges from the start. Before she was born, her mother ran away from home at age 13 to live on the streets. Then when she was 9, her father was sentenced to life in prison for committing murder. In this world, with an absent father and a mother who struggled to survive and to recognize value in herself and her daughter, Donique lacked role models who could guide her. She had to learn to self-parent, and her anger often got the best of her, leading to difficulties in high school including frequent absences and low performance.

Despite her challenges and stubborn attitude, Donique's school counselor, Travis Pinckney, saw something special in her. Encouraging her to move beyond her past, he began to work with her to help her develop hope and a vision for the goals she could achieve. He advised her to retrain her focus on attendance, academic performance, and college entrance tests. She got it. She began to work tirelessly, retaking whole credit courses she had failed, starting grade recovery, mentoring at-risk ninth graders, and retaking the SAT, all while working at the local library. During that period she used her passion for writing to create a short film to help other students learn from her academic and social mistakes. But could she persist enough to gain entrance to college and thrive there?

(to be continued ...)

Many students find it challenging to persist past the obstacles that challenge them. You'll learn more about Donique's experience at the end of the chapter.

Working through this chapter will help you to:

Text and photo used by permisison of Donique Wray.

persist
Keep moving ahead toward what you want from school and life so you can *finish strong*.

How Can College Get You Where You Want to Go? *(and if you have no clue where you are going, how can college help you figure it out?)*

Persistence is what helps you do what you have to do to get where you want to go—and you are already building it. Whether you've just completed high school or its equivalent or are returning to school after staying home with young children, whether you've worked in one or more jobs or served in the armed forces, you have persisted through the experience. Now you have decided to pursue a degree, enrolled in college, found a way to pay for it, and signed up for coursework. Game on: Now it's up to you to finish strong so that you reap the benefits of your time and efforts.

From the simplest possible perspective, college success is about accomplishing tasks and responsibilities: Show up (either in person or virtually) to class, pay attention and participate, do your best work, and turn assignments in on time. But issues and distractions can make it tough to persist on a day-to-day basis. Many students wonder, "Why am I doing this?" It's an important question to ask yourself. As you begin to answer, knowing more about how college will help you in the workplace can help you stay in motion toward your goals.

What you learn in specific coursework is important, especially in courses related to your major and what you want to pursue in your career. But even more importantly, **college is a training ground for life**. It is an opportunity to build skills and habits that you need to survive in this era of rapid change, when:

- Many formerly domestic jobs have moved overseas.
- Graduates working in the United States now compete with and work with people who live in different time zones, speak different languages, and come from different cultures.
- Technological development continues at an ever-faster pace, demanding constant learning and training.
- Global media and communication technology enable exposure to different people, places, values, cultures, beliefs, and perspectives.
- **Knowledge work**, such as Internet technology, is on the rise while labor-based jobs, such as factory work, are in shorter supply.

Knowledge work
work that is primarily concerned with information rather than manual labor.

What you need to achieve your goals in this world, where you may compete for information-based jobs with highly trained and motivated people from around the globe, is different from what workers needed even one generation ago. In addition to specific skills and consistent hard work, you need *transferable skills*—skills and qualities that can transfer to any job or career area—like these:

- A commitment to lifelong learning
- The ability to work in a team
- Problem solving and critical thinking
- Self-management skills, including time management
- Communication, both in person and in writing
- Flexibility in the face of change

Look at Key 1.1 for the results of a recent survey of employers, showing what they most value in potential employees (note the high number of transferable skills).

College provides multiple opportunities for you to gather and hone the tools you need to succeed, tools such as the following:

Skills specific to academic subjects and career paths. At the most basic level, your coursework trains you in areas that link to the workplace opportunities you aim for.

 Key 1.1 Employers rate the importance of candidate qualities and skills.

What employers look for in people they hire, ranked by the percentage of employers who value each quality or skill

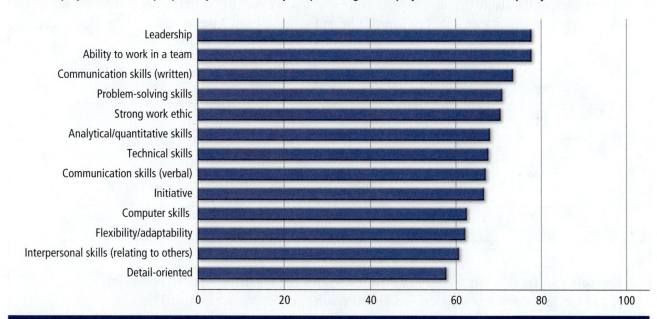

Source: Based on NACE Research: Job Outlook 2105 (https://www.naceweb.org/s11122014/job-outlook-skills-qualities-employers-want.aspx).

Experience as a learner. You know those core requirement courses that don't seem to relate to your career goals? They train you in how to learn. In today's workplace, where rapid change means that employees frequently have to learn new ideas, techniques, and technology, knowing how to learn is an essential skill for anyone who wants to keep a job.

Opportunities to grow as a team player and social being. The modern workplace values teamwork above almost all other qualities. Whether you go to class online or in person, you interact with others. The more practice you have working with people—instructors, fellow students, co-workers—the more marketable you will be.

Opportunities to give back to those around you. One of the best ways to develop valuable skills, both transferable and task specific, is through giving to others. Explore any volunteering opportunities your college may coordinate or offer, including service learning courses.

Think about yourself *right now*. Complete the short assessment in this chapter's *All About You*, a self-awareness building exercise. Then consider: Would you hire yourself? If you answered no, all is not lost: The work you do in this course will prepare you to succeed in college and get the job you want after graduation. If you answered yes, this course will help you improve even more.

College is a transition for any student. Take a look at what the transition means and the resources that can support you.

ALL ABOUT YOU

If you were a hiring manager and could only hire one person in your small company this year, what qualities would you most want in that employee? For example, would you require strong communication skills, excellent teamwork, or the ability to problem solve? Write your top five qualities in the spaces that follow and rank their levels of importance from 1 to 5, with 1 being the highest and 5 the lowest.

Quality	Ranking
_____	_____
_____	_____
_____	_____
_____	_____
_____	_____

Compare your list with lists from one or more classmates. Ask the following questions: What qualities from other lists would you include on your own? Would you change your rankings?

How Can You Transition to College-Level Work? *(and step up your game no matter your starting point?)*

The so-called typical path of the student—graduating from high school at 18, attending college for 2 to 4 years, and then finding a job right after graduation—is no longer typical. Today, students follow a variety of paths and time schedules to reach their goals. However, whether high school graduation was last year, 10 years ago, or achieved by working toward a GED, every student faces the challenge of transitioning to college work and culture.

Knowing what to expect will help you prepare. Here are two significant differences everyone will face (spend some time with your college's student handbook to get informed about details specific to your school).

More independence and responsibility. Perhaps the single most significant difference between high school and college is the extent to which you are responsible for your actions. You will be expected to make the following—and more—happen on your own:

- Buy books and other assigned materials.
- Use your syllabi to set up your schedule for the term.
- Keep on top of assignment deadlines and exam dates.
- Get help when you need it.
- Complete assigned coursework.
- Set up study group meetings.
- Be present, on time, and with needed materials, whether in a classroom or on a computer.
- Manage your out-of-class time effectively.

Increased workload. College means more work per course, and more challenging work, than you completed in high school. You will be required to read more material and to move faster through those materials. Your brain will need to both recall information and think critically about it (analyze, compare and contrast, evaluate, and more). To manage all this, you need adequate study time. A rule of thumb is to study at least 2 hours for each hour of class time, meaning that if your classes are in session for 9 hours a week, you need to schedule at least 18 hours of study and work time through the week, every week.

You are not alone as you face these challenges. Look to the people around you, the technology available to you, and this course for support.

© Courtesy of Sarah Lyman Kravits

People Can Help

Faculty and staff are among the most valuable—but underused—sources of help. A recent survey of college freshmen indicated that only 25% of students asked a teacher for advice after class throughout the term, and only 8% considered seeking counseling.[1] That means that 75% did not ask their instructor for help and 92% would never seek counseling, no matter the need.

Don't let these important sources of support go untapped. Connect with instructors, teaching assistants, advisors, tutoring centers, and counselors throughout your college career.

Instructors and Teaching Assistants

You have frequent contact with instructors, whom you may see in person or connect with online one or more times a week. Consult them to:

- Clarify material presented in class.
- Help with homework.
- Find out how to prepare for a test.
- Ask about a paper while you are working on it.
- Find out why you received a particular grade on a test or assignment.
- Get advice about the department—courses, majoring—or related career areas.

Before or after class works well for a quick question. When you want to have a longer conversation, make an appointment to talk during in-person or virtual office hours, start up an exchange using e-mail, or request a phone call by leaving a voice mail message.

Office hours.   Instructors' regular office hours appear on your syllabi, on websites for individual courses, and on instructors' or departmental web pages. Always make an appointment for a conference. Online instructors may offer videoconferences through Skype or other platforms. Adjunct instructors who have no permanent office space may prefer phone calls.

E-mail.   Instructors' e-mail addresses appear on your syllabi and on the course sites. Use e-mail to clarify assignments and assignment deadlines, to ask questions about lectures or readings, and to clarify what will be covered on tests.

Voice mail.   If something comes up at the last minute and your instructor has provided a phone number on the syllabus, leave a short, specific message. Adjunct instructors without a school-sponsored phone number may provide a cell number, or they may only be reachable by e-mail.

Academic Advisors, Tutors, and Academic Centers

An academic advisor is a student's personal connection with the college, and most colleges assign an advisor to each student. Your advisor will help you choose courses, plan your overall academic program, and understand college regulations, including graduation requirements. Although you may only be required to meet with your advisor once per term, you can schedule additional meetings if you need.

Tutors can give you valuable and detailed help on specific academic subjects. Most campuses have private tutoring available, and many schools offer free peer tutoring. If you feel you could benefit from the kind of one-on-one work a tutor can give, ask your instructor or your academic advisor to recommend a tutor.

Academic centers, including reading, writing, math, and study-skills centers, offer consultations and tutoring to help students improve skills at all levels. If your school has one or more academic centers, you may be able to find a tutor there.

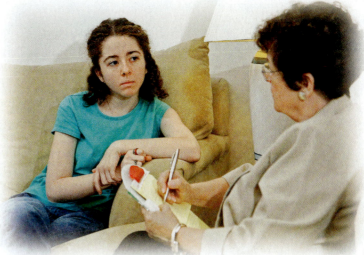

© Lisa F. Young/Fotolia

Therapists at your school's counseling center can help you manage a variety of personal challenges.

Counseling

College counseling services can help you address academic problems, stress, and psychological issues. As stated on the website of one school's counseling services, "counseling services are designed to assist students with addressing the difficulties that they encounter during these years and to promote greater overall wellness within the student population."[2]

Counseling is confidential, focused on your particular needs, and directed toward helping you handle what is bothering you. In most cases it is not ongoing, and it ends when you have achieved the goals that you and your counselor have defined.

Knowing How to Use Technology Can Help

Technology permeates college life. In a given day you might access a syllabus online, work on a team project with fellow students using a document-sharing platform, use the Internet to tap into a library database, draft an assignment on a computer, and e-mail a paper to an instructor. An increasing number of campuses have wireless networks, and of course some courses take place completely online. Some schools use a "paperless" system in which all student notifications are sent via e-mail. Here are some ways to smooth the transition using technology:

Get connected. Register for a school e-mail account and connect to the college network. Learn how to operate your school's learning management system (LMS) and explore your course sites in the LMS. Register your cell phone number with the school to receive emergency alerts.

Use computers to find information. Frequent the college website, and use library databases. If they are available, download podcasts of lectures.

Be a cautious user. Save your work periodically onto a primary or backup hard drive, CD, or flash drive. In addition, install an antivirus program and update it regularly.

Stay on task. During study time, try to limit Internet surfing, direct messaging, visiting Facebook pages, and playing computer games.

Follow guidelines when contacting instructors via e-mail. When you submit assignments, take exams, or ask questions electronically, rules of etiquette promote civility and respect. Try these suggestions the next time you e-mail an instructor:

- **Use your school account.** Instructors may delete unfamiliar e-mails.
- **Don't ask for information you can find on your own.** Check the syllabus and the course website for answers first.
- **Write a clear subject line.** State exactly what the e-mail is about.
- **Start with a greeting using the instructor's name and title.** "Hello, Professor Smith," or "Hi, Dr. Reynolds," is better than "Hey" or having no greeting at all.
  - **Be clear and comprehensive.** First, state your question or problem and what you want to achieve. If necessary, support your position. End with a thank you and sign your full name.
  - **Use complete sentences, correct punctuation, and capitalization.** Avoid abbreviations, acronyms, and other styles more suitable to texting.
  - **Give the instructor time to respond.** Many instructors state on course materials that they will respond within a specific time period, often 24 hours. If you hear nothing after a couple of days, send a follow-up note that contains the full text of your first message.

This Course Can Help

The goal of this course is to help you build the skills and habits that will propel you successfully into your future.

- **With your instructor and fellow students,** you will build teamwork skills as well as your ability to get along with others.
- **With your coursework and text,** you will improve your study skills, critical and creative thinking skills, and learning strategies, as well as your ability to self-manage.
- **With your electronic interactions,** whether on your course site, a MyLab, or other electronic materials, you will increase your skill as a user of technology.

Where do habits fit in? Productive, positive habits make skill building and goal achievement possible. The skills you build will serve you only if you are in the habit of using them. Take a look at how habits affect your life.

Understanding how to use research and communication technology is as important for day-to-day college activities as it is for the workplace.

© Courtesy of Sarah Lyman Kravits

What Is a Habit and How Can It Help? *(how can you actually follow through on changing habits?)*

Habits affect much of your day-to-day life including what you eat, what you wear, what you do and when, where you put things, and much more. People perform habits over and over again without really thinking about what they are doing.

> **Habit**
> *a regular pattern of behavior that has become almost involuntary.*

Bad and Good Habits

What makes a habit "bad" or "good"? *Bad habits* have negative effects. Some, like alcohol and drug abuse, are destructive to your health and well-being. Other bad habits prevent you from reaching important goals. A common example: Leaving studying until late in the evening after classes, your work shift, and social time may leave you with almost no energy to do schoolwork well or on time. *Good habits,* in contrast, have positive effects. If you are in the habit of keeping study materials with you throughout the day and turning to them whenever you have a block of time, you'll be more able to stay on top of your assignments.

Although some habits have the same effect on almost everyone, what makes many habits good or bad often depends on individual circumstances. Writing papers in the evenings might work well for one student and be labeled a "bad habit" by another who can't write well at that hour. The collection of habits that work best for you will be as individual as you are.

Most students begin college with a set of habits they have had for years. The first step is self-knowledge: Identify your particular habits and analyze whether each has positive or negative effects on your life. Then the larger challenge is to adjust or set aside the habits that have negative effects and improve or add habits that foster success.

How to Improve Your Habits

Adjusting habits is a challenge for anyone, but determination combined with self-knowledge can bring change. In fact, recent brain research shows that when people work to change old habits and solidify new habits, they actually create new brain cells and new neural pathways that move currents from cell to cell.[3] There are two ways to improve your habits:

Replace or change an existing habit. When an existing habit has negative effects, it is not enough to just ditch it. You have to substitute something in its place, says Scott H. Young, a student who is a habits expert: "If you opened up your computer and started removing hardware, what would happen? Chances are your

© 123RF

computer wouldn't work. Similarly, you can't just pull out habits without replacing the needs they fulfill."[4] For example, if you try to stop eating sugar in high-stress situations, you will need to come up with a healthier stress-response action.

Begin a new habit.   When you create a new habit, you are starting from the ground up, deciding on the specific nature of the habit as well as when, where, and how to use it.

Whether replacing or generating a habit, use the following steps to make the change:[5]

1. **Identify what you want to change and why.**   What do you want to accomplish? Are you changing an existing habit or beginning a new habit? Write it down in specific terms. Use positive language: "I will use my time between classes to study" is more motivating than "I need to stop wasting time between classes."

2. **Name specific, short-term actions related to this habit change.**   For example, if you aim to use between-class time to study, a specific behavior might be, "Bring my psychology book on Tuesdays so I can study between algebra and lunch."

3. **Set up support.**   You are more likely to succeed if your friends or family help you stay on track. Set up a progress-report plan with someone. Maybe once a week you'll call or post a note on Facebook. Consider asking your support person to send motivating texts or e-mails.

4. **Get started, and keep it up for at least 21 days—maybe 30.**   Habits experts note that it takes at least 21 days of consistently performing a new or changed habit to get it to stick. Personal development expert Steve Pavlina, noting how software companies give consumers 30 days to try out a new product, recommends that you follow that lead and beef up your "trial period" to 30 days.

5. **Be accountable as you go.**   Note your actions and your progress in writing. Use whatever works for you—your planner, a separate notebook, e-mails, a computer document.

6. **Evaluate your progress.**   Step back and evaluate how the process is going, and ask your support person or people to give you feedback if possible.

7. **If necessary, switch gears.**   Not everyone responds well to drastic change. If a new habit isn't sticking or your attempts to change are making you want to give up, go back and adjust your habit goal. For example, a student who has always pulled all-nighters before exams might not be able to cut out *all* late-night cramming. Instead, she could build in 3 hours of study time the night before the exam as part of a week-long study schedule.

As you work to establish new habits, keep it simple. Work on only one or maybe two habits at a time. If you attempt more, you run the risk of overloading and not successfully changing any of them. Over time and through trial and error, you will find what works for you.

TAKE ACTION

Work to Change a Habit

Think of a habit of yours that you think might get in the way of your ability to succeed in college. Write it here: _____

_____

_____

Why do you want to change this habit—in other words, what negative effect does it have on your academic performance? _____

_____

Describe the new or changed habit you would like to adopt. _____

_____

Name two specific, short-term actions you will take to make this change.

1. _____

2. _____

Identify the start date and end date (21 days later) of the period of time when you will focus on this change on a daily basis. _____ / _____

Name someone who will support your efforts. _____

Describe how you will track your progress.

_____

Finally, put your two actions to work every day for 21 days. Describe the result here. What is different, if anything? Evaluate the effect this process had and whether you achieved your goal of positive change.

_____

_____

_____

Now that you know more about habits, examine the set of habits that you will explore throughout this text. Any of them that you make your own will benefit you throughout your life.

What Habits Drive Success?
(and how can you make success-building habits your own?)

Being able to solve problems effectively is a key ingredient of academic, career, and life success. Art Costa, professor emeritus of education at California State University, Sacramento, and co-director of the Institute for Intelligent Behavior in El Dorado Hills, California, studied how students respond to problems and handle unfamiliar information and situations. He found that students who solved problems most effectively tended to rely on a certain group of habits. These positive habits promote success when used regularly and consistently.

The Habits for Success

To help you solve problems successfully and achieve your college and life goals, *Keys to Effective Learning* features 11 Habits for Success based on Costa's work (see Key 1.2). Practicing these habits will help you:

- Work more effectively toward the grades you want.
- Manage yourself—your time, money, and responsibilities.
- Maximize your learning potential.
- Work well with others at school and elsewhere.
- Succeed in your coursework for your major.
- Graduate and thrive in the workplace.

The chapters of *Keys to Effective Learning* introduce you to these habits and give you opportunities to explore them. Each chapter features a habit and builds that habit in connection with the chapter topics, through both what you read and the exercises you complete. In the last chapter, you will have the opportunity to revisit all 11 habits—to apply each, evaluate your development, and plan how to make progress in the future.

HABIT	CORRESPONDING CHAPTER	APPLY IT TO THE CHAPTER...	APPLY IT TO LIFE...
PERSIST. Stick with it until you complete it. Finish strong.	*Chapter 1 Habits for Success*	Stick to your goal of earning a college degree.	Persist in working on a relationship that means a lot to you.
LEARN. Be a lifelong learner, always seeking to know more. Take initiative and be self-directed.	*Chapter 2 Learning Preferences*	As your strengths and challenges change over time, self-directed learning allows you to respond to those changes.	Be ready to learn new skills and knowledge to stay employable in an era of rapid workplace change.
ANTICIPATE. Design a plan of action and define specific goals before beginning.	*Chapter 3 Time and Money*	Plan out your class meetings, work times, and other responsibilities at the beginning of each week.	Before rushing into a big purchase such as a car, research what will get you the most bang for your buck.
COMMUNICATE. Ask for help and give help when you can. Connect with others with a purpose in mind.	*Chapter 4 Setting and Reaching Goals*	Friends and classmates can help hold you accountable for steps toward an important goal.	Ask for ideas about how others manage stress through food and exercise choices.
IMAGINE. Expand your thinking to create new and useful ideas, solutions, and techniques.	*Chapter 5 Critical and Creative Thinking*	Brainstorm possible ways to get the courses you need to fulfill requirements.	Risk trying out a new idea in your home life, and let it be okay if you make a mistake.
INQUIRE. Use questions to build knowledge. Excavate problems so you can solve them before they grow out of control.	*Chapter 6 Reading and Studying*	Ask questions before reading (while skimming material) or during reading (in margins) in order to maximize your understanding of what you read.	In any conversation, take time to ask questions that help you understand the situation and the person better.

(continued)

HABIT	CORRESPONDING CHAPTER	APPLY IT TO THE CHAPTER...	APPLY IT TO LIFE...
CONTRIBUTE. Use your past knowledge and experiences to add value to problem solving.	*Chapter 7 Reading Across the Disciplines*	Concepts in one course can apply to another; for example, you can use psychology ideas when analyzing a character in a book.	When you are stopped short by a problem, recall and use how you've approached similar problems in the past.
LISTEN. Consider what others have to say, and work to understand perspectives that differ from yours.	*Chapter 8 Active Listening and Note Taking*	When classmates speak up in class, listen to and consider their questions and ideas as you would those of your instructor.	Let co-workers have a say when a situation comes up, and consider their ideas carefully.
PERCEIVE. Build awareness of the information that comes your way through sensory pathways.	*Chapter 9 Memory*	Use senses-based mnemonic devices to remember science and math facts.	Engage your vision, hearing, and other senses to strengthen your ability to remember procedures and people's names on the job.
RISK. Take productive risks. Extend your limits wisely.	*Chapter 10 Test Taking I: Test Preparation and Objective Tests*	Use test preparation strategies to make the risk of test taking a responsible one, with a strong likelihood of success.	Before making a drastic life change, consider whether your chances of success are good enough for you to take the plunge.
ADJUST. Have the flexibility to shift your actions. Optimize how you react to a changing situation.	*Chapter 11 Test Taking II: Getting Results on Essay Tests and Graded Projects*	When you encounter a tricky essay question, a flexible mind will help you approach it comprehensively.	When a health problem throws you a curve ball, optimize your actions to promote successful problem solving.

Source: Adapted with permission from *Discovering & Exploring Habits of Mind* (pp. 22–37), by Arthur L. Costa and Bena Kallick. Alexandria, VA: ASCD. © 2000 by ASCD. Learn more about ASCD at www.ascd.org.

Here is a list of the Habits for Success. First, rate each based on how much you think you have and use that habit right now–from 1 (I don't have it at all) to 10 (I live this habit).

_____Persist	_____Inquire
_____Learn	_____Contribute
_____Anticipate	_____Listen
_____Communicate	_____Risk
_____Imagine	_____Adjust
_____Perceive	

Next, underline what you consider to be your three strongest habits. Then, circle what you consider the three habits that need the most work.

As you learn about each habit through your work in this book, consider the following: How have your three strongest habits improved your life? How would your life change if you developed your three weakest habits? Remember, with work you can improve and strengthen your habits. You will have a chance to revisit this assessment in the last chapter and measure your progress.

You can use one or more of the Habits for Success to confront academic challenges you will face in college—from learning to understand difficult texts to listening from the perspective of your instructor. In many cases you will use more than one habit at a time. For example, when working with a study group, you may connect with purpose, contribute to the work, and listen to other perspectives. With more practice, the habits will become simpler to apply no matter what the situation and will become an essential part of how you operate in school, in the workplace, and in your personal life. The chapter features and exercises will help you persist in habit exploration throughout the term.

Coaching to Build Habits for Success

What is coaching? To begin to answer this question, consider a basketball team playing a game. Although the coach has run the practices and drills, at game time he or she gives support from the sideline. The players are in the spotlight, accountable for their performance. Coaching gives the players the tools to succeed, the power to generate ideas, and the motivation to act so that they can perform at game time.

© Stephen Coburn/Fotolia

persist

?

STUDENT TO STUDENT

People attend college for technical training, for the sake of learning, for increased earning power, and for many other reasons. Pair up with a fellow student. Take turns asking each other:

What are your reasons for attending college? Consider the Habit for Success that opened this chapter: Which of the reasons you have for attending college seem most likely to help you persist, and why?

Like the basketball team, you are accountable for your actions. An academic or career or life coach can help you build habits that promote success. Through in-person conversations involving powerful questions that inspire thinking and generate action, a coach can prepare you to perform when your time in the spotlight arrives.

Coaching can apply to any area of your life, and many different people can use coaching tools—instructors, advisors, and more. The personal relationship is key to building trust and producing results. In each chapter of this text, you will have two opportunities to benefit from coaching.

Inside Tips from Sarah, Academic Coach

Think about what happens when you are unable to follow through on a goal. What is the cost to you? Does it deplete opportunities, relationships, self-esteem, or something else?

Now consider a specific, school-related action you want to do more consistently. What does it cost you to be inconsistent? How would you benefit if you were to perform this action consistently? What are you willing to do to persist more effectively?

Come up with one specific way to increase your persistence with this action (it could be as simple as writing a reminder down where you will see it every day without fail). Holding the goal of persistence in your mind, put that action into practice and observe whether you experience an improvement.

- With the Powerful Questions exercises, you team up with a fellow student and coach each other.
- With the Inside Tips feature, one of the authors coaches you in a way that matches her expertise.

Carol Carter is your career coach. Carol was a vice president in the corporate world and now is president of her own company. She has hired hundreds of graduates and has worked with many interns throughout her 30-year career. She will give you guidance on what employers look for in people they hire, so that you can work to build these much-needed skills in school.

Sarah Lyman Kravits is your college coach. Sarah is a student success instructor. She will coach you on how to solidify the study and self-management skills you have, improve the ones you struggle with, and use these skills to improve academic performance now and throughout college. She will also help you see the connection between school and life success.

How willing are you to work hard to reach your definition of success? It will take effort to rid yourself of habits that limit you and to develop habits that empower you—but if you are willing to put forth that effort, you will reap the benefit. Your opportunity to create positive change is now. This book and course will give you the chance to change your reality, creating opportunities and opening doors to the rest of your life.

HABIT IN ACTION WRAP-UP

What happened with Donique? After raising her scores and GPA and joining the Hicks Prep Club, Donique was accepted to the University of North Florida (UNF) and awarded the Hicks Scholarship—4 years of tuition, room and board, and meals worth $80,000. She made a strong start, especially considering her past. Donique set academic goals with Assistant Director of UNF Foundation Scholarships, Probyn Inniss, and chose to spend time with friends who nurtured her. She also camped out regularly at the Writing Center at UNF, revising and improving her papers, working to improve her writing on the way to one of her life goals—writing books and blogs that can help others.

Donique understands the persistence it takes to advocate for yourself, to fight for the people, resources, and opportunities that promote success. She does not yet know whether she will focus on criminal justice, sociology, or English literature. But she has the inner wisdom to know that regardless of what she majors in, being true to her own passion and vision will help her finish strong. As she says, "You can't get to a better place without enduring the difficulty of the challenges on the path."

Connect this story to your life: Where do you need to advocate for yourself, and in pursuit of what goal? Identify an action you will take as a self-advocate. Who can you call on to help you finish strong? Identify a person who can support you and what help you will request.

Building Skills

Note the Important Points

Describe an important goal that college helps students achieve. _____
_____
_____

Name two challenges students face as they adjust to college culture. _____
_____
_____

Define a *habit* and describe what makes it "bad" or "good." _____
_____
_____

Name two strategies a person can use to change or replace a problematic habit. _____
_____
_____

According to Art Costa's research, what do the Habits for Success help people to do more effectively?
_____
_____
_____

Critical Thinking

Target Challenges at the Start

Students come to college coursework with a variety of levels of preparation. Examine how prepared you are by answering the following questions on paper or a computer document.

Gather information: How well do you think your high school experience prepared you for college work? Do you feel that you lack skill in reading, writing, math, or any other area?

Generate ideas for what might help: When you have addressed academic or workload challenges in the past, what has worked and what has not? Flip through the text: What chapters or sections may help you with a particular shortcoming?

Take action: Commit to addressing a particular challenge using book strategies, a careful eye toward your syllabus, and a campus resource. Define specific details by filling in the blanks below. Then, put your plan to work starting now.

Your challenge: _____

Book strategy #1 _____ on page _____

Book strategy #2 _____ on page _____

Syllabus dates/weeks to watch: _____ and _____

Campus resource: _____

Location: _____ Phone/e-mail: _____

Contact resource by: _____ Goal of contact: _____

Team Building

collaborative solutions

Shifting to College-Level Work

In person or online, gather a group of three to five students. Generate a list of transition challenges that can affect performance in class, outside of class, or both. When you have as many challenges as you have group members, each person should choose one.

Look at the challenge assigned to you. On your own and in conversation with friends or family, generate as many practical ideas about how to overcome it as you can. E-mail your list to everyone else in your group.

After everyone has sent and received ideas, come together in person or online and discuss them. Which ideas may work better than others? Are there new ideas group members might add? In your discussion, narrow down to a "top three" ideas for each transition challenge.

The last step: Identify one of the transition challenges you face yourself. Make a plan to put one or more of the top three ideas to work. Evaluate whether it helped you cope.

persist

Persistence Brings Test and Life Success

Preparation for tests scheduled at any time in the term starts on the first day of class. Everything you do for a course—every fact and idea that you hear, every concept you read, every assignment you generate, and every topic you discuss—builds your knowledge, preparing you to finish strong by showing what you know on test day. And all of it prepares you to face the tests that will come your way at work and in life.

Make a plan to persist toward test success starting now. Looking at the syllabi for the courses you are taking this semester, determine which test is coming up first. Fill in the following in relation to this test:

Course: _____

Test date and time (note in calendar or planner): _____

From what you can tell from the syllabus, topic(s) covered on the test: _____

_____

_____

Time each week you will study for this test (for example, every Thursday from 3:00 to 4:30):

_____ (note in calendar or planner)

_____

_____

Office hours for the instructor who teaches this course: _____

Use this information to prepare—honor your weekly study times, consult with your instructor, and stay aware of the test date. After the test, evaluate: Describe whether these strategies helped you persist and finish strong.

_____

_____

_____

2

learning preferences

building and using self-knowledge

AUSTIN YELLEN, *student,*
University of Colorado at Boulder

As a child, Austin Yellen believed that his father had graduated from Harvard. Having been assured by his parents that doing well in school was largely a function of genetics, he was confident that learning would come relatively easily to him. The confidence brought early success, which fed his drive to continue to excel.

At the age of 12, though, Austin discovered that his father had not attended Harvard and in fact had not even finished his sophomore year of high school. He learned the truth—not one member of his family, immediate or extended, had earned a college degree. After this, the drive Austin once had toward schoolwork was shifted to athletics, and his confidence gradually mutated into an attitude that he didn't have to work much to do well academically. School became a game with simple rules: Attempt to get a B in each class while putting in as little effort as possible. He became an expert at assessing how much to work on assignments based on how they counted toward his overall grade.

Even with the attitude that classes were just something to get through, Austin was able to graduate high school and gain admittance to the University of Colorado at Boulder. Having resisted guidance in the application process, he mistakenly entered the school of Arts and Sciences, although he intended to earn a degree in business. With his habit of exhibiting minimal effort in classes, would he be prepared for the challenge of college?

(to be continued . . .)

The modern world demands lifelong learning—and learning throughout life requires you to self-direct. You'll learn more about Austin's experience at the end of the chapter.

Working through this chapter will help you to:

- Assess learning preferences. p. 26

- Investigate how you prefer to interact with information and people. p. 33

- Identify in-class and study strategies that work effectively with particular preferences. p. 36

- Build lesser-developed learning preferences. p. 36

- Determine ways to adjust to different teaching styles. p. 37

- Identify and manage learning disabilities. p. 42

Text and photo used by permission of Austin Yellen.

learn Strive to know more, to understand something new about the world, yourself, and others. Take initiative to learn throughout your life and to *self-direct*.

Why Explore Who You Are as a Learner? *(what does it matter?)*

College is an ideal time to think about how you learn, think, and function in the world. The more you know yourself, the more you will be able to self-direct—to analyze courses, evaluate potential study partners, and choose what, how, and where to study, all with an eye toward what works best for you.

Your Abilities Can Change and Develop

Each person in the world is born with particular levels of ability and potential in different areas. What one person finds easy, another may experience as very difficult. Over time, individuals develop unique **learning preferences**, which often lead to labels ("slacker," "quiet," "disorganized," and so on) coming from others or from within.

Instead of letting a label define you, know that you can move beyond labels. Brain studies show that humans of any age can learn new ideas and skills and that this learning actually changes the structure and function of the cells in the brain. This means that intelligence can grow when you work to keep learning.

Picture a bag of rubber bands of different sizes. Some are thick, and some are thin; some are long, and some are short—*but all of them can stretch*. A small rubber band, stretched out, can reach the length of a larger one that lies unstretched. In other words, with effort and focus, you can grow to some extent whatever raw material you start with.

To begin thinking about where you can go, ask yourself: Who am I right now? Where would I like to be in 5 years? In 10 years? Self-assessments allow you to gather information about yourself that will help you answer some of these big questions and stretch your rubber band as far as it can go.

Self-Knowledge Gives You the Power of Choice

There may be much about yourself, your surroundings, and your experiences that you cannot control. However, self-knowledge gives you tools to choose how you *respond* to circumstances. For example, even though you cannot

Learning preference
a way in which a person most effectively receives and processes information.

© Courtesy of Sarah Lyman Kravits

control the courses you are required to take or how your instructors teach, an understanding of your strengths, weaknesses, and preferences can help you self-direct as you respond to those courses and instructors in a way that allows you to learn.

The two assessments in this chapter—Multiple Pathways to Learning and the Personality Spectrum—will give you insight into those preferences, strengths, and weaknesses. The material following the assessments show you how to maximize what you do well and compensate for challenging areas by making specific choices about what you do in class time, when studying, and in the workplace. Understanding yourself as a learner will also help you choose how to respond to others in a group situation. Whether in an academic or a workplace situation, each team member takes in material in a unique way. You can improve communication and teamwork by using what you know about yourself as well as others.

What Tools Can Help You Assess How You Learn and Interact with Others? (is this a test?)

The two assessments in this chapter have different objectives. Multiple Pathways to Learning focuses on learning preferences and areas of potential. In contrast, the Personality Spectrum helps you evaluate how you react to people and situations.

Following each assessment is information about the typical traits of each intelligence or personality spectrum dimension. As you will see from your scores, you have abilities in all areas, though some are more developed than others. Remember: This is not a test of your knowledge as you would take for one of your courses. There are no "right" answers, no "best" scores. Completing a self-assessment is like wearing glasses to correct blurred vision. The glasses do not create new paths and possibilities, but they help you to see more clearly the ones in front of you at this moment.

Assess Your Multiple Intelligences with Pathways to Learning

In 1983, Howard Gardner changed the way people perceived intelligence and learning with his theory of multiple intelligences. Gardner believed that the traditional view of **intelligence**, based on mathematical, logical, and verbal measurements that make up an "intelligence quotient" (IQ), did not reflect the spectrum of human ability. He focused on the idea that humans possess a number of different areas of natural ability and potential that he called *multiple intelligences*.

Intelligence
as defined by Howard Gardner, an ability to solve problems or create products that are of value in a culture.

© Reflektastudios/Fotolia

The Theory of Multiple Intelligences

Gardner's research led him to believe that there are eight unique "intelligences," or areas of ability. These include the areas traditionally associated with the term *intelligence*—logic and verbal skills—but go beyond, to encompass a range of human ability.[1] These intelligences almost never function in isolation. You will almost always use several at a time for any significant task.[2]

Look at Key 2.1 for descriptions of each intelligence along with examples of people who have unusually high levels of ability in each intelligence. Everyone has some level of ability in each intelligence. Your goal is to identify what your levels are and to work your strongest intelligences to your advantage.

The way Gardner defines intelligence emphasizes how different abilities have value in different arenas. In Tibet, for example, mountain dwellers prize the bodily kinesthetic ability of a top-notch Himalayan mountain guide, while in Detroit, automakers appreciate the visual-spatial talents of a master car designer.

Your Own Eight Intelligences

Gardner believes that all people possess some capacity in each of the eight intelligences, but each person has developed some intelligences more fully than others. When you find a task or subject easy, you are probably using a more fully developed intelligence. When you have trouble, you may be using a less developed intelligence.[3]

Gardner also believes your levels of development in the eight intelligences can grow or recede throughout your life, depending on effort and experience. For example, although you may not become a world-class pianist if you have limited musical ability, with focus and work you can develop what you have. Conversely, even a highly talented musician will lose ability without practice. The brain grows with learning and becomes sluggish without it.

Use the Multiple Pathways to Learning assessment to determine where you are right now in the eight intelligence areas. Then look at Key 2.2, immediately following the assessment, to identify specific skills associated with each area. Elsewhere in your text, you may find information about how to apply your learning preference knowledge to key success skills and to specific areas of study.

INTELLIGENCE	DESCRIPTION AND SKILLS	HIGH-ACHIEVING EXAMPLE
Verbal– Linguistic	Ability to communicate through language; listening, reading, writing, speaking	▪ Author J. K. Rowling ▪ Orator and President Barack Obama
Logical– Mathematical	Ability to understand logical reasoning and problem solving; math, science, patterns, sequences	▪ Physicist Stephen Hawking ▪ Mathematician Svetlana Jitomirskaya
Bodily– Kinesthetic	Ability to use the physical body skillfully and to take in knowledge through bodily sensation; coordination, working with hands	▪ Gymnast Nastia Liukin ▪ Survivalist Bear Gryllis
Visual– Spatial	Ability to understand spatial relationships and to perceive and create images; visual art, graphic design, charts and maps	▪ Artist Walt Disney ▪ Designer Stella McCartney
Interpersonal	Ability to relate to others, noticing their moods, motivations, and feelings; social activity, cooperative learning, teamwork	▪ Media personality Ellen Degeneres ▪ Former Secretary of State Colin Powell
Intrapersonal	Ability to understand one's own behavior and feelings; self-awareness, independence, time spent alone	▪ Animal researcher Jane Goodall ▪ Philosopher Friedrich Nietzsche
Musical	Ability to comprehend and create meaningful sound; sensitivity to music and musical patterns	▪ Singer and musician Alicia Keys ▪ Composer Andrew Lloyd Webber
Naturalist	Ability to identify, distinguish, categorize, and classify species or items, often incorporating high interest in elements of the natural environment	▪ Social activist Wangari Maathai ▪ Bird cataloger John James Audubon

MULTIPLE PATHWAYS TO LEARNING

Each intelligence has a set of numbered statements. Consider each statement on its own. Then, on a scale from 1 (lowest) to 4 (highest), rate how closely it matches who you are right now and write that number on the line next to the statement. Finally, total each set of six questions. Enter your scores in the grid on page 31.

1. rarely   2. sometimes   3. usually   4. always

1. _____ I enjoy physical activities.
2. _____ I am uncomfortable sitting still.
3. _____ I prefer to learn through doing.
4. _____ When sitting I move my legs or hands.
5. _____ I enjoy working with my hands.
6. _____ I like to pace when I'm thinking or studying.
_____ TOTAL for **BODILY–KINESTHETIC**

1. _____ I enjoy telling stories.
2. _____ I like to write.
3. _____ I like to read.
4. _____ I express myself clearly.
5. _____ I am good at negotiating.
6. _____ I like to discuss topics that interest me.
_____ TOTAL for **VERBAL–LINGUISTIC**

1. _____ I use maps and diagrams easily.
2. _____ I draw pictures/diagrams when explaining ideas.
3. _____ I can assemble items easily from diagrams.
4. _____ I enjoy drawing or photography.
5. _____ I do not like to read long paragraphs.
6. _____ I prefer a drawn map over written directions.
_____ TOTAL for **VISUAL–SPATIAL**

1. _____ I like math in school.
2. _____ I like science.
3. _____ I problem-solve well.
4. _____ I question how things work.
5. _____ I enjoy planning or designing something new.
6. _____ I am able to fix things.
_____ TOTAL for **LOGICAL–MATHEMATICAL**

1. _____ I listen to music.
2. _____ I move my fingers or feet when I hear music.
3. _____ I have good rhythm.
4. _____ I like to sing along with music.
5. _____ People have said I have musical talent.
6. _____ I like to express my ideas through music.
_____ TOTAL for **MUSICAL**

1. _____ I need quiet time to think.
2. _____ I think about issues before I want to talk.
3. _____ I am interested in self-improvement.
4. _____ I understand my thoughts and feelings.
5. _____ I know what I want out of life.
6. _____ I prefer to work on projects alone.
_____ TOTAL for **INTRAPERSONAL**

1. _____ I like doing a project with other people.
2. _____ People come to me to help settle conflicts.
3. _____ I like to spend time with friends.
4. _____ I am good at understanding people.
5. _____ I am good at making people feel comfortable.
6. _____ I enjoy helping others.
_____ TOTAL for **INTERPERSONAL**

1. _____ I like to think about how things, ideas, or people fit into categories.
2. _____ I enjoy studying plants, animals, or oceans.
3. _____ I tend to see how things relate to, or are distinct from, one another.
4. _____ I think about having a career in the natural sciences.
5. _____ As a child I often played with bugs and leaves.
6. _____ I like to investigate the natural world around me.
_____ TOTAL for **NATURALISTIC**

Source: Developed by Joyce Bishop, PhD, Golden West College, Huntington Beach, CA. Based on Howard Gardner, *Frames of Mind: The Theory of Multiple Intelligences*, New York: Harper Collins, 1993.

MULTIPLE PATHWAYS TO LEARNING

Scoring Grid for Multiple Pathways to Learning

For each intelligence, shade the box in the row that corresponds with the range where your score falls. For example, if you scored 17 in bodily-kinesthetic intelligence, you would shade the middle box in that row; if you scored a 13 in visual-spatial, you would shade the last box in that row. When you have shaded one box for each row, you will see a "map" of your range of development at a glance.

A score of 20–24 indicates a high level of development in that particular type of intelligence, 14–19 a moderate level, and below 14 an underdeveloped intelligence.

	20–24 (Highly Developed)	14–19 (Moderately Developed)	Below 14 (Underdeveloped)
Bodily-Kinesthetic			
Visual-Spatial			
Verbal-Linguistic			
Logical-Mathematical			
Musical			
Interpersonal			
Intrapersonal			
Naturalistic			

Verbal–Linguistic	- Remembering terms easily - Mastering a foreign language - Using writing or speech to convince someone to do or believe something
Musical–Rhythmic	- Sensing tonal qualities - Being sensitive to sounds and rhythms in music and in spoken language - Using an understanding of musical patterns to hear music
Logical–Mathematical	- Recognizing abstract patterns - Using facts to support an idea and generating ideas based on evidence - Reasoning scientifically (formulating and testing a hypothesis)
Visual–Spatial	- Recognizing relationships between objects - Representing something graphically - Manipulating images
Bodily–Kinesthetic	- Strong mind–body connection - Controlling and coordinating body movement - Using the body to create products or express emotion
Intrapersonal	- Accessing your internal emotions - Understanding your own feelings and using them to guide your behavior - Understanding yourself in relation to others
Interpersonal	- Seeing things from others' perspectives - Noticing moods, intentions, and temperaments of others - Gauging the most effective way to work with individual group members
Naturalistic	- Ability to categorize something as a member of a group or species - Understanding of relationships among natural organisms - Deep comfort with, and respect for, the natural world

Source: Adapted from David Lazear, *Seven Pathways of Learning*, Tucson: Zephyr, 1994.

Assess Your Style of Interaction with the Personality Spectrum

The concept of dividing human beings into four basic "personality types" goes as far back as the ancient Greek philosophers. Personality assessments help you understand how you respond to the world around you—people, work, and school—and guide you as you explore majors and careers. The Personality Spectrum self-assessment in this chapter is based on the Myers–Briggs Type Indicator (MBTI), developed by Katharine Briggs and her daughter, Isabel Briggs Myers (www.myersbriggs.org). as well as the Keirsey Sorter, a condensed four-temperament version of the 16 MBTI types that was created by David Keirsey and Marilyn Bates (www.keirsey.com).

Personality Spectrum assessment creator Joyce Bishop adapted and simplified the Keirsey Sorter and MBTI material into four personality types—Thinker, Organizer, Giver, and Adventurer. Like the assessments on which it is based, the Personality Spectrum helps you identify the kinds of interactions that are most, and least, comfortable for you. Complete the Personality Spectrum assessment and then plot your results on the scoring diagram. As with multiple intelligences, these results may change over time as you experience new things and change and continue to learn. Key 2.3 shows the skills associated with each personality type.

Key 2.3 Particular abilities and skills are associated with each Personality Spectrum dimension.

Thinker	
	• Solving problems
	• Developing models and systems
	• Analytical and abstract thinking

Organizer	
	• Responsibility, reliability
	• Neatness, organization, attention to detail
	• Comprehensive follow-through on tasks

Giver	
	• Successful, close relationships
	• Making a difference in the world
	• Negotiation, promoting peace

Adventurer	
	• Courageous and daring
	• Hands-on problem solving
	• Active and spontaneous style

Source: ©2001, Joyce Bishop, in *Keys to Success*, 3rd ed., Upper Saddle River, NJ: Pearson Prentice Hall, 2001.

PERSONALITY
SPECTRUM

STEP 1 Rank-order all four responses to each question from most like you (4) to least like you (1) so that for each question you use the numbers 1, 2, 3, and 4 one time each. Place numbers in the boxes next to the responses.

4. most like me   3. more like me   2. less like me   1. least like me

1. I like instructors who
   a. ☐ tell me exactly what is expected of me.
   b. ☐ make learning active and exciting.
   c. ☐ maintain a safe and supportive classroom.
   d. ☐ challenge me to think at higher levels.

2. I learn best when the material is
   a. ☐ well organized.
   b. ☐ something I can do hands-on.
   c. ☐ about understanding and improving the human condition.
   d. ☐ intellectually challenging.

3. A high priority in my life is to
   a. ☐ keep my commitments.
   b. ☐ experience as much of life as possible.
   c. ☐ make a difference in the lives of others.
   d. ☐ understand how things work.

4. Other people think of me as
   a. ☐ dependable and loyal.
   b. ☐ dynamic and creative.
   c. ☐ caring and honest.
   d. ☐ intelligent and inventive.

5. When I experience stress I would most likely
   a. ☐ do something to help me feel more in control of my life.
   b. ☐ do something physical and daring.
   c. ☐ talk with a friend.
   d. ☐ go off by myself and think about my situation.

6. I would probably not be close friends with someone who is
   a. ☐ irresponsible.
   b. ☐ unwilling to try new things.
   c. ☐ selfish and unkind to others.
   d. ☐ an illogical thinker.

7. My vacations could be described as
   a. ☐ traditional.
   b. ☐ adventuresome.
   c. ☐ pleasing to others.
   d. ☐ a new learning experience.

8. One word that best describes me is
   a. ☐ sensible.
   b. ☐ spontaneous.
   c. ☐ giving.
   d. ☐ analytical.

STEP 2 Add up the total points for each letter.

TOTAL FOR   a. _____ Organizer   b. _____ Adventurer   c. _____ Giver   d. _____ Thinker

STEP 3 Plot these numbers on the brain diagram on page 35.

Scoring Diagram for Personality Spectrum

Write your scores from page 34 in the four squares just outside the brain diagram—Thinker score at top left, Giver score at top right, Organizer score at bottom left, and Adventurer score at bottom right.

Each square has a line of numbers that go from the square to the center of the diagram. For each of your four scores, place a dot on the appropriate number in the line near that square. For example, if you scored 15 in the Giver spectrum, you would place a dot between the 14 and 16 in the upper right-hand line of numbers. If you scored a 26 in the Organizer spectrum, you would place a dot on the 26 in the lower left-hand line of numbers. Connect the four dots to make a shape that gives you a visual representation of your level of development in each dimension.

THINKER

Technical
Scientific
Mathematical
Dispassionate
Rational
Analytical
Logical
Problem Solving
Theoretical
Intellectual
Objective
Quantitative
Explicit
Realistic
Literal
Precise
Formal

ORGANIZER

Tactical
Planning
Detailed
Practical
Confident
Predictable
Controlled
Dependable
Systematic
Sequential
Structured
Administrative
Procedural
Organized
Conservative
Safekeeping
Disciplined

GIVER

Interpersonal
Emotional
Caring
Sociable
Giving
Spiritual
Musical
Romantic
Feeling
Peacemaker
Trusting
Adaptable
Passionate
Harmonious
Idealistic
Talkative
Honest

ADVENTURER

Active
Visual
Risking
Original
Artistic
Spatial
Skillful
Impulsive
Metaphoric
Experimental
Divergent
Fast-paced
Simultaneous
Competitive
Imaginative
Open-minded
Adventuresome

The more balanced the shape (closer to a square), the more equally developed the four spectrums of your personality. However, many people's shapes show one or two areas that are more developed than the others.

For the Personality Spectrum,
26–36 indicates a strong tendency in that dimension
14–25 indicates a moderate tendency
0–13 indicates a minimal tendency

Source for brain diagram: Morris, Charles G., *Understanding Psychology*, 3rd, ©1996. Electronically reproduced by permission of Pearson Education, Inc.

How Can You Use Your Self-Knowledge? *(how does this all translate into daily life?)*

As you analyze learning preferences through completing assessments, you develop a clearer picture of who you are and how you interact with others. Now—and most importantly—focus on how you can use your self-knowledge to self-direct and choose effective strategies during class time, when studying, and as you pursue a career.

Class Time Choices

The opportunity for choice lies in how you interact with your instructor and function in the classroom. Because it is impossible for instructors to tailor classroom presentation to 15, 40, or 300 unique learners, you may find yourself in sync with one teacher and mismatched with another. Sometimes, the way the class is structured can have more of an effect on your success than the subject matter; for example, a strong interpersonal learner who has trouble writing may unexpectedly do well in a composition course emphasizing group work.

After several class meetings, you should be able to assess each instructor's dominant teaching styles (see Key 2.4). Because the word-focused lecture (either in person or in a video or text online) is still the most common way instructors deliver information, the traditional course generally works best for verbal or logical learners and Thinkers and Organizers.

Your preferences might not match up with how one or more of your instructors teach. You might have many lecture-based classes but lack strength in verbal intelligence or Organizer qualities. You might find it challenging to adjust from course to course based on how different each experience is from another. What can you do?

Play to your strengths. For example, if you're a kinesthetic learner, you might rewrite or type your lecture notes, make flash cards, or take walks while saying important terms and concepts out loud. Likewise, if you are a Giver with an instructor who delivers straight lectures, consider setting up a study group to go over details and fill in factual gaps.

Work to strengthen weaker areas. As a visual learner reviews notes from a structured lecture, he could use logical-mathematical strategies such as outlining notes or thinking about cause-and-effect relationships within the material. An Organizer, studying for a test from notes delivered by an instructor with a random presentation, could organize the material in different formats, including tables and timelines.

Broaden your educational experience by interacting with instructors outside of class time, either virtually or in person.

© Pixland/Getty Images

Key 2.4   Instructors often prefer one or more teaching styles.

TEACHING STYLE	WHAT TO EXPECT IN CLASS
Lecture, verbal focus	Instructor speaks to the class for the entire period, with little class interaction. Lesson is taught primarily through words, either spoken or written on the board, on PowerPoints in class or online, with handouts or text, or possibly through podcasts.
Lecture with group discussion	Instructor presents material but encourages class discussion.
Small groups	Instructor presents material and then breaks class into small groups for discussion or project work.
Visual focus	Instructor uses visual elements such as PowerPoint slides, diagrams, photographs, drawings, transparencies, in-class or "YouTube for Schools" videos, or movies.
Logical presentation	Instructor organizes material in a logical sequence, such as by steps, time, or importance.
Random presentation	Instructor tackles topics in no particular order, and may jump around a lot or digress.
Conceptual presentation	Instructor spends the majority of time on the big picture, focusing on abstract concepts and umbrella ideas.
Detailed presentation	Instructor spends the majority of time, after introducing ideas, on the details and facts that underlie them.
Hands-on presentation	Instructor uses demonstrations, experiments, props, and class activities to show key points.

Ask your instructor for additional help.   Connect through e-mail or during office hours. Building a relationship with an instructor or a teaching assistant can be rewarding, especially in large lectures where you are anonymous unless you speak up. For example, a visual learner might ask the instructor to recommend figures or videos to study that illustrate the lecture.

Get help from technology.   If your course has an online course page, look on that page for accessible resources that may supplement your in-class experience. If you can or should use a computer during class time, you can use a platform like Google Docs or Evernote to take notes. Platforms like Pinterest allow you to incorporate visual elements with text, which can benefit someone with strong visual-spatial intelligence. Smartpens or Voice Memo can allow you to record a lecture if you benefit from hearing it back repeatedly.

The adjustments you make for your instructor's teaching style will build the flexibility that you need for career and life success. Just as you can't hand pick your instructors, you will rarely, if ever, be able to choose your work colleagues. You will have to adjust to them, and they to you. Keep in mind, too, that research shows a benefit from learning in a variety of ways—kind of like cross-training for the brain. Knowing this, some instructors may challenge you to learn in ways that aren't comfortable for you.

A final point: Some students try to find out more about an instructor by asking students who have already taken the course or looking up comments that appear online. Be careful: You may not know or be able to trust an anonymous poster who comments on an instructor, and even if you hear a review from a friend you do trust, every student–instructor relationship is unique. An instructor your friend loved may turn out to be a bad match for you, or vice versa. Prioritize taking the courses that you need, and know that you will find a way to make the most of what your instructors offer, no matter who they are.

Study Choices

Because you have more control over your study time than over your class time, studying presents an exceptional opportunity for self-direction. Start now to use what you have learned about yourself to choose your best study techniques. For example, if you tend to learn successfully from a linear, logical presentation, look for order (for example, a timeline of information organized by event dates) as you review notes. If you are strong in intrapersonal intelligence, you could find quiet, solitary spaces to study whenever possible.

Make choices that improve weak areas.   When faced with a task that challenges your weaknesses, use strategies that boost your ability. For example, if you are an Adventurer who does *not* respond well to linear information, try applying your strengths to the material using a hands-on approach. Or you can try developing your area of weakness by using study skills that work well for Thinker-dominant learners.

Understand other team members.   When studying in a group, understanding one another's learning preferences will help you work more effectively and promote better communication. Certain tasks in a group project will be suited to specific team members based on their preferences, and if people have the opportunity to put their strengths to work, good results are more likely.

Use tech tools.   There is a digital way to use almost any study strategy you prefer, and new technology appears all the time (making the habit of continual learning even more valuable). You can create digital flash cards, use Skype to work with a study partner, organize notes with a digital note-taking app, and more. If you know that technology interests and motivates you, incorporate it into your routine. If you discover that you are less comfortable with technology but need to improve, look at how your strengths can serve

First, on paper or on a computer, summarize yourself as a learner in a paragraph or two. Focus on what you learned about yourself from the chapter assessments. Done? Check here. _____

Next, schedule a meeting with your academic advisor (use your interpersonal intelligence).

Name of advisor: _____

Time/date of meeting: _____

Give the advisor an overview of your learning strengths and challenges, based on your summary. Ask for advice about courses that might interest you and majors that might suit you. Take notes.

Indicate two courses to consider in the next year:

1. _____

2. _____

Indicate two possible majors:

1. _____

2. _____

Finally, create a separate to-do list of how you plan to explore one course offering and one major. Set a deadline for each task.

---

you. For example, an interpersonal learner may ask for help from a tech-savvy classmate, and a Thinker may prefer an online tutorial.

Key 2.5 shows study strategies that suit each intelligence, and Key 2.6 shows study strategies that suit each Personality Spectrum dimension. Because you have some level of ability in each area, and because you will sometimes need to boost your ability in a weaker area, you may find useful suggestions under any of the headings. Try different techniques. Pay attention to what works best for you. You may be surprised at what you find useful.

Key 2.5 Choose study techniques to maximize each intelligence.

Verbal-Linguistic

- Read text; highlight selectively
- Use a computer to retype and summarize notes
- Outline chapters
- Recite information or write scripts/debates

Musical-Rhythmic

- Create rhythms out of words
- Beat out rhythms with hand or stick while reciting concepts
- Write songs/raps that help you learn concepts
- Write out study material to fit into a wordless tune you have on a CD or MP3 player; chant or sing the material along with the tune as you listen

Logical-Mathematical

- Organize material logically; if it suits the topic, use a spreadsheet program
- Sequentially explain material to someone
- Develop systems and find patterns
- Analyze and evaluate information

Visual-Spatial

- Develop graphic organizers for new material
- Draw "think links" (mind maps)
- Use a computer to develop charts and tables
- Use color in your notes for organization

Bodily-Kinesthetic

- Move while you learn; pace and recite
- Rewrite or retype notes to engage "muscle memory"
- Design and play games to learn material
- Act out scripts of material

Intrapersonal

- Reflect on personal meaning of information
- Keep a journal
- Study in quiet areas
- Imagine essays or experiments before beginning

Interpersonal

- Study in a group
- As you study, discuss information over the phone or send instant messages
- Teach someone else the material
- Make time to discuss assignments and tests with your instructor

Naturalistic

- Break down information into categories
- Look for ways in which items fit or don't fit together
- Look for relationships among ideas, events, facts
- Study in a natural setting if it helps you focus

Source: Adapted from David Lazear, *Seven Pathways of Learning*, Tucson: Zephyr, 1994.

Thinker		• Convert material into logical charts, flow diagrams, and outlines • Reflect independently on new information • Learn through problem solving • Design new ways of approaching material or problems
Organizer		• Define tasks in concrete terms • Use a planner to schedule tasks and dates • Organize material by rewriting and summarizing class and/or text notes • Create, or look for, a well-structured study environment
Giver		• Study with others in person, on the phone, or using instant messages • Teach material to others • Seek out tasks, groups, and subjects that involve helping people • Connect with instructors, advisors, and tutors
Adventurer		• Look for environments/courses that encourage nontraditional approaches • Find hands-on ways to learn • Use or develop games or puzzles to help memorize terms • Fight boredom by asking to do something extra or perform a task in a more active way

Source: ©2001, Joyce Bishop, in *Keys to Success*, 3rd ed., Upper Saddle River, NJ: Pearson Prentice Hall, 2001.

Workplace Choices

Knowing how you learn and interact with others will help you work more effectively and make more targeted and productive career planning choices. How can a self-directed employee or job candidate benefit from self-awareness?

Better performance and teamwork. When you understand your strengths, you can find ways to use them on the job more readily, as well as determine how to compensate for tasks that take you out of your areas of strength. In addition, you will be better able to work with others. For example, a team leader might offer an intrapersonal team member the chance to take material home to think about before attending a meeting; an Adventurer might find ways to spearhead new projects, while delegating the detailed research to a Thinker on the team.

Inside Tips from Carol, Career Coach

Many different sources can introduce you to careers. Some students get interested in careers through watching TV shows, for example. However, if *NCIS* or *Criminal Minds* is your favorite show, it doesn't necessarily mean you are up for a career in forensics. Build understanding of yourself and your interests by asking specific questions. Someone interested in forensics might ask: Am I good in math and science? Am I a strong detail person? Can I deal with the seamy and scary?

If your exploration leads you to want to pursue a career interest, develop a list of places where you might intern or work, so that you can find out if the job or field makes sense for you. If you don't try out a field or profession, it is like marrying someone without ever dating. Experiment with all kinds of things to find out what feels right and energizes you.

POWERFUL QUESTIONS

STUDENT TO STUDENT

It is now common to have more than one career, and perhaps several, over your lifetime. Whether you change careers because you don't like what you're doing, you lose your job in an economic downturn, or new technology creates a significant shift, you may have to learn new skills. Pair up with a fellow student. Imagine yourself in development training several years after finishing college as you ask each other these questions:

Do you prefer a stable career trajectory, or are you more comfortable with change and instability? What are you willing to do to acquire new knowledge: On-the-job training? Going back to school for an additional degree? Self-study? What actions can you take now to help you build the Habit for Success of lifelong learning so that you can weather the ups and downs of life and work?

Better career planning.   Exploring ways to use your strengths in school will help you make better choices about what **internships**, jobs, or careers will suit you. For most college students, majors and internships are more immediate steps on the road to a career. Internships can give you a chance to "try out" your major in a workplace setting. You might even discover you don't have an interest in a career in that area, which could lead to switching majors.

Key 2.7 links majors and internships to the eight intelligences. This list represents only a fraction of the available opportunities. Use what you see here to inspire thought and spur investigation. If something from this list or elsewhere interests you, consider looking for an opportunity to "shadow" someone (i.e., follow an individual for a day to see what he or she does) to see if you might want to commit to an internship or major.

Internship
a temporary work program that allows you to gain supervised, practical experience in a job and career area.

How Can You Identify and Manage Learning Disabilities? *(and how are they different from regular challenges?)*

Although all students have areas of strength and weakness, some challenges are more significant and are diagnosed as learning disabilities. These merit specific attention. Focused assistance can help students who are learning disabled manage their conditions and excel in school.

MULTIPLE INTELLIGENCE		CONSIDER MAJORING IN	THINK ABOUT AN INTERNSHIP AT A
Bodily-Kinesthetic		■ Massage or physical therapy ■ Kinesiology ■ Construction engineering ■ Sports medicine ■ Dance or theater	■ Sports physician's office ■ Physical or massage therapy center ■ Construction company ■ Dance studio or theater company ■ Athletic club
Intrapersonal		■ Psychology ■ Finance ■ Computer science ■ Biology ■ Philosophy	■ Accounting firm ■ Biology lab ■ Pharmaceutical company ■ Publishing house ■ Computer or Internet company
Interpersonal		■ Education ■ Public relations ■ Nursing ■ Business ■ Hotel/restaurant management	■ Hotel or restaurant ■ Social service agency ■ Public relations firm ■ Human resources department ■ Charter school
Naturalistic		■ Geology ■ Zoology ■ Atmospheric sciences ■ Agriculture ■ Environmental law	■ Museum ■ National park ■ Environmental law firm ■ Zoo ■ Geological research firm
Musical		■ Music ■ Music theory ■ Voice ■ Composition ■ Performing arts	■ Performance hall ■ Radio station ■ Record label or recording studio ■ Children's music camp ■ Orchestra or opera company
Logical-Mathematical		■ Math ■ Physics ■ Economics ■ Banking/finance ■ Computer science	■ Law firm ■ Consulting firm ■ Bank ■ Information technology company ■ Research lab
Verbal-Linguistic		■ Communications ■ Marketing ■ English/literature ■ Journalism ■ Foreign languages	■ Newspaper or magazine ■ PR/marketing firm ■ Ad agency ■ Publishing house ■ Network TV affiliate
Visual-Spatial		■ Architecture ■ Visual arts ■ Multimedia designs ■ Photography ■ Art history	■ Photo or art studio ■ Multimedia design firm ■ Architecture firm ■ Interior design firm ■ Art gallery

Identifying a Learning Disability

The National Center for Learning Disabilities (NCLD) states that learning disabilities:[4]

- Are neurological disorders that interfere with one's ability to understand or use language, spoken or written.
- *Do not* include intellectual disability, autism, behavioral disorders, impaired vision, hearing loss, or other physical disabilities.
- *Do not* include attention-deficit disorder and attention-deficit/hyperactivity disorder, although these problems are often associated with learning disabilities.[5]
- Often run in families and are lifelong conditions, although specific strategies can help people with learning disabilities manage and even overcome areas of challenge.

How can you determine if you should be evaluated for a learning disability? According to the NCLD, persistent issues in any of the following areas may indicate one is present:[6]

- Reading or reading comprehension
- Math calculations, understanding language and concepts
- Social skills or interpreting social cues
- Following a schedule, being on time, meeting deadlines
- Reading or following maps
- Balancing a checkbook
- Following directions, especially on multistep tasks
- Writing, sentence structure, spelling, and organizing written work

Details on specific learning disabilities appear in Key 2.8. For an evaluation, contact your school's learning center or student health center for a referral to a licensed professional. A professional diagnosis is required for a person with learning disabilities seeking to receive federally funded aid.

Managing a Learning Disability

If you are diagnosed with a learning disability, you can maximize your ability to learn by being both self-directed and willing to continue to learn about yourself. Keep in mind that you are in charge of if and when you tell people about your disability. You may disclose it prior to enrollment, at the time of enrollment, or during a course, or you may choose not to discuss it at all if you believe you can cope on your own.[7] Here are ways to manage:

Be informed about your disability. Search the library and the Internet—try NCLD at www.ncld.org or LD Online at www.ldonline.org, or call NCLD at 1-888-575-7373. If you have an Individualized Education Program (IEP)—

DISABILITY OR CONDITION	WHAT ARE THE SIGNS?
Dyslexia and related reading disorders	Problems with reading (spelling, word sequencing, comprehension, reading out loud) and with translating written language into thought or thought into written language
Dyscalculia (developmental arithmetic discorders)	Difficulty recognizing numbers and symbols, memorizing facts, understanding abstract math concepts, applying math to life skills (time management, handling money), and performing mental math calculations
Developmental writing disorders	Difficulty composing sentences, organizing a writing assignment, or translating thoughts coherently to the page
Handwriting disorders (dysgraphia)	Distorted or incorrect language, inappropriately sized and spaced letters, wrong or misspelled words, difficulty putting thoughts on paper or grasping grammar, large gap between spoken language skills and written skills
Speech and language disorders	Problems with producing speech sounds, using spoken language to communicate, or understanding what others say
LD-related social issues	Problems recognizing facial or vocal cues from others, understanding how others are feeling, controlling verbal and physical impulsivity, and respecting others' personal space
LD-related organizational issues	Difficulty scheduling and organizing personal, academic, and work-related materials

Source: LD Online: LD Basics, http://www.ncld.org/content/view/445/389, © 2009.

a document describing your disability and recommended strategies—read it and make sure you understand it.

Seek assistance from your school.   Speak with your advisor about getting a referral to the counselor who can help you get specific accommodations in your classes. Services mandated by law for students with learning disabilities include:

- Extended time on tests
- Note-taking assistance (for example, having another student take notes for you)
- Assistive technology devices (MP3 players, tape recorders, laptop computers)
- Modified assignments
- Alternative assessments and test formats

Other services that may be offered include tutoring, study-skills assistance, and counseling.

Be a dedicated student. Be on time and attend class. Read assignments before class. Sit where you can focus. Review notes soon after class. Spend extra time on assignments. Ask for help.

Understand your learning preferences. Students with learning disabilities can use their strengths to compensate. For example, a strong Organizer who has trouble processing heard language can reinforce learning through retyping notes or summarizing textbook materials.

Finally, build a positive attitude. Focus on what you have achieved and on how far you have come. Rely on support from others, knowing it will give you the best possible chance to succeed.

HABIT IN ACTION WRAP-UP

© Courtesy of Austin Yellen

What happened with Austin?

Early on, Austin had a fortunate experience while rushing his fraternity. During a mandatory study session, an older fraternity brother remarked: "High school is a place where knowledge is spoon-fed to you. College is a place where you come to seek knowledge." This statement had a profound effect on Austin, changing his entire attitude toward school and learning. He realized he had the freedom to learn whatever he wanted and to take his education where he wanted it to go.

Austin began sitting in the front of every class, whether in a 20-student room or a 300-person lecture hall. Observing other students' strategies, he learned how to take effective notes. He spoke up in class to stay engaged. These simple actions had significant results—his GPA at the end of his first year was two letter grades higher than his high school GPA.

Investigating how he could transfer into the business school, Austin found he would have to get a B or better in five specific courses. While he passed the first four, a combination of difficulty in math and stress from the loss of a close friend led to his failing calculus. Instead of giving up at that point, he redoubled his efforts, going to his professor's office hours and seeking tutoring from friends. He passed the course and is now in business school majoring in Finance, always keeping in mind what his fraternity brother told him.

Connect this story to your life: What are you driven to learn, and what are you willing to do to learn it? Identify a learning goal that you are willing to put effort into. Describe the specific ways in which you will self-direct and take initiative to achieve that goal.

Building Skills

for successful learning

Note the Important Points

Define the term *learning preference*. _____
_____
_____

Name two benefits of getting to know yourself as a learner. _____
_____
_____

Describe what the multiple intelligences assessment can help you discover. _____
_____
_____

What are the four dimensions of the Personality Spectrum assessment? _____
_____
_____

Name one way to use your understanding of how you learn . . .

. . . during class time. _____

. . . when studying. _____

. . . in the workplace. _____

Name two facts about learning disabilities. _____
_____
_____

Critical Thinking

Maximize Your Classroom Experience

Considering what you know about yourself as a learner and about your instructors' teaching styles this term, decide which class situation is the most challenging for you. Identify it here:

Course: _____   Instructor style: _____

Your view of the problem: _____

_____

_____

Describe three learning-preference-based actions you can take to improve the situation.

1. _____

_____

2. _____

_____

3. _____

_____

Finally, choose one action and put it to work. Briefly note what happened: Were there improvements as a result?

_____

_____

_____

_____

_____

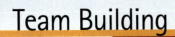

Team Building

collaborative solutions

Ideas About Personality Types

Divide into groups according to the four types of the Personality Spectrum–Thinker-dominant students in one group, Organizer-dominant students in another, Giver-dominant students in a third, and Adventurer-dominant students in the fourth. If you have scored the same in more than one of these types, join whatever group is smaller. With your group in person or through digital communication, generate lists as follows:

1. The strengths of this type

2. The struggles, or things that cause stress, for this type

3. Career areas that tend to suit this type

4. Types of people this type works well with

5. Types of people that cause stress for this type

If possible, each group can present this information in class or on a course website; this will boost understanding and acceptance of diverse ways of relating to information and people.

Learn More about Your Test-Taking Self Using a Self-Portrait

Complete the following on separate sheets of paper or electronically (if you can use a graphics program).

Getting ready for tests means more than just learning your material—it also requires the kind of self-knowledge that helps you make the best study choices. Build your ability to self-direct by combining what you've learned about yourself as a student into a comprehensive "self-portrait."

Design your portrait in "think-link" or mind-map style. A think link is a visual presentation of related ideas, similar to a map or web, which represents your thought process. Put your ideas inside geometric shapes (boxes or circles) and attach related ideas and facts using lines (you may find additional information about visual note-taking styles elsewhere in your text).

To get started, try using the style shown in Key 2.9. Put your main idea ("Me") in a shape in the center and then create a wheel of related ideas coming off that central shape, with lines connecting the thoughts that go with each idea. Describe your dominant multiple intelligences, Personality Spectrum dimensions, preferred teaching styles and classroom settings, preferred study situations (times, locations, company), abilities and interests, and anything else relevant to who you are as a test-taker.

After creating your self-portrait, make one new choice regarding how you will prepare for tests this term, to take advantage of a strength in a particular intelligence or Personality Spectrum dimension. Will you change your study location or time? Will you try a new study strategy?

_____

_____

_____

_____

You will change as you continue to learn. Revisit your self-portrait in the future—next term or even next year. Revise it to reflect what you've learned and how you've changed.

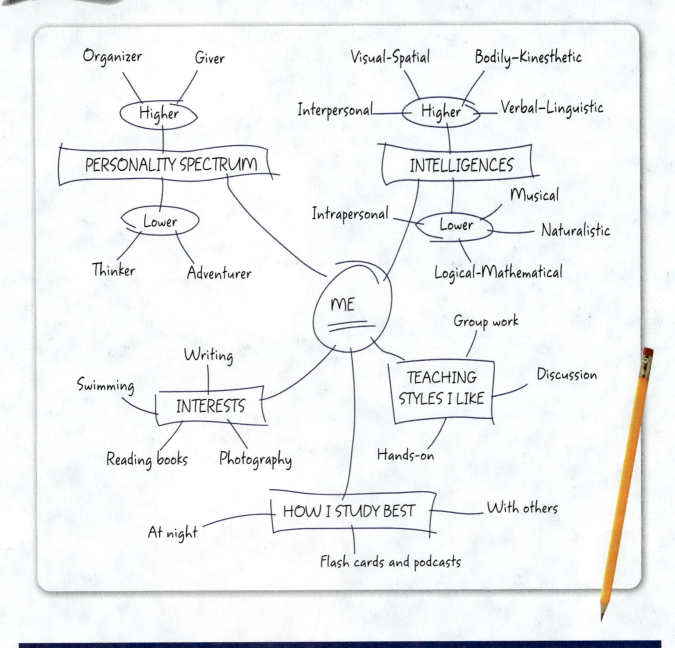

Organizer   Giver

Higher

PERSONALITY SPECTRUM

Lower

Thinker   Adventurer

Visual-Spatial   Bodily-Kinesthetic

Interpersonal   Higher   Verbal-Linguistic

INTELLIGENCES

Musical

Intrapersonal   Lower   Naturalistic

Logical-Mathematical

ME

Writing

Swimming   INTERESTS

Reading books   Photography

Group work

TEACHING
STYLES I LIKE   Discussion

Hands-on

HOW I STUDY BEST   With others

At night

Flash cards and podcasts

3

time and money

managing important resources

MISA GONZALES, *educational consultant and founder of MindFULL Learning Institute*

In school and in her working life, Misa Gonzales has found that following her vision leads to detours off traditional paths. Born and raised in Tucson, Arizona, she began assisting her parents—both art teachers—in the classroom at the age of 12 and later worked part-time teaching art for the Parks and Recreation Department. When her boss wanted to increase her hours, she signed a contract to work full time at the age of 16, attending a charter school 4 hours a day 4 days a week to accommodate her work commitments. At 17, during her junior year, she began taking community college coursework.

After graduation, busy with her job and her son who was born when she was 18, Misa set aside college plans temporarily. When she was 24 and now a single parent of two, the City of Tucson cut her job out of the budget. She began studying at Pima Community College, where she did well. However, through her coursework she noticed she was missing important knowledge, such as how to take useful notes and what a "thesis" is.

Misa completed her general education degree and started coursework at the University of Arizona in the business management program. After a semester, she told her advisor that she didn't belong there and asked where she might be better suited. Her advisor moved her to the College of Education and the English Department. Surprised by this abrupt change and struggling with the building blocks of effective writing, Misa felt far away from the plan she had anticipated. How would she get to where it all made sense?

(to be continued ...)

For nearly every student, college brings changes and challenges that you could not have anticipated—but planning, when you can, will help you manage. You'll learn more about Misa's experience at the end of the chapter.

Working through this chapter will help you to:

- Understand who you are as a time and money manager. p. 54
- Explore ways to build a schedule and prioritize tasks. p. 57
- Manage procrastination and time traps. p. 61
- Use a budget to evaluate and adjust spending and income. p. 63
- Investigate how to increase income through work and financial aid. p. 65
- Analyze the cost of credit and adjust credit use. p. 70

Text and photo used by permission of Misa Gonzales

anticipate

Thinking ahead about your time and your budget will help you cope with obstacles in your path. Anticipating roadblocks, *plan* a set of actions that will lead you toward your goals.

Who Are You as a Time and Money Manager? *(and how does that affect success in school?)*

Astudent may seem to have everything it takes to succeed in school—skill and talent, a well-chosen college and major, a strong support system, and the best of intentions. However, without time to study or money to pay tuition and expenses, success may be out of reach.

Time and money are essential resources for college students. Time is limited to 24 hours a day for everyone, and you need it to attend classes, study, and work on projects and assignments. Money is limited for most students, and you need it to pay for tuition, books, and other expenses. The key is to make smart decisions about how you use each.

These valuable resources are linked in several ways. For example, many students need time to work, so that they can earn the money to pay for expenses. Additionally, if you work, the money you spend costs you the time you spent earning it. For example, if you have a job that pays $10 an hour, a $200 purchase costs you 20 hours of work. Before making a purchase, it's wise to ask yourself if it's worth the time it took to earn the cost.

Another link between time and money is that it takes money to pay for time spent in college. Many students cannot afford to go to college full time, straight through the 2 or 4 years it takes to graduate. Such students make money-saving choices like attending part time while working, taking some or all courses online, or taking a year off to earn money for tuition.

Going to college may cost more hours of work than almost any other purchase. However, the tuition and time you spend will improve your earning power. Look at the statistics in Key 3.1 to see how college graduates tend to earn more in the workplace than nongraduates. Anticipate the benefit of your efforts, and see college as part of your plan for career success.

Effective time and money management plans are based on self-knowledge, so start by thinking about how you interact with these resources.

Who You Are as a Time Manager

Body rhythms and habits affect how each person deals with time. For example, while some people are night owls, others function best in the morning.

Key 3.1 More education is likely to mean more income.

Median annual income of persons with income 25 years old and over, by gender and highest level of education, 2009

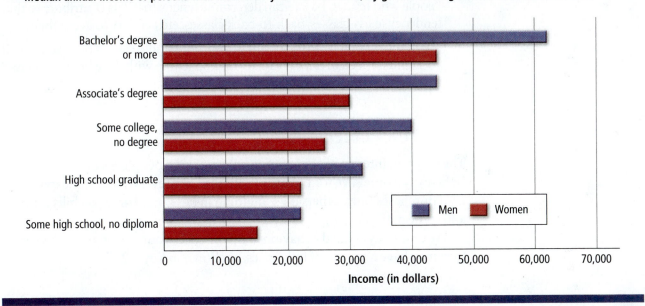

Source: U.S. Census Bureau, "Income, Poverty, and Health Insurance Coverage in the United States, 2009," *Current Population Reports*, Series P60-238, September 2010.

The more you understand your time-related behaviors, the better you can plan a schedule that maximizes strengths and reduces stress. To help time work for you rather than against you, do the following:

Create a personal time "profile." Ask yourself the following questions:

- At what time or times of day do I have the most energy? The least energy?
- Do I tend to be early, on time, or late?
- Do I focus well for long stretches or need regular breaks?

ALL ABOUT YOU

For each question, circle the number in the range that most applies to you.

My energy is best in the . . .	morning	1 2 3 4 5	evening
I tend to be . . .	always on time	1 2 3 4 5	always late
I focus best . . .	for long periods	1 2 3 4 5	for short periods
I'm most likely to . . .	save money	1 2 3 4 5	spend money
I put money toward . . .	things now	1 2 3 4 5	future needs
I would borrow money . . .	anytime	1 2 3 4 5	never

Consider your profile when creating a schedule.   For example:

- Early birds may try to schedule early classes; people whose energy peaks later may look for classes in the afternoons or evenings.

- People who tend to be late can determine what situations contribute to this tendency (early classes, back-to-back classes, etc.) and try to avoid them.

- If you focus well for long stretches, you can handle classes back to back; if you tend to need breaks, try to set up a schedule with time between class meetings.

How You Perceive and Use Money

The way you interact with money is unique. Some people spend earnings right away, some save for the future. Some charge everything, some make cash purchases only, others do something in between. Some pay bills online and some mail checks.

Your money-related behaviors tend to reflect your values and goals, and they may have a variety of influences, as shown in Key 3.2.

Key 3.2   **Many factors affect how you manage money.**

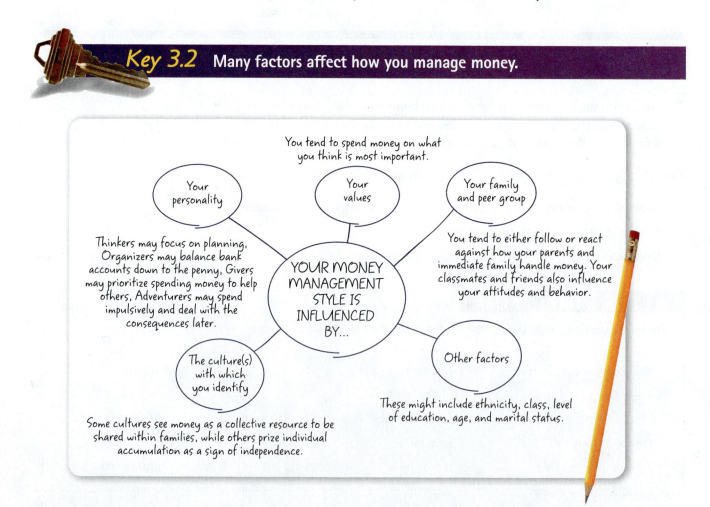

You tend to spend money on what you think is most important.

Your personality

Your values

Your family and peer group

YOUR MONEY MANAGEMENT STYLE IS INFLUENCED BY...

Thinkers may focus on planning, Organizers may balance bank accounts down to the penny, Givers may prioritize spending money to help others, Adventurers may spend impulsively and deal with the consequences later.

You tend to either follow or react against how your parents and immediate family handle money. Your classmates and friends also influence your attitudes and behavior.

The culture(s) with which you identify

Other factors

Some cultures see money as a collective resource to be shared within families, while others prize individual accumulation as a sign of independence.

These might include ethnicity, class, level of education, age, and marital status.

Improving how you handle money requires that you analyze your attitudes and behaviors. Says money coach Connie Kilmark, "If managing money was just about math and the numbers, everyone would know how to manage their finances sometime around the fifth grade."[1] Once you take a hard look at your approach to money, you can make real-life money decisions based on what works best for you.

Now that you are thinking about your tendencies, take a closer look at your resources. First explore time, the resource accessible to everyone.

How Can You Manage Your Time?
(when there seems to be so little of it?)

Consider each day as a jigsaw puzzle: You have all the pieces (seconds, minutes, hours) in a pile, and your task is to anticipate how you want your day to look. Start by building the schedule that works best for you.

Build a Schedule

Schedules help you gain control of your life in two ways: They provide segments of time for things you have to do, and they remind you of events, due dates, responsibilities, and deadlines. Your first step is to find a planner that will help you achieve the control a schedule can provide.

Choose a Planner

Get a planner that works for how you live. There are two major types:

- A book or notebook, showing either a day or a week at a glance, where you note your commitments.

- A program on an electronic planner or smartphone. Basic functions allow you to schedule days and weeks, note due dates, and make to-do lists. If your electronic planner has a companion computer program, which many do (examples include iCal and Google Calendar), you can back up your schedule on a computer and view it there.

Although electronic devices are handy, powerful, and capable of all kinds of functioning, they are not cheap, the software can fail, and batteries can die. Analyze your preferences and finances and choose the best tool for you. A blank notebook, used every day, may work as well for some students as a top-of-the-line smartphone.

© Courtesy of Sarah Lyman Kravits

Schedule and Prioritize Tasks, Events, and Commitments

Prioritizing helps you focus the bulk of your energy and time on your most important tasks. Since many top-priority items (classes, work) occur at designated times, prioritizing helps you anticipate these activities and plan less urgent tasks around them.

You can use a system of levels to prioritize your tasks.

- **Priority 1.** These are crucial, high-stakes items that you must do, usually at a specific time. They may include attending class, working at a job, caring for a child or parent.

- **Priority 2.** These are important items that have some flexibility in scheduling. Examples include study time and exercising.

- **Priority 3.** These are less crucial items. Examples include calling a friend or downloading songs onto your iPod.

Next, use the following steps to lay everything out in your planner:

1. **Enter Priority 1 items in your planner first.** This means class times and days for the term, including labs and other required commitments; work hours; and essential personal responsibilities such as health-related appointments or childcare.

2. **Enter key dates from your course syllabi.** When you get your syllabi for the term, enter all test and quiz dates, due dates for assignments, presentation dates for projects, holidays, and breaks in your planner.

3. **Enter dates of events and commitments.** Put commitments in your schedule where you can see and plan for them. Include club and organizational meetings, in-person or online events you need to attend, and personal commitments such as medical appointments, family events, work obligations, or important social events.

4. **Schedule Priority 2 items around existing items.** Once you have the essentials set, put in study time, workouts, study group meetings, and other important but flexible items. Schedule class prep time—reading and studying, writing, and working on assignments and projects—in the planner as you would any other activity. As a rule, schedule at least 2 hours of preparation for every hour of class—that is, if you take 12 credits, you'll spend 24 hours or more a week on course-related activities in and out of class.

5. **Include Priority 3 items where possible.** Schedule these items, such as social time or doing errands, around the items already locked in.

Once your schedule is filled out, decide on a visual way to indicate priority level. Some people use numbers or letters (A, B, C). Others write different priority items in different-colored pens (red for Priority 1, blue for Priority 2, etc.). Electronic planners may allow you to color-code or flag items according to priority.

Key 3.3 shows parts of a daily schedule and weekly schedule.

Prioritize
to arrange or deal with tasks in order of importance.

Monday, March 14

Time	Tasks	Priority
6:00 A.M.		
7:00		
8:00	Up at 8am — finish homework	
9:00		
10:00	Business Administration	
11:00	Renew driver's license @ DMV	
12:00 P.M.		
1:00	Lunch	
2:00	Writing Seminar (peer editing to...	
3:00	↓	
4:00	check on Ms. Schwartz's office h...	
5:00	5:30 work out	
6:00	↳ 6:30	
7:00	Dinner	
8:00	Read two chapters for	
9:00	Business Admin.	
10:00		
11:00		
12:00		

Monday, March 28

8		Call: Mike Blair	1
9	BIO 212	Financial Aid Office	2
10			3
11	CHEM 203	EMS 262 *Paramedic	4
12		role-play*	5
Evening	6pm yoga class		

Tuesday, March 29

8	Finish reading assignment!	Work @ library	1
9			2
10	ENG 112	(study for quiz)	3
11	↓		4
12			5
Evening		until 7pm	

Wednesday, March 30

8		Meet w/advisor	1
9	BIO 212		2
10		EMS 262	3
11	CHEM 203 *Quiz		4
12		Pick up photos	5
Evening	6pm Dinner w/study group		

Make Your Schedule Work for You

Once your schedule is written, it's time to put it to use. These strategies will help.

Plan regularly.   Set aside regular periods: each day to plan the next day and the weekend to plan the next week. Keep your planner with you at all times, and check it periodically.

Look at your term or semester all at once.   Finals week is *not* the only busy week you'll face. If you map out your biggest responsibilities from the beginning to the end of the term, you can see where your work-heavy weeks come up and can anticipate how to handle them. For example, a student with three tests and a presentation in one week in November may adjust a work schedule, arrange extra child care, or plan extra blocks of study time.

Make and use to-do lists. Use a *to-do* list to record the things you want to accomplish on a busy day or for a particular challenge like exam week or a major project. Write items on separate paper, prioritize the list, and then transfer the items you plan to accomplish each day to open time slots in your planner.

Post monthly calendars at home. Use a monthly wall calendar for an overview of your major commitments and upcoming events. If you live with family or friends, create a group calendar to stay on top of plans and avoid scheduling conflicts. Try having each person write commitments in a particular color.

Schedule downtime. Taking time off—to watch a show, text friends, go for a walk with someone, work out, take a nap—will refresh you and actually improve your productivity when you get back on task. Even small 10-minute breathers within study sessions can help you find more of a balance between work and play.

Manage time traps. Everyone experiences *time traps*—situations and activities that eat up time you could spend in a more productive way. Note what

TAKE ACTION
Make a To-Do List

Make a to-do list for your busiest day this coming week. Note tasks and events, including class and study time, and activities you would like to do (exercising, lunch with a friend) if you have extra time. Then use a coding system to categorize your list according to priority.

Date: _____

1. _____

2. _____

3. _____

4. _____

5. _____

6. _____

7. _____

8. _____

9. _____

10. _____

11. _____

12. _____

Now record this day's schedule in your planner, including items from this list where they fit. At the end of the day, evaluate this system. If the to-do list helped you manage your time and tasks effectively, try using it on a daily or weekly basis or on your busiest days.

distracts you most (Facebook, Instagram, Funny or Die videos, sending messages to friends, and so on) and make conscious decisions about when and how long you do these activities so that they don't derail your most important goals. This is not to say you should eliminate all fun from your schedule —just control it, so it doesn't control you.

Be flexible. Sudden changes can and will upset your plans. For changes that occur frequently, such as a job that tends to run into overtime, set up a backup plan (or two) ahead of time. For sudden changes, such as car breakdowns or health issues, use problem-solving skills to help you through (your course this term may include more detailed information about problem solving). Your academic advisor, counselor, dean, financial aid advisor, and instructors can provide ideas and assistance.

© LifeBound, LLC

Balance means getting your work done as well as finding time to have fun with friends.

Fight Procrastination

It's human, and common for busy students, to leave difficult or undesirable tasks until later. However, if taken to the extreme, **procrastination** can cause serious problems. For example, workplace procrastinators who don't finish tasks may prevent others from doing their work, sabotage a project, or even lose a job because of it. Procrastinating takes the power away from the habit of anticipating and planning, because it stops you from putting your plans into action.

If procrastination can cause such major issues, why do it? One reason people procrastinate is to avoid the truth about what they can achieve. "As long as you procrastinate, you never have to confront the real limits of your ability, whatever those limits are,"[2] say procrastination experts Jane B. Burka and Lenora Yuen, authors of *Procrastination: Why You Do It and What to Do About It.*

Here are some strategies that can help you avoid procrastination and its negative effects.

> **Procrastination**
> the act of putting off a task until another time.

- **Analyze the effects.** What benefit will remain out of reach if you continue to put off a task? Chances are you will gain more in the long term by facing the task head-on.

- **Set reasonable goals.** Because unreasonable goals can immobilize, take manageable steps. If you concentrate on achieving one small step at a time, the task becomes less burdensome.

- **Get started whether you "feel like it" or not.** Break the paralysis of doing nothing by doing something—anything. Most people, once they start, find it easier to continue.

Inside Tips from Sarah, Academic Coach

Technology can save you a tremendous amount of time, but it can also be an enormous time drain, as when you start texting friends or surfing YouTube on a study break and look up to see that an hour has passed. Ask yourself: What does it cost me to spend an hour, or two, or three, on social media? What amount gives me the fun and connection I need while not affecting my academic goals? Use your self-knowledge and scheduling skills to control your social tech time. One idea that works for some students is to read for 25 minutes and spend 5 minutes on social media time every half-hour, using an alarm to get back on task.

- **Ask for help.** Once you identify what's holding you up, find someone to help you face the task. Another person may come up with an innovative method to get you moving again.

- **Don't expect perfection.** People learn by approaching mistakes with a growth mindset. Richard Sheridan, president of Menlo Innovations, fosters a culture of exploration by telling his employees to "make mistakes faster."[3]

- **Acknowledge progress.** When you accomplish a task, celebrate with whatever feels like fun to you.

The Myth of Multitasking

Although many believe that multitasking is a crucial skill, research has shown that the human brain is biologically capable of doing only one thinking task at a time. When you try to do two tasks at once (like talking on the phone while reading e-mail), you are actually "switch-tasking," meaning that your brain works on one thing at a time, interrupting the first activity with the second and then switching back. The time it takes to switch from one activity to another is called *switching time*.[4]

POWERFUL QUESTIONS

anticipate

STUDENT TO STUDENT

Think about what leads you to procrastinate—a particular kind of assignment, a certain course, instructions from a person you find difficult. Pair up with a fellow student. Take turns asking each other:

What do you tend to put off, and what happens because of it? How can anticipating what happens when you act—or fail to act—help you face your responsibilities? What is an upcoming task you need to accomplish, and what is your plan to get it done without procrastinating?

According to two researchers, David Meyer and Dr. John Medina, switching time increases errors and the amount of time it takes to finish the tasks you are working on by an average of 50%. This means the more switching you do, the longer it takes to complete your activities, and the more mistakes you make.[5] The cost to the quality of your work may not be worth the juggling.

If you want to succeed, consider the words of Tony Schwarz: "Difficult as it is to focus in the face of the endless distractions we all now face, it's far and away the most effective way to get work done."[6] Focusing on one task at a time will save you time, mistakes, and stress.

Focus is as necessary for money management as it is for time management. Paying attention to where your money goes will help you make the most of what you have.

How Can You Manage Your Money?
(when costs just keep going up?)

According to the American Psychological Association, nearly three out of four Americans cite money as the number one stressor in their lives.[7] The cost of college tuition continues to rise more quickly than the rate of inflation, and books and other college expenses take a large toll on bank accounts. Self-supporting students pay for living and family expenses on top of college costs. Students who take longer than expected to complete a degree or certificate often pay more for the additional time in school. Add in the growing wage gap between the highest earners and the majority of the workers in the U.S., and it adds up to challenging financial situations for the vast majority of college students.

Your challenge is to come up with enough money to pay for college and expenses, without working so many hours that you have no time to study or taking out so many loans that you can't dig yourself out of debt for years. The solution requires the habit of anticipating and planning, and may involve a combination of applying for financial aid, holding a job, effective budgeting, and avoiding credit card debt.

© Palmer Kane LLC./Shutterstock

Explore and Apply for Financial Aid

Financing your education—alone or with the help of your family—involves gathering financial information and making decisions about what you can afford and how much help you need. Here are some roadblocks that stand in the way of getting help:

Students don't apply. One recent report indicated that almost 40% of full-time community college students do not fill out a federal aid application, including 29% of students with incomes under $10,000 per year. These students may be intimidated by the application process or simply believe that they won't qualify for aid.[8]

The economy has an effect. When the economy is struggling, private banks are less likely to grant loans, and federal programs like the Pell Grants (see Key 3.4) have less money. Also, in tough economic times, more students apply for grants, so recipients get smaller pieces of the pie.[9]

Colleges vary in what they offer. State colleges provide fewer opportunities for aid when their funding is reduced. In addition, some smaller colleges no longer offer federal loans to their students.

Find your way around these roadblocks by becoming informed about what is available. Then take initiative to go out and get it.

Types of Aid

Aid comes in the form of student loans, grants, and scholarships. *Almost all students are eligible for some kind of need-based or merit-based financial assistance.*

Student loans. Student loan recipients are responsible for paying back the amount borrowed, plus interest, according to a payment schedule that may stretch over a number of years. The federal government administers or oversees all student loans. To receive aid from a federal program, you must be a citizen or eligible noncitizen and be enrolled in a program that meets government requirements.

Grants. Unlike student loans, grants do not require repayment. Grants are funded by federal, state, or local governments as well as private organizations. They are awarded to students who show financial need.

Scholarships. Scholarships are awarded to students who show talent or ability in specific areas (academic achievement, sports, the arts, citizenship, or leadership). They may be financed by government or private organizations, employers (yours or your parents'), schools, religious organizations, local and community groups, credit unions, or individuals. They do not require repayment.

Key 3.4 Understand federal loan and grant programs.

GRANTS	LOANS
■ **Pell.** Need-based, available to undergraduates with no other degrees. In 2010–2011, approximately 9.1 million undergraduates received Pell Grants. ■ **Federal Supplemental Educational Opportunity (FSEOG).** Need-based, only available at participating schools. ■ **Work–study.** Need-based, pays an hourly wage for selected jobs.	■ **Stafford.** For students enrolled at least half-time. In 2010–2011, approximately 10.3 million students received Stafford Loans. ■ **Perkins.** For those with exceptional financial need. ■ **PLUS.** Available to students claimed as dependents by their parents.

Sources: "Student Aid on the Web." U.S. Department of Education, January 31, 2012. From http://studentaid.ed.gov/PORTALSWebApp/students/english/index.jsp; and College Board Advocacy and Policy Center. *Trends in Student Aid 2011.* New York, NY: The College Board, 2011, p. 3.

Key 3.4 lists federal grant and loan programs. Additional information about each is available in various federal student aid publications, which you can find at your school's financial aid office, request by phone (800-433-3243), or access online at http://studentaid.ed.gov.

Looking for Aid

The following aid search strategies demand that you energize the habit of anticipation and planning.[10]

Ask, ask, ask. Visit the financial aid office more than once. Ask what you are eligible for. Alert the office to any change in your financial situation. Search libraries and the web, including your school's website, for information on everything that is possible.

Apply for government aid. Fill out the Free Application for Federal Student Aid (FAFSA) form electronically through your college's financial aid office, the FAFSA website (www.fafsa.ed.gov), or the U.S. Department of Education's website (www.ed.gov/finaid.html). You will create a personal portfolio called MyFSA on the site, where you will enter and store information, including your FAFSA form and any other pertinent forms. The U.S. Department of Education has an online tool called FAFSA Forecaster to help you estimate how much aid you qualify for. You will need to reapply every year for federal aid. *Note:* This is a *free* tool. If you hear about services that charge a fee for completing your FAFSA for you, avoid them.

Seek private aid. Search libraries and your school's website, go through books that list scholarships and grants, talk with a financial aid advisor, and check scholarship search sites such as Scholarships.com and Fastweb .com. Know details that may help (you or your family's military status, ethnic background, membership in organizations, religious affiliation, and so on). However, be wary of private loans, which can have higher interest rates than federal loans, less flexible terms of repayment, and tougher consequences for late payments or defaults.

Consider a range of options. Compare loans using websites like www.estudentloan.com. Evaluate majors for job prospects and earning potential. Consider transferring to a less expensive school—you may be able to get a comparable education while escaping postgraduation debt.

Applying for Aid

Apply by the deadline or, even better, early. The earlier you complete the process, the greater your chances of being considered for aid, especially when you are vying for part of a limited pool of funds. Here are some additional tips from financial aid experts Arlina DeNardo and Carolyn Lindley of Northwestern University:[11]

- **Know what applications you need to fill out.** FAFSA is required at all colleges, but some also require a form called the CSS/Financial Aid Profile.

- **Note the difference between merit-based and need-based aid.** While some aid is awarded based on financial need, other aid is merit-based, meaning that it is linked to specifics such as academic performance, a particular major, or ethnic origin.

- **Be aware of the total cost of attending college.** When you consider how much money you need, add books, transportation, housing, food, and other fees to tuition.

- **If you receive aid, pay attention to the award letter.** Know whether the aid is a grant or a loan that needs to be repaid. Follow rules such as remaining in academic good standing. Note reapplication deadlines and meet them (many require reapplication *every year*).

Finally, don't take out more money than you need. If you max out on your total aid too early in your college career, you could run into trouble as you approach graduation. Look at your needs year by year, and make sure you are only taking out what is absolutely necessary.

Many students are able to fit part-time work into their schedules if they stay local. Look for jobs at nearby businesses and organizations.

© Paul Vasarhelyi/Shutterstock

Juggle Work and School

More than two-thirds of college students have some kind of job while in school. If you want to or need to work, try to balance it with your academic work and goals.

Establish Your Needs

Anticipate what you need from a job. Ask questions like these:

- How much money do I need to make—weekly, per term, for the year?
- What time of day is best for me? Should I consider night or weekend work?
- Can my schedule handle a full-time job, or should I look for part-time work?
- Do I want hands-on experience and/or connections in a particular field?
- How flexible a job do I need?
- Can I, or should I, find work at my school or as part of a work-study program?

Analyze the Impact

Working while in school has both positive and negative effects. Think through these pros and cons when considering or evaluating any job.

PROS OF WORKING WHILE IN SCHOOL	CONS OF WORKING WHILE IN SCHOOL
• Gain general and career-specific experience. • Develop contacts. • Enhance your school performance (although full-time work can be problematic, working up to 15 hours a week may actually improve efficiency). • Earn money.	• Have less time to study due to time commitment for your job. • Have less time for nonacademic activities. • Must shift gears mentally from work to classroom. • May stretch yourself too thin; can become fatigued and anxious.

Identify Options, Make a Choice, and Evaluate

With the information you have gathered and analyzed, look carefully at what is available on and off campus, and apply for the job or jobs that suit your needs best. Sometimes work-study programs are a good place to start because they are flexible, typically provide employment on campus (less commute time), and may offer college credit along with pay.

Continue to evaluate whether the pros of your job are worth it. Are your studies suffering? Are you making enough money? Are you getting enough sleep? If the job doesn't benefit you as much as you anticipated, consider making a change—perhaps you can renegotiate your job duties and schedule, or maybe you need to change jobs. Plan careful, well-considered choices that bring you what you need most.

Manage Income and Expenses Through Budgeting

Creating a practical monthly **budget** that works means that you take these steps:

1. Gather information about what you earn (money flowing in).
2. Figure out your expenditures (money flowing out).
3. Calculate and analyze the difference between earnings and expenditures.
4. Adjust spending or earning with the goal of coming out even or ahead.

> **Budget**
> a plan to coordinate resources and expenditures; a set of goals regarding money.

Your biggest expense right now is probably tuition. However, if you have taken out student loans that you don't begin to pay until after you earn your degree, that expense may not hit you fully until after you finish school. For now, as you consider your budget, include only the part of the cost of your education you are paying for while you are still in school.

Figure Out What You Earn

To determine what is available to you on a monthly basis, start with the money you earn in a month's time at any regular job. Then, if you have savings set aside for your education or any other source of income, determine how much of it you can spend each month and add that amount. For example, if you have a grant for the entire year, divide it by 12 (or by how many months you are in school over the course of a year) to see how much you can use each month.

Figure Out What You Spend

First, note regular monthly expenses like rent, phone, and cable (look at past checks and electronic debits to estimate what the month's bills will be). Some expenses, like automobile and health insurance, may be billed only once or twice a year. In these cases, divide the yearly cost by 12 to see how much you spend every month. Then, over a month's time, keep a spending log in a small notebook to record each day's cash or debit card expenditures. Be sure to count smaller purchases if they are frequent (for example, one or two pricey coffees a day add up over time). By the end of the month, you will have a good idea of where your dollars go.

Key 3.5 lists common sources of income as well as expenses for students. Use the total of all your monthly expenses as a baseline for other months, realizing that spending will vary depending on events in your life or factors such as seasons. For example, if you pay for heating, that cost will be far greater in cold weather.

Personal finance software programs like Quicken, or online or app-based money managers such as Mint or Moneytrackin', can help you track spending and saving and categorize expenses. With software, you can create reports about how much you spend on groceries in a 1-month period or how much you earned from work in a year's time. Also, if you manage bank and credit accounts online, you can easily access information about what you are earning and spending over a period of time.

Analyze the Difference

Once you know what you earn and what you spend, calculate the difference: Subtract your monthly expenses from your monthly income. Ideally, you have money left over to save or spend. However, if you are spending more than you take in, examine these areas of your budget.

- **Expenses.** Did you forget to budget for recurring expenses such as the cost for semiannual dental visits or car insurance? Or was your budget derailed by an emergency expense?
- **Spending patterns and priorities.** Did you spend money wisely during the month, or did you overspend on wants rather than needs?
- **Income.** Do you bring in enough money? Do you need another income source or better job?

Adjust Spending or Earning

If you spend more than you are earning, plan to earn more, spend less, or better yet, do both. To increase resources, consider taking a part-time job,

Key 3.5 Where money comes from . . . and where it goes.

Common Sources of Income	Common Expenses
■ Take-home pay from a full-time or part-time job	■ Tuition you are paying now
■ Take-home pay from summer and holiday employment	■ Books and other course materials
■ Money earned from work-study or paid internship	■ Rent or mortgage
■ Money from parents or other relatives	■ Utilities (electric, gas, oil, water)
■ Scholarships	■ Telephone (cell phone and/or landline)
■ Grants	■ Food
■ Loans	■ Clothing, toiletries, household supplies
	■ Transportation and auto expenses (gas, maintenance, service)
	■ Credit cards and other payments on credit (car payment)
	■ Childcare
	■ Entertainment (cable TV, movies, eating out, books and magazines, music downloads)
	■ Computer-related expenses, including online service costs
	■ Insurance (health, auto, homeowner's or renter's, life)
	■ Miscellaneous expenses

© Leungchopan/Fotolia

increasing hours at a current job, or finding aid. There are several ways to decrease spending. One is to think before you buy: Do I really need this? Is the expense worth it? Here are other ways to manage spending:

- Share living space.
- Take advantage of free on-campus entertainment (movies and events).
- Rent movies or borrow them from friends or the library.
- Eat at home more often.
- Set up automatic bill payments so your needs are taken care of before your wants.
- Take advantage of sales, use coupons, buy store brands, and buy in bulk.
- Use your student ID for savings on entertainment, food, and other purchases (consult your school for a full list of available discounts).

- Walk or use public transport.
- Bring lunch from home.
- Shop in secondhand stores or swap clothing with friends.
- Make coffee at home instead of buying it at expensive coffee shops.
- Reduce credit hours.
- Ask a relative to help with child care or create a babysitting co-op.

Cutting back on day-to-day expenses can make a significant difference over time (see Key 3.6). Ask yourself: Would you rather spend your money on coffee or put it toward next term's tuition?

Call on your dominant multiple intelligences when planning your budget. For example, visual learners may want to create a chart, and bodily-kinesthetic learners may want to dump receipts into a big jar and tally them at the end of the month. Personal finance software can accommodate different types of learners with features such as written reports (verbal-linguistic, logical-mathematical) and graphical reports (visual). Consider using online tools such as Mint.com or Thrive.com. See the Multiple Intelligence Strategies for Financial Management for more MI-based ideas on how to manage your money.

Manage Credit Card Use

Credit card companies target college students with dozens of offers. Credit cards are a handy alternative to cash and can help build a strong credit history if used carefully, but they also can plunge you into debt, affecting your credit rating and making it difficult to get loans or finance car or home purchases. Tough economic times often mean more people rely on credit to get by. Recent statistics show how college students use credit cards:[12]

Key 3.6 Put your wallet away today to save money for tomorrow.

DAY-TO-DAY EXPENSE	APPROXIMATE COST	POTENTIAL SAVINGS
Gourmet coffee	$4 per day, 5 days a week, totals $20 per week	$80 per month; $960 for the year. Invested in a 5% interest account for a year, would amount to over $1,000.
Alcohol	Two drinks plus tip total about $20 per night, two nights per week amounts to $40 per week	$160 per month; $1,920 for the year. Invested in a 5% interest account for a year, would amount to over $2,000.
Ordering in meals	$15 per meal, twice per week, totals $30 per week	$120 per month; $1,440 for the year. Invested in a 5% interest account for a year, would amount to nearly $1,550.

MULTIPLE INTELLIGENCE STRATEGIES

For Financial Management

Name a significant upcoming expense: _____

In the right-hand column, record specific ideas for how MI strategies can help you afford it.

Intelligence	Use MI Strategies to Manage Your Money	Identify MI Strategies that can Help you Make a Purchase
Verbal–Linguistic	• Talk over your financial situation with someone you trust. • Write out a detailed budget outline. If you can, store it on a computer file so you can update it regularly.	
Logical–Mathematical	• Focus on the numbers; with a calculator and amounts that are as exact as possible; determine your income and spending. • Calculate how much you'll have in 10 years if you start now to put $2,000 in a 5% interest-bearing IRA account each year.	
Bodily–Kinesthetic	• Create a set of envelopes, each for a different budget item—rent, dining out, phone, and so on. Each month, put money, or a slip with a dollar amount, in each envelope to represent what you can spend. When the envelope is empty or the number on the paper is reduced to zero, stop spending.	
Visual–Spatial	• Set up a budgeting system that includes color-coded folders and colored charts. • Create color-coded folders for papers related to financial and retirement goals—investments, accounts, and so on.	
Interpersonal	• Whenever money problems come up, discuss them right away with a family member, partner, or roommate. • Generate a 5-year financial plan with one of your friends.	
Intrapersonal	• Schedule quiet time to plan how to develop, follow, and update your budget. Consider financial management software, such as Quicken. • Think through where your money should go to best achieve your long-term financial goals.	
Musical	• Include a category of music-related purchases in your budget—going to concerts, buying CDs—but keep an eye on it to make sure you don't go overboard.	
Naturalistic	• Analyze your spending by using a system of categories. Your system may be based on time (when payments are due), priority (must-pay bills versus extras), or spending type (monthly bills, education, family expenses).	

© Courtesy of Sarah Lyman Kravits

To maintain an accurate view of where your money goes, keep credit card receipts and include those purchases as you track expenses.

- 84% of college students hold at least one credit card. The average number of cards is 4.6, and 50% have four or more.

- Students who hold credit cards carry an average outstanding balance of $3,173.

- 90% of students pay for some type of education expense on credit, including 76% who charge textbooks and 30% who use cards to pay tuition.

Many college students charge a wide variety of expenses like car repairs, food, and clothes in addition to school costs. Before they know it, they are deeply in debt. It's hard to notice trouble brewing when you don't see your wallet taking a hit.

How Credit Cards Work

Every time you charge a purchase, you create a debt that must be repaid. The credit card issuer earns money by charging interest on unpaid balances. Here's an example: Say you have a $3,000 unpaid balance on your card at an annual interest rate of 18%. If you make the $60 minimum payment every month, it will take you eight years to pay off your debt, *assuming that you make no other purchases*. By the time you finish, you will repay nearly twice your original debt:

- Original debt—$3,000

- Cost to repay credit card loan at an annual interest rate of 18% for 8 years—$5,760

- Cost of using credit—$5,760 – $3,000 = $2,760

The first step in avoiding debt is to know as much as you can about credit cards, starting with the important concepts in Key 3.7.

Managing Credit Card Debt

The majority of American citizens have some level of debt, and many people go through periods when they have a hard time paying bills. A few basics will help you stay in control.

- **Choose your card wisely.** Look for cards with low interest rates, no annual fee, a rewards program, and a grace period (no penalty for late payments up to a certain number of days).

- **Pay bills on time, and make at least the minimum payment.** Set up a reminder system that activates a week or so before the due date. You can create an e-mail alert through your card account, make a note in your datebook, or set an alarm on your electronic planner.

- **Ask questions before charging.** Would you buy that item if you had to pay cash? Can you pay the balance at the end of the billing cycle?

Map Out Your Budget

Use this exercise to see what you take in and what you spend. Then decide what adjustments you need to make. Consider using an online calculator for this task, such as www.calculatorweb.com.

Before you begin. Keep a spending log for 1 week or 1 month, whatever you have time for (if you use 1 week, multiply weekly by four to determine estimated monthly expenses in Step 1, and enter amounts for bills you pay each month). Include purchases made by cash, check, debit card, and credit card.

Step 1: Expenses. Based on your spending log, estimate your current expenses in dollars per month, using the following table. The grand total is your total monthly expenses. If any expense comes only once a year, enter it in the "Annual Expenses" column and divide by 12 to get your "Monthly Expenses" figure for that item.

Expenses	Monthly Expenses	Annual Expenses
School supplies including books and technology		
Tuition and fees		
Housing: Dorms, rent, or mortgage		
Phone (cell and/or landline)		
Cable TV, Internet		
Gas and electric, water		
Car costs: monthly payment, auto insurance, maintenance, repairs, registration, inspections		
Travel costs: gas, public transportation, parking permits, tolls		
Vacations, trips home		
Food: Groceries, meal plan cafeteria, eating out, snacks		
Health insurance		
Health maintenance costs: gym, equipment, sports fees, classes		
Medical costs: doctor and dentists visits, vision, prescriptions, counseling		
Entertainment: movies, music purchases, socializing		
Laundry costs: supplies, service		
Clothing purchases		
Household supplies		
Payments on credit card debt		
Student loan or other loan repayment		
Donations to charitable organizations		
Childcare		
Other: emergencies, hobbies, gifts		
TOTAL EXPECTED EXPENSES		

Step 2: Gross Income. Calculate your average monthly income. As with expenses, if any source of income arrives only once a year, enter it in the annual column and divide by 12 to get the monthly figure. For example, if you have a $6,000 scholarship for the year, your monthly income would be $500 ($6,000 divided by 12).

Income/resources	Monthly Income	Annual
Employment (after federal/state taxes)		
Family contribution		
Financial Assistance: grants, federal and other loans		
Scholarships		
Interest and dividends		
Other gifts, income, and contributions		
Total Expected Income		

Step 3: Net Income (Cash Flow). Subtract the grand total of your monthly expenses from the grand total of your monthly income. The result is your net income.

INCOME PER MONTH	
Total expected expenses	
Total expected income	
NET INCOME (INCOME – EXPENSES)	

Source: Adapted from Julie Stein, California State University, East Bay.

Step 4: Adjustments. If you end up with a negative number, indicating that you are spending more than you earn, what would you change? Examine your budget and spending log to look for problem areas. Remember, you can increase income, decrease spending, or both. List two workable ideas about how you can get your cash flow back to a positive number.

_____

_____

Creditor
a person or company to whom a debt is owed, usually money.

- **Stay on top of problems.** If you get into trouble, call the **creditor** and see if you can set up a payment plan. Then, going forward, try to avoid the same mistakes. Organizations such as the National Foundation for Credit Counseling (www.nfcc.org) can help you solve problems.

- **Reduce opportunities to spend.** Cut up a credit card or two if you have too many. Remember that even when you destroy a card, the debt remains until you've paid it off in full.

WHAT TO KNOW ABOUT . . .	. . . AND HOW TO USE WHAT YOU KNOW
Account balance. A dollar amount that includes any unpaid balance, new purchases and cash advances, finance charges, and fees. Updated monthly.	Charge only what you can afford to pay at the end of the month. Keep track of your balance. Hold on to receipts and call customer service if you have questions.
Annual fee. The yearly cost that some companies charge for owning a card.	Look for cards without an annual fee or, if you've paid your bills on time, ask your current company to waive the fee.
Annual percentage rate (APR). The amount of interest charged yearly on your unpaid balance. This is the cost of credit if you carry a balance in any given month. The higher the APR, the more you pay in finance charges.	Shop around (check Studentcredit.com). Also, watch out for low, but temporary, introductory rates that skyrocket to over 20% after a few months. Always ask what the long-term interest rate is and look for fixed rates (guaranteed not to change).
Available credit. The unused portion of your credit line, updated monthly on your bill.	It is important to have credit available for emergencies, so avoid charging to the limit.
Cash advance. An immediate loan, in the form of cash, from the credit card company. You are charged interest immediately and may also pay a separate transaction fee.	Use a cash advance only in extreme emergencies because the finance charges start as soon as you complete the transaction and interest rates are greater than the regular APR. It is a very expensive way to borrow money.
Credit limit. The debt ceiling the card company places on your account (e.g., $1,500). The total owed, including purchases, cash advances, finance charges, and fees, cannot exceed this limit.	Credit card companies generally set low credit limits for college students. Owning more than one card increases the credit available, but most likely increases problems as well. Try to use only one card.
Delinquent account. An account that is not paid on time or one where the minimum payment has not been met.	Always pay on time, even if it is only the minimum payment. If you do not pay on time, you will be charged substantial late fees and will risk losing your good credit rating, which affects your ability to borrow in the future. Delinquent accounts remain part of your credit records for years.
Due date. The date your payment must be received and after which you will be charged a late fee.	Avoid late fees and finance charges by paying at least a week in advance.
Finance charges. The total cost of credit, including interest, service fees, and transaction fees.	The only way to avoid finance charges is to pay your balance in full by the due date. If you keep your balance low, you will be more able to pay it off.
Minimum payment. The smallest amount you can pay by the statement due date. The amount is set by the credit card company.	Making only the minimum payment each month can result in disaster if you charge more than you can afford. When you make a purchase, think in terms of total cost.
Outstanding balance. The total amount you owe on your card.	If you carry a balance over several months, additional purchases are hit with finance charges. Pay cash for new purchases until your balance is under control.
Past due. Your account is considered "past due" when you fail to pay the minimum required payment on schedule.	Look for past due accounts on your credit history by getting a credit report from one of the credit bureaus (Experian, TransUnion, and Equifax) or myFICO or Credit Karma.

If you use credit wisely while in school, anticipating the effects of your spending and planning accordingly, you are likely to carry this effective habit into a brighter financial future.

© Courtesy of Misa Gonzales

What happened with Misa?

It took a year for Misa to be on board with the idea of becoming a teacher. First, she had to gain confidence with writing. She did her own online research about thesis statements, research strategies, and informational literacy. Having two children and a heavy course load forced her to learn to plan out her time. When she received a syllabus, she mapped out test and paper due dates in a calendar book. She wrote assignments on thin sticky note strips and put them in the calendar book several days before they were due, moving them each day until she completed them, at which point she would fold them over and write DONE on them. She graduated with a degree in Secondary Education Extended English.

The confidence and motivation she built served Misa well in her student teaching at Desert View High School in Tucson, where her mentor teacher Liz Denbo provided support and strategies that took her talents to the next level. Before the year was over, the principal offered her a contract. That next year she taught in the school's new freshman academy, in a new wing where every freshman had a laptop. Working with students to learn the new tools, she discovered a passion for using technology to expand educational possibilities and increase efficiency. The next year found her training teachers on the technology. When then-Education Secretary Arne Duncan visited Tucson, he nominated Misa as one of 10 ConnectED Champions of Change, and she was invited to the White House along with 9 other educators noted for their innovative use of technology in education.

Continuing to anticipate the future of technology in education, Misa has founded a company called MindFULL Learning Institute, which trains teachers in what she refers to as STEAM education—Science, Technology, English, Arts, and Mathematics. Her strategies get students involved in building, construction, and design, along with filming, editing, and using social media to market creations. She helps students plan for success as digital citizens in a world that is more changed and more closely connected every day.

Connect this story to your life: What do you anticipate can happen in your future if you devote time, effort, and focus to it? Describe a specific plan you can follow to move toward and reach what you anticipate.

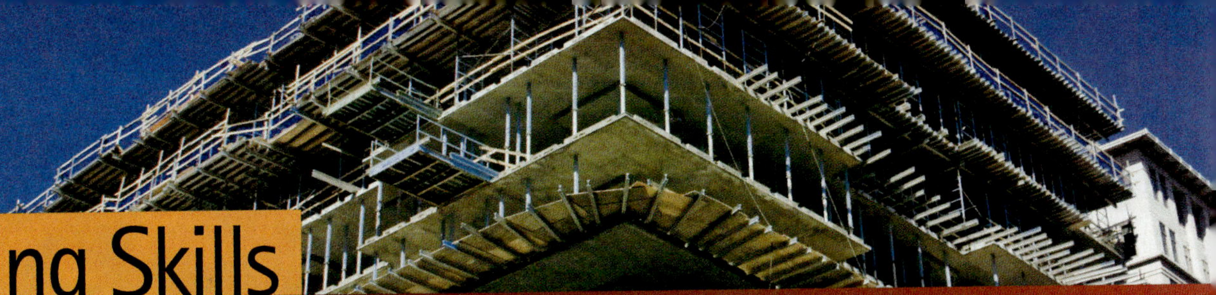

Building Skills

for successful learning

Note the Important Points

Explain two ways in which your key resources–money and time–are connected.

List two influences on how you manage money.

What does it mean to prioritize?

Name two strategies that can help you put your schedule to work.

Describe two actions you can take to find financial aid.

Define what it means to "budget," including listing the four steps.

Critical Thinking

applying learning to life

Discover How You Spend Your Time

Use the in-text grids to record data. Answer questions and write additional thoughts on separate paper or in digital format.

Everyone has exactly 168 hours in a week. How do you spend your hours? Start by guessing or estimating the time you spend on three particular activities. How much time do you spend on each of these activities in a week?

Studying? _____ hours

Sleeping? _____ hours

Interacting with media and technology (computer, online services, apps, texting, video games, television) for nonacademic purposes? _____ hours

To find out the real story, record how you actually spend your time for 7 days. The Weekly Time Log chart has blocks showing half-hour increments. As you go through the week, write down what you do each hour, indicating when you start and when you stop. Include sleep and leisure time. Record your *actual* activities instead of the activities you think you *should* be doing. There are no wrong answers.

After a week, note how many hours you spent on each activity using the Weekly Summary chart. Round off the times to half-hours—if you spent 31 to 44 minutes on an activity, mark it as a half-hour; if you spent 45 to 59 minutes, mark it as 1 hour. Log the hours in the boxes in the chart using tally marks, with a full mark representing 1 hour and a half-size mark representing a half-hour. In the third column, total the hours for each activity. Finally, add the totals in that column. Your grand total should be approximately 168 hours (if it isn't, go back and check your calculations and fix any errors you find). Leave the Ideal Time in Hours column blank for now.

TIME	MONDAY activity	TUESDAY activity	WEDNESDAY activity	THURSDAY activity
6:00 A.M.				
6:30 A.M.				
7:00 A.M.				
7:30 A.M.				
8:00 A.M.				
8:30 A.M.				
9:00 A.M.				
9:30 A.M.				
10:00 A.M.				
10:30 A.M.				
11:00 A.M.				
11:30 A.M.				
12:00 P.M.				
12:30 P.M.				
1:00 P.M.				
1:30 P.M.				
2:00 P.M.				
2:30 P.M.				
3:00 P.M.				
3:30 P.M.				
4:00 P.M.				
4:30 P.M.				
5:00 P.M.				
5:30 P.M.				
6:00 P.M.				
6:30 P.M.				
7:00 P.M.				
7:30 P.M.				
8:00 P.M.				
8:30 P.M.				
9:00 P.M.				
9:30 P.M.				
10:00 P.M.				
10:30 P.M.				
11:00 P.M.				
11:30 P.M.				
12:00 A.M.				
12:30 A.M.				
1:00 A.M.				
1:30 A.M.				
2:00 A.M.				

TIME	FRIDAY activity	SATURDAY activity	SUNDAY activity
6:00 A.M.			
6:30 A.M.			
7:00 A.M.			
7:30 A.M.			
8:00 A.M.			
8:30 A.M.			
9:00 A.M.			
9:30 A.M.			
10:00 A.M.			
10:30 A.M.			
11:00 A.M.			
11:30 A.M.			
12:00 P.M.			
12:30 P.M.			
1:00 P.M.			
1:30 P.M.			
2:00 P.M.			
2:30 P.M.			
3:00 P.M.			
3:30 P.M.			
4:00 P.M.			
4:30 P.M.			
5:00 P.M.			
5:30 P.M.			
6:00 P.M.			
6:30 P.M.			
7:00 P.M.			
7:30 P.M.			
8:00 P.M.			
8:30 P.M.			
9:00 P.M.			
9:30 P.M.			
10:00 P.M.			
10:30 P.M.			
11:00 P.M.			
11:30 P.M.			
12:00 A.M.			
12:30 A.M.			
1:00 A.M.			
1:30 A.M.			
2:00 A.M.			

ACTIVITY	TIME TALLIED OVER ONE-WEEK PERIOD	TOTAL TIME IN HOURS	IDEAL TIME IN HOURS
Example: Class	卌 卌 卌 ǀǀ	16.5	
Class			
Work			
Studying			
Sleeping			
Eating			
Family time/childcare			
Commuting/traveling			
Chores and personal business			
Friends and important relationships			
Telephone time			
Leisure/entertainment			
Spiritual life			
Other			

Look over your results, paying special attention to how your *estimated* hours for sleep, study, and technology activities compare to your *actual* logged activity hours for the week. Use a separate sheet of paper or electronic file to answer the following questions:

- What surprises you about how you spend your time?

- Do you spend the most time on the activities that represent your most important values—or not?

- Where do you waste the most time? What do you think that is costing you?

- On which activities do you think you should spend *more* time? On which should you spend *less* time?

Go back to the Weekly Summary chart and fill in the Ideal Time in Hours column with the number of hours you think would make the most sense. Consider the difference between your actual hours and your ideal hours. What changes are you willing to make to get closer to how you want to ideally spend your time? Write a short paragraph describing, in detail, two changes you plan to make this term to focus more of your time on your most important goals.

Team Building

Everyday Ways to Save Money

- In person or online, gather a group of three or four students. Think about the ways you spend money in a typical month, and share your list with each student. Looking at the lists, determine two areas of spending that you have in common.

- On your own, take 5 minutes to generate ideas about how to reduce spending in those two areas. What expense can you reduce or do without? Where can you look for savings? Can you exchange a product or service for one that a friend can provide?

- Come together as a group again to share your ideas. Discuss which ones you would be most able and likely to put into action. Write your three most workable ideas here.

1. _____

2. _____

3. _____

On your own, try these ideas to see how they can help you put some money toward your savings. After you have seen the results, circle the strategy that is helping you the most.

_____

anticipate

Plan to Prepare for Midterm/Exam Week

It is never too early to prepare for a big exam week (choose either midterm or finals week, depending on which is more challenging for you). Look at your schedule now, and note the date exactly 3 weeks before your first midterm or final exam. Write that date here.

_____

Your goal is to find *3 hours per day for each day of those 3 weeks* to study for your exams. First, set aside the hours allotted to Priority 1 activities—class, work, caring for children or others, and sleep. Then look at what is left. For each day in the calendar below, write the date and indicate your planned study hours in whatever combination works for you—for example, "2–5 p.m," or "10–11 a.m. and 9–11 p.m.," or even "1–2 p.m., 5–6 p.m., and 9–10 p.m." If on any day you don't have three hours available, aim for at least two.

Month: _____						
SUN	MON	TUES	WED	THURS	FRI	SAT

Enter this schedule into your planner, and do your best to stick to it. If life gets in the way of any of your study sessions, commit to finding other times for them rather than giving them up.

4
setting and reaching goals
using values, stress management, and teamwork

ELISE TRAN, *student,*
Colorado School of Mines

Elise Tran craved connection from a young age. Her parents worked all the time, and she struggled to relate to her two older brothers. When she was in the fourth grade, her parents divorced, and her mother continued to work long hours day and night to support her children. Noticing that she wasn't herself, Elise's peers and their parents took action to connect with her, inviting her to dinner and providing transportation to events. Although this created community for Elise, she continued to struggle in school.

Elise and her mother didn't know how to register for high school and encountered complications because of her grades and change of school districts. The principal of her previous school reached out to a parent, a counselor at a local high school, who saw something in Elise and did whatever he could to get her into the school. Amazed by his kindness, Elise became determined to succeed academically.

Over her high school experience, teachers mentored Elise, encouraging her to join clubs and get involved in the community. Their help led to her membership in the National Honor Society and a local internship. Elise made a point to reach out to counselors and teachers, knowing that as the first in her family to graduate from high school as well as a first-generation college student, she had fewer resources and less of an understanding of what it takes to succeed in higher education. Would her ability to connect help her overcome these disadvantages and make the most of college?

(to be continued...)

It's one thing to connect with others in all the possible ways—and another thing to connect with purpose, having a goal in mind for what you want out of the connection. You'll learn more about Elise's experience at the end of the chapter.

Working through this chapter will help you to:

- Explore values in connection with goals. p. 86
- Work toward goal achievement and use the SMART goal system. p. 89
- Recognize and analyze causes of stress. p. 93
- Explore stress management strategies. p. 95
- Build teamwork skills. p. 104
- Communicate effectively. p. 107

Text and photo used by permission of Elise Tran

communicate Goals are often easier to reach with help from those around you. *Connect with purpose* to others and their ideas to maximize your chances of success.

What Do You Value? *(and why do values matter when setting goals?)*

To set the goals that are best for you—and, even more importantly, to move ahead toward achieving them—you need to identify the **core values** that motivate you. This chapter will show you how to set S.M.A.R.T. goals (specific, measurable, achievable, realistic, and time bound) based on these values. It will also give you tools to manage the stress that can hinder your efforts to reach your target, and strengthen your ability to work with others so you can achieve goals more effectively than if you worked alone.

Values are influenced by family, friends, culture, media, school, work, neighborhood, religion, world events, and more. Your strongest values are often linked to childhood experiences and family, but values may shift as you acquire knowledge and experiences and build new relationships. For example, a student whose family and friends were there for him after a serious accident may place greater value on relationships than he did before the accident.

Values help you to:

- **Understand what you want out of life.** Your top goals reflect what you value most.

- **Choose how to use your time.** When your day-to-day activities align with what you think is most important to do, you gain greater fulfillment from them.

- **Build "rules for life."** Values form the foundation for decisions and behavior. You will return repeatedly to them for guidance, especially in unfamiliar situations.

For the best chance at success, your core values should inform your goals and choices. The stronger the link between your values and your long-term goals, the happier, more motivated, and more successful you are likely to be in setting and achieving those goals. If your choice to pursue a college degree reflects a belief that a college education will help you get ahead, for example, you may be more likely to persist.

> **Core values**
> the principles and qualities that inform your beliefs and actions.

Rate each of the following values on a scale from 1 to 5, 1 being least important to you and 5 being most important. Write each rating next to the corresponding value.

Knowing yourself _____

Self-improvement _____

Physical/mental health _____

Leadership/teamwork skills _____

Getting a good job _____

Pursuing an education _____

Connecting to family _____

Helping others _____

Reading _____

Taking risks _____

Being with friends _____

Political involvement _____

Being organized _____

Spiritual/religious life _____

Health and fitness _____

Community involvement _____

Time for fun/relaxation _____

Being liked by others _____

Time to yourself _____

Lifelong learning _____

Competing and winning _____

Financial stability _____

Making a lot of money _____

Creative/artistic pursuits _____

Other (write in below) _____

_____

_____

Write your top three values here:

1. _____

2. _____

3. _____

Choose one top value that has affected an educational choice you have made. Explain the choice and how the value was involved. Example: A student who values financial stability takes a personal finance course.

_____

_____

_____

How Do You Set and Achieve Goals?
(and what about when you just don't feel motivated to get there?)

When you set a **goal**, you focus on what you want to achieve and create a path to get you there, whether in a long-term or short-term time frame. *Long-term* goals are broader objectives you want to achieve over a long period of time, perhaps a year or more. *Short-term* goals are smaller steps that move you toward a long-term goal, making it manageable and achievable, piece by piece (see Key 4.1).

Goal
an end toward which you direct your efforts.

Set Long-Term Goals

What do you want your life to look like in 5 or 10 years? What degree do you want to earn, what kind of job do you want, where do you want to live? Answers to questions like these help identify long-term goals.

Some long-term goals have an open-ended time frame. For example, if as a nursing student your long-term goal is to stay on top of developments in medicine, you will pursue this goal throughout your professional life. Other goals, such as completing the required courses for your degree, have a more definite end and often fewer options for getting there.

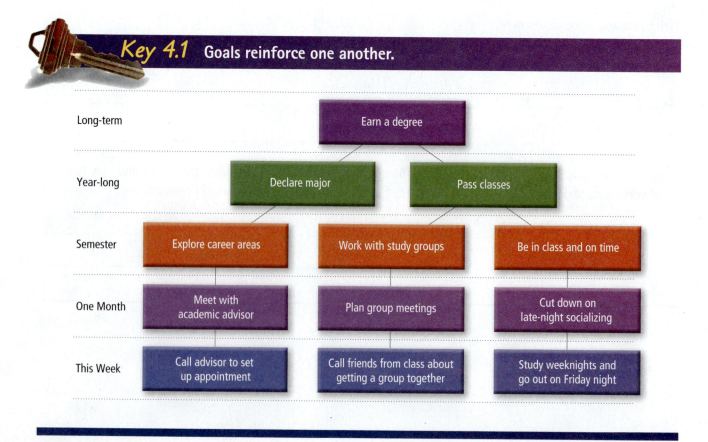

Key 4.1 Goals reinforce one another.

Long-term		Earn a degree	
Year-long	Declare major		Pass classes
Semester	Explore career areas	Work with study groups	Be in class and on time
One Month	Meet with academic advisor	Plan group meetings	Cut down on late-night socializing
This Week	Call advisor to set up appointment	Call friends from class about getting a group together	Study weeknights and go out on Friday night

One way to make long-term goals real is to put them in writing. For example:

My goal is to become a nurse practitioner, emphasizing preventive medicine in my work at a clinic in an underserved community.

To determine your long-term goals, think about what you want to accomplish while in school and after you graduate.

© LifeBound, LLC

Set Short-Term Goals

Lasting as short as an hour or as long as several months, *short-term* goals help you narrow your focus and encourage progress toward long-term goals. The student aiming to be a nurse practitioner might set supporting short-term goals like these for her second year of college:

- Choose courses that keep me on track to complete premed requirements.
- Locate a medical practice serving an underprivileged community and apply for a summer internship.
- Research graduate schools that offer a nurse-practitioner degree.

Getting more specific, this student may set these short-term goals for the next 6 months:

- I will learn the names and functions of every human bone and muscle.
- I will work with a study group to understand the muscular-skeletal system.

These goals can be broken down into even shorter time frames. Here are 1-month goals:

- I will work with on-screen tutorials of the muscular-skeletal system.
- I will spend 3 hours a week with my study partners.

Your short-term goals may last a week, a day, or even a couple of hours. Here's how a student with children might use short-term goals to support a month-long goal to set up weekend childcare:

- **By the end of today:** Text and e-mail friends to see if they know of available sitters or are looking to pick up some extra cash themselves.
- **One week from now:** Have at least two potential sitters to contact.
- **Two weeks from now:** Have spoken to potential sitters and evaluated the possibilities.
- **Four weeks from now:** Have plan in place for regular help for at least one weekend day.

Your Syllabus: A Powerful Goal-Achievement Tool

For each course you take, your syllabus provides a clear layout of the goals you will target throughout the term and when you need to achieve them. Keep paper syllabi where you can refer to them frequently, and note where to access electronic syllabi if your instructors post them online. Key 4.2 shows a portion of an actual syllabus with important items noted.

Set Up a Goal-Achievement Plan

At any given time, you are working toward goals of varying importance. Prioritize your goals so that you can put the bulk of your energy and time toward those that matter most. Then draw up a plan, using the S.M.A.R.T. system to make your goals Specific, Measurable, Achievable, Realistic, and Time Bound. See Key 4.3 on p. 93 for the parts of a S.M.A.R.T. goal and an example.

Setting goals is only the start. The real work is in working toward them, and the real benefit is in reaching them. Follow these steps, noting where your S.M.A.R.T. system actions fit in.

Step 1: Define an achievable, realistic goal. What do you want? Write out a clear description.

Step 2: Define an action plan. How will you get there? Brainstorm different paths. Choose one; then map out its steps. Break a long-term goal into short-term subgoals.

Step 3: Make sure your goal is time bound. When do you want to accomplish your goal? Define a realistic time frame. Create specific deadlines for each step on the path.

Step 4: Identify resources and support. What and who will keep you on track? Use helpful websites or apps. Communicate with people who will push you in a positive way.

Step 5: Be accountable. How will you assess your progress? Create a system to measure how you move toward your goal, keeping your time frame in mind.

Step 6: Prepare to get unstuck. What will you do if you hit a roadblock? Anticipate problems and define strategies for handling them. Connect with purpose to people who can help. Remind yourself of the benefits of your goal.

Step 7: Take action. How will you persist? Follow the steps in your plan until you achieve your goal.

Step 8: Celebrate! How will you recognize your accomplishments? Appreciate your hard work with something you enjoy—a movie night, an outing with friends, something you've been wanting to buy, maybe even a long nap.

It will take work and persistence to pursue your goals, and most people find it tough to stay motivated consistently. The changes—positive or negative—that happen along the way are likely to cause some stress. With effort, stress can be effectively managed on the way to your goals. Examine potential sources of stress and strategies for dealing with them.

ENG 122 Spring 2017

Instructor: Jennifer Gessner
Office Hours: Tue & Thur 12:30–1:30 (or by appointment) in DC 305
Phone: 303-555-2222
E-mail: jg@abc.xyz

How to connect with the instructor

Required Texts: *Good Reasons with Contemporary Arguments,* Faigley and Selzer
A Writer's Reference, 5th ed., Diana Hacker

Required Materials:
- a notebook with lots of paper
- a folder for keeping everything from this class
- an active imagination and critical thinking

Books and materials to get ASAP

Course Description: This course focuses on argumentative writing and the researched paper. Students will practice the rhetorical art of argumentation and will gain experience in finding and incorporating researched materials into an extended paper.

Writer's Notebook: All students will keep, and bring to class, a notebook with blank paper. Throughout the semester, you will be given writing assignments to complete in this book. You must bring to class and be prepared to share any notebook assignment. Notebook assignments will be collected frequently, though sometimes randomly, and graded only for their completeness, not for spelling, etc.

Course coverage, expectations, responsibilities

Grading:
- Major Writing Assignments worth 100 points each.
- Final Research Project worth 300 points.
- Additional exercises and assignments range from 10 to 50 points each.
- Class participation: Based on the degree to which you complete the homework and present this in a thoughtful, meaningful manner in class.
- Attendance: Attendance is taken daily and students may miss up to three days of class without penalty, but will lose 5 points for each day missed thereafter.
- Late work: All work will lose 10% of earned points per class day late. No work will be accepted after five class days or the last class meeting.

How grades are determined for this course

Final Grade: The average of the total points possible (points earned divided by the total possible points).100–90% = A; 89–80% = B; 79–70% = C (any grade below 70% is not passing for this class).

Academic Integrity: Students must credit any material used in their papers that is not their own (including direct quotes, paraphrases, figures, etc.). Failure to do so constitutes plagiarism, which is illegal, unethical, <u>always recognizable</u>, and a guaranteed way to fail a paper. The definition of plagiarism is "to steal and use (the writings or ideas of another) as one's own."

Reflects school's academic integrity policy

Week 4
2/1   <u>The Concise Opinion.</u>
             HW: Complete <u>paper #1 Rough Draft (5–7 pages double-spaced)</u>

Topic of that days class meeting

Notice of due date for paper draft

2/3   How Professionals Argue
             HW: <u>Read Jenkins Essay (p 501 of Good Reasons) and Rafferty Essay (p 525)</u>; compare argumentative style, assess and explain efficacy of arguments.

Notice of reading assignments to complete

Week 5
2/15   Developing an Argument
             Essay Quiz on Jenkins and Rafferty Essays
             HW: Chap 5 of *Good Reasons;* based on components of a definition of argument, write a brief explanation of how your argument might fit into this type.

Notice of quiz

2/17   Library Workday: Meet in Room 292
             PAPER #1 DUE

Notice of final due date for paper

Source: Excerpt from "A Syllabus Helps you Stay on Schedule and Fulfill Responsibilities" by Jennifer Gessner, Community College of Denver. Used by permission of Jennifer Gessner.

Name a general area in which you want to change or improve this year.

_____

Identify a specific goal in this area. Starting from number 1 at the bottom of this figure and working your way up, use the S.M.A.R.T. system to plan how you will achieve it.

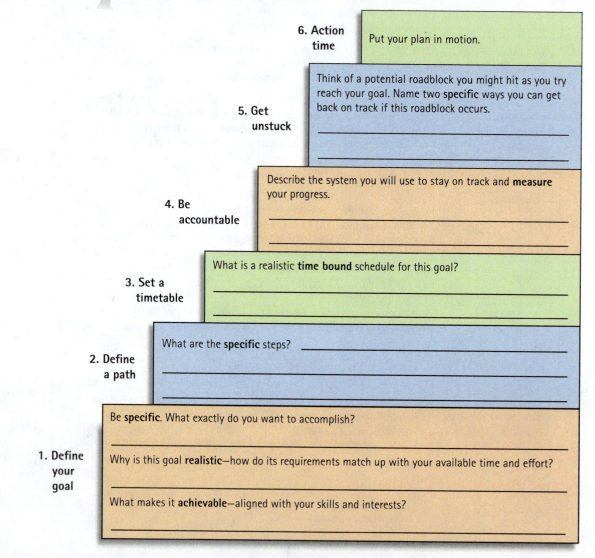

6. Action time — Put your plan in motion.

5. Get unstuck — Think of a potential roadblock you might hit as you try reach your goal. Name two **specific** ways you can get back on track if this roadblock occurs.

_____

_____

4. Be accountable — Describe the system you will use to stay on track and **measure** your progress.

_____

_____

3. Set a timetable — What is a realistic **time bound** schedule for this goal?

_____

_____

2. Define a path — What are the **specific** steps? _____

_____

_____

1. Define your goal — Be **specific**. What exactly do you want to accomplish?

_____

Why is this goal **realistic**—how do its requirements match up with your available time and effort?

_____

What makes it **achievable**—aligned with your skills and interests?

_____

Define your path using the schedule from number 3. Use this grid to assign estimated dates to specific steps.

Step				
Date done				

Work S.M.A.R.T. toward an important goal.

GOAL: To raise my algebra grade from a C to a B.

MY GOAL IS . . .	MEANING . . .	EXAMPLE
Specific	Defined concretely with as many details as possible.	I plan to study algebra at least an hour a day. I will contact the math center and set up weekly appointments with a tutor.
Measurable	Structured in a way you can measure, including a specific way to evaluate progress.	I will note weekly quiz grades to evaluate my progress. I will take practice tests using the textbook exercises and use the answer key to grade my work.
Achievable	Aligned with your interests and values as well as with available skills and resources.	I'm driven to improve my grade because I want to keep my GPA high enough to retain my financial aid. I have access to tutoring and I have time available.
Realistic	Reasonable and calculated in terms of both effort and time necessary.	With two-thirds of the term left, one letter grade increase is a reasonable expectation.
Time Bound	Set up within specific time boundaries so that you have just enough time pressure to motivate you (and not paralyze you).	I can set up tutoring by the end of the week. I have two months and probably seven or eight quizzes' worth of grades available to contribute to a higher overall grade.

How Can You Manage Stress?
(especially when it creates roadblocks on the way to goals?)

If you feel **stress** as you try to reach your goals, you are not alone. Stress levels among college students have increased, with challenging effects (see Key 4.4). Handling stress effectively involves identifying stressors (things that cause stress for you), using day-to-day stress management strategies, and maintaining a healthy body and mind.

For nearly every student, dealing with stress is an everyday challenge. Stress levels that rise too high can take a toll on health and goal achievement. However, a moderate amount of stress can motivate you to do well on tests, finish assignments on time, or prepare for a presentation. Key 4.5 shows that stress can be helpful or harmful, depending on how much you experience.

Stress
physical or mental strain produced in reaction to pressure.

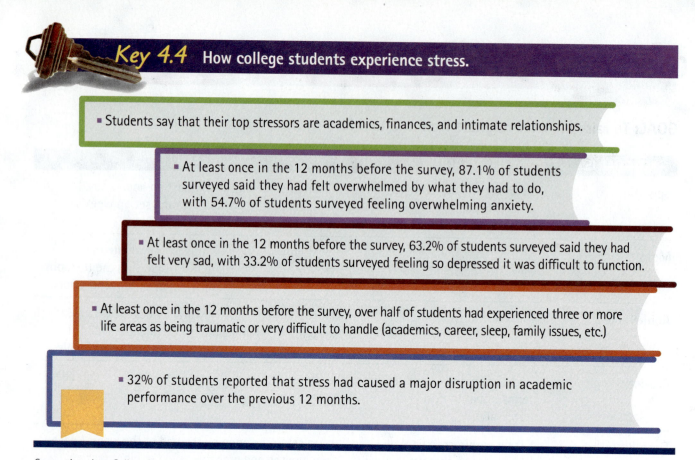

Key 4.4   How college students experience stress.

- Students say that their top stressors are academics, finances, and intimate relationships.

- At least once in the 12 months before the survey, 87.1% of students surveyed said they had felt overwhelmed by what they had to do, with 54.7% of students surveyed feeling overwhelming anxiety.

- At least once in the 12 months before the survey, 63.2% of students surveyed said they had felt very sad, with 33.2% of students surveyed feeling so depressed it was difficult to function.

- At least once in the 12 months before the survey, over half of students had experienced three or more life areas as being traumatic or very difficult to handle (academics, career, sleep, family issues, etc.)

- 32% of students reported that stress had caused a major disruption in academic performance over the previous 12 months.

Source: American College Health Association National College Health Assessment II, Undergraduate Reference Group, Spring 2014. http://www.acha-ncha.org/docs/NCHA-II_WEB-PAPER_SPRING2014_UNDERGRAD_REFERENCEGROUP_EXECUTIVESUMMARY.pdf

Key 4.5   Stress levels can help or hinder performance.

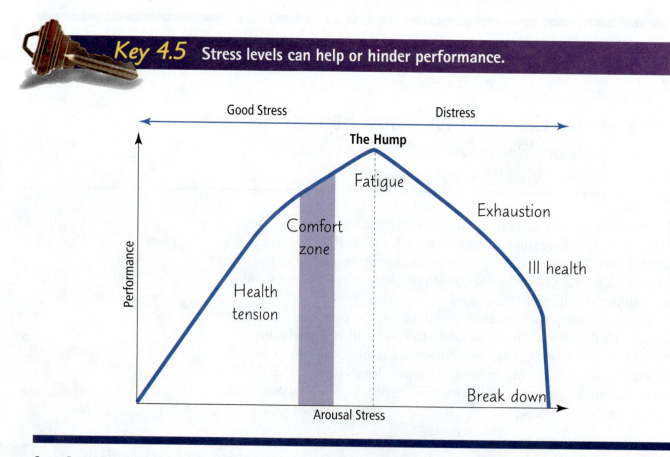

Source: Excerpt from "What is Stress?" Copyright © 2006 by The American Institute of Stress. Used by permission of The American Institute of Stress.

As you read on about how to cope with stress, keep in mind:

- **The goal-setting strategies in this chapter are stress-management strategies.** When you set S.M.A.R.T. goals and pursue them step by step with focus, connecting to others with purpose along the way, you reduce stress.

- **Time-management strategies are stress-management strategies.** When you create and follow a schedule, complete to-do list items, and avoid procrastinating, you reduce stress.

Identify and Address Stressors

All sorts of situations and experiences—both positive and negative—can cause stress during college. Furthermore, everyone has a unique response to any potential stressor. You can explore how you currently respond to various stressors using the *All About You* self-assessment.

Evaluating your "stress score" can help you decide how to handle ongoing pressures as well as adjust to temporary periods of particularly high stress. Here are some ways to manage:

Be realistic about commitments. There are only so many hours in a day, and an overload of work, school, and/or other activities can create stress. Set up a plan that works for you. If you need to work, find a job with obligations you can reasonably meet. If extracurricular commitments become too much, cut back. If family obligations present a challenge, recruit help.

Know yourself. Using self-knowledge to reduce stress means making the best choices for you wherever you can. If you are a night person, for example, try to schedule study time in the evening. If exercise calms and focuses you, make time for it between classes. If you have trouble ignoring alerts on your Snapchat or Twitter when you study, put your phone in a drawer.

Have some fun. Doing things you enjoy can take the edge off of stress. Moderation is the key. Choose what you find fun (meeting up with friends, binge-watching a favorite TV show, and so on) and include it in your schedule in a way that doesn't affect your ability to get work done.

© LifeBound, LLC

Try to find productive, healthful ways to manage stress levels. This student has chosen to spend time outdoors, eat a salad, and connect with a friend on the phone.

ALL ABOUT YOU

Using a scale from 1 to 10, with 1 being the lowest possible level of stress and 10 being the highest possible level, rate each item based on how much stress it causes you right now:

_____ 1. Increased independence and responsibility

_____ 2. Family relationships

_____ 3. Friend relationships

_____ 4. Academic relationships (instructors, student peers, administration, etc.)

_____ 5. Boyfriend/girlfriend/spouse/partner relationships

_____ 6. Managing time and schedule

_____ 7. Managing money

_____ 8. Performance on assignments

_____ 9. Performance on tests

_____ 10. Physical health and fitness

_____ 11. Mental health and balance

_____ 12. Academic planning (major, etc.)

_____ 13. Career planning and vision for future

_____ 14. Work situation, if you have a job on or off campus

_____ 15. Current living situation (home with family, apartment with a friend, etc.)

Total your points here: _____

The lowest possible score is 15, and the highest possible is 150. The higher your score, the more stress you perceive you are currently experiencing. Think about:

- What your total says about your life right now. A score over 100 may indicate stress reduction should be a top priority. A score under 50 may indicate tolerable, and even productive, levels of stress.

- How to address areas that you rated the highest. You can focus on any area that you rated a 7 or higher, or if your ratings are all under 7, look at your three highest-rated areas.

Connecting with purpose to school and community resources can help you manage stressors. On a separate sheet of paper or digital file, write down names, locations, hours, phone numbers, URLs, and any other pertinent information for the following resources:

- Free counseling offered to students

- Exercise facility

- Sexual assault center

- Other resource

Source: Adapted in part from Kohn, P. M., K. Lafreniere, and M. Gurevich, "The Inventory of College Students Recent Life Experiences: A Decontaminated Hassles Scale for a Special Population." *Journal of Behavioral Medicine, 13*(6), 1990, pp. 619–630.

Actively manage your schedule.   Get in the habit of checking your planner throughout the day. Schedule small steps toward big goals. If you can take even one tiny step toward a goal, do it.

Try relaxation techniques.   Techniques that will help you relax and increase your awareness of your physical body can help calm you. These include various breathing techniques (some based in yoga), meditation (while still and quiet or while in motion), and visualization (focusing on a place that you find calming).

Check things off.   Use a physical action when you complete a task—check off the item, delete it from your task list, crumple up the Post-It note. A physical act can relieve stress and highlight the confidence that comes from getting something done.

Manage family responsibilities.   Students with elderly parents, relatives with health care issues, or young children often have to juggle family responsibilities as they try to study (see Key 4.6 for helpful suggestions on childcare issues).

When you need help, ask for it.   Calling on family and friends to help you in specific ways is a key way to connect with purpose. Switch shifts at work to free up study time, ask a friend to take your kids the day before a test, or have a family member help you study.

Keep Your Body Healthy

Even the most driven goal achiever has trouble moving ahead when illness or injury hits. If you do your best to eat well, get exercise and sleep, and avoid substances that can throw you off your game, you will be in shape to stay in motion.

Eat Well

Eating well and getting exercise can be tough for students. The *food environment* in college is often filled with unhealthy choices,[1] and students tend to sit a lot, grab meals on the run, and eat as a reaction to stress. Healthy eating requires *balance* (varying your diet) and *moderation*

Inside Tips from Sarah, Academic Coach

Think about how your health habits affect your academic performance: What helps you, and what sets you back? To reach goals that are new to you as a college student, you may need to change your approach to personal wellness. Ask yourself: What improvement will benefit you? Decide on a concrete change that you think will help (go to bed an hour earlier, send your last text at 11 p.m., go without refined sugar). Put this change in place for a couple of weeks. If it makes a difference, keep it up—and maybe add another.

STUDYING WITH CHILDREN

- **Keep them up to date on your schedule.** Kids appreciate being involved, even though they may not understand entirely. Let them know when you have a big test or project due and what they can expect of you.
- **Find help.** Know your schedule and arrange for child-care if necessary. Consider offering to help another parent in exchange for babysitting, hiring a sitter, or using a day care center.
- **Utilize techonology.** You may be able to have a study session over the phone, through instant messaging, by e-mail, or over social networking sites. Additionally, some sites offer tools that allow multiple users to work on a document or project remotely.
- **Be prepared and keep them active.** Consider keeping some toys, activities, or books that only come out during study time. This will make the time special for children.
- **Plan for family time.** Offset your time away from your children with plans to do something together such as a movie or ice cream. Children may be more apt to let you study when they have something to look forward to.

STUDYING WITH INFANTS

- **Utilize your baby's sleeping schedule.** Study at night if your baby goes to sleep early or in the morning if your baby sleeps late.
- **Make time in the middle.** Study during nap times if you aren't too tired yourself.
- **Talk to your baby.** Recite your notes to the baby. The baby will appreciate the attention, and you will get work done.
- **Keep them close.** Put your baby in a safe and fun place while you study, such as a playpen, motorized swing, or jumping seat.

©(l)WavebreakmediaMicro/Fotolia; (r)Sborisov/Fotolia

(eating reasonable amounts). Here are some ways to incorporate both into your life:

- **Vary what you eat and reduce portion size.** For guidance about the different types and amounts of food you should be eating, explore the information and helpful tools at www.choosemyplate.gov. The graphic shown on this website indicates an ideal balance of food groups. Balance your diet so that you get the nutrients you need.

- **Limit fat, cholesterol, sugar, white flour, and alcohol.** Try to eliminate *trans fats*, which increase the risk of heart disease. Minimize candy, desserts, sugar-filled drinks, and alcohol, which is calorie-heavy.

- **If you need to lose weight, communicate.** A campus counselor can help you find a support group, such as Weight Watchers or an on-campus organization, to help you stay on target. Set reasonable weight-loss goals and work toward them gradually (1–2 pounds a week).

Exercise Regularly

Being physically fit increases your energy, helps you cope with stress, and keeps you goal-directed. Here are some ways to make exercise a regular part of your life:

- If you attend school on a campus, walk to classes and meetings.
- Use stairs wherever possible—at home, at school, and elsewhere.
- Use local or school-sponsored fitness facilities.
- Play team recreational sports at school or in your community.
- Find activities you can do on your own time, such as running or yoga.
- Work out with friends or family to combine socializing and exercise.

Being fit is a lifelong pursuit that is never "done." Furthermore, since your body is constantly changing, reevaluate your exercise program on a regular basis to maximize its benefits.

Get Enough Sleep

The average student sleeps only 6 to 7 hours a night—and often gets much less.[2] Overwhelmed students often prioritize schoolwork over sleep, staying up until the wee hours of the morning to study or pulling "all-nighters" to get through a tough project or paper. Although sleep needs vary according to age and other factors, getting fewer hours than you need constitutes sleep deprivation.

Being sleep deprived hinders your ability to concentrate, raises stress levels, and makes you more susceptible to illness. For the sake of your health, your goals, and your GPA, find a way to get the sleep you need. Sleep expert Gregg D. Jacobs, Ph.D., has the following practical suggestions:[3]

- **Reduce consumption of alcohol and caffeine.** Caffeine may keep you awake, especially if you drink it late in the day. Alcohol can prevent you from sleeping deeply.
- **Exercise regularly.** Exercise, especially in the afternoon or early evening, promotes sleep.
- **Nap.** Taking short afternoon naps can reduce the effects of sleep deprivation.
- **Be consistent.** Try to establish a regular sleep time and wake-up schedule.
- **Transition to sleep.** Give yourself a chance to wind down—read, listen to music, drink herbal tea.

Finally, try to avoid staring at a screen in the last half hour or so before you go to sleep. Studies show that the blue-tinged light emitted by screens can cause the human brain to suppress sleep-inducing hormones, especially in teenagers, which contributes to more difficulty falling asleep as well as less restful sleep.[4]

Avoid Alcohol and Drug Abuse

Some students choose to use alcohol and other potentially addictive substances to alleviate stress temporarily or for other reasons. Actually, using

having five or more drinks (for men) or four or more (for women) at one occasion.

these substances can affect your life in ways that *increase* stress. Overuse and abuse of these substances can have potentially serious consequences, including sending you way off the track that leads to your goals.

Alcohol is a depressant and the most frequently used, and abused, drug on campus. Of all alcohol consumption, **binge drinking** is associated with the greatest problems. Students who binge drink are more likely to miss classes or work, perform poorly, experience physical problems (memory loss, headache, stomach issues), become depressed, and engage in unplanned or unsafe sexual activity.[5] Even a few drinks affect muscle coordination and, more importantly, the ability to reason and make sensible decisions. Any of these effects can send stress levels through the roof.

College students may use drugs to relieve stress, connect with particular social groups, or just to try something new. In most cases, the negative consequences of drug use outweigh any temporary high. Drug use violates federal, state, and local laws, and you may be arrested, tried, and imprisoned for possessing even a small amount of drugs. You can jeopardize your reputation and your student status if you are caught using drugs or if drug use impairs your performance. Finally, long-term drug use can damage your body and mind. Every consequence of drug use has the potential to prevent you from achieving the goals that mean the most to you.

If you drink or take drugs, think carefully about the effects on your health, safety, and academic performance. Consider the positive and negative effects of your choice. If you believe you have a problem, communicate and connect with purpose to people who can help. College and community resources can help you generate options for recovery and better health.

Keep Your Mind Healthy

Staying positive about who you are, making hopeful plans for the future, and building resilience to cope with setbacks will promote good mental health. However, some people experience emotional disorders that make it more difficult than usual to calm the stress response and cope. If you recognize yourself in any of the following descriptions, contact your student health center or campus counseling center for help or a referral to a specialist. Emotional disorders include:

- **Anxiety disorders.** Disorders such as generalized anxiety disorder (GAD) and obsessive-compulsive disorder (OCD) create high-stress responses that are difficult to control.
- **Post-traumatic stress disorder.** Past trauma (rape, war experiences, assault, loss, illness) triggers flashbacks, irritability, emotional distance, and sometimes violence.

STUDENT TO STUDENT

Consider how your health habits affect your goals. Pair up with a fellow student. Take turns asking each other:

Is there anything about the way you eat, exercise, sleep, or use substances that is causing unmanageable stress? Are your health habits moving you toward or away from your goals? If you are unhappy with where you are at, who can help you change? Name two people with whom you can communicate, and describe how you will connect purposefully with them.

- **Eating disorders.** *Anorexia nervosa* (severe restriction of eating), *bulimia* (eating excessive amounts of foods followed by purging), or *binge-eating disorder* (bingeing on foods without purging) cause serious health problems.

- **Clinical depression (depressive disorder).** At varying levels of severity, this illness dampens energy and motivation and sometimes leads to threats of suicide.

Of these disorders, depression in particular has become fairly common on college campuses, due in part to the wide range of stressors that students experience. Recent research reports that nearly half of surveyed students reported feelings of depression at some point, with more than 30% saying that the level of depression made it difficult to function at times.[6] Key 4.7 on page 103 shows possible causes of depression as well as some typical symptoms and offers helpful coping strategies.

At its worst, depression can lead to suicidal thoughts and attempts. If you recognize severe depression or suicidal thoughts in someone you know, do everything you can to convince the individual to see a health professional. If you are struggling with severe depression or are thinking of suicide, get help. There are people who care and can assist you. The right help can change—or even save—a life.

For Stress Management

Name a current task or situation that is causing a high level of stress: _____.
In the right-hand column, record specific ideas for how MI strategies can help you manage that stress.

Intelligence	Use MI Strategies to Manage Stress	Identify MI Strategies that Can Help You Manage and Reduce Stress
Verbal-Linguistic	• Keep a journal of what situations, people, or events cause stress. • Write letters or e-mail or text friends about your problems.	
Logical-Mathematical	• Think through problems using a problem-solving process, and devise a detailed plan. • Analyze the negative and positive effects that may result from a stressful situation.	
Bodily-Kinesthetic	• Choose a physical activity that helps you release tension—running, yoga, team sports—and do it regularly. • Plan physical activities during free time—go for a hike, take a bike ride, go dancing with friends.	
Visual-Spatial	• Enjoy things that appeal to you visually—visit an exhibit, see an art film, shoot photos with your camera. • Use a visual organizer to plan out a solution to a stressful problem.	
Interpersonal	• Communicate with people who care about you and are supportive. • Shift your focus by being a good listener to others who need to talk about their stresses.	
Intrapersonal	• Schedule downtime when you can think through what is causing stress. • Allow yourself 5 minutes a day of meditation where you visualize a positive way for a stressful situation to resolve.	
Musical	• Listen to music that relaxes, inspires, and/or energizes you. • Write a song about what is bothering you.	
Naturalistic	• See whether the things that cause you stress fall into categories that can give you helpful ideas about how to handle situations. • If nature is calming for you, interact with it—spend time outdoors, watch nature-focused TV, read books or articles on nature or science.	

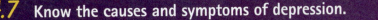

Key 4.7 Know the causes and symptoms of depression.

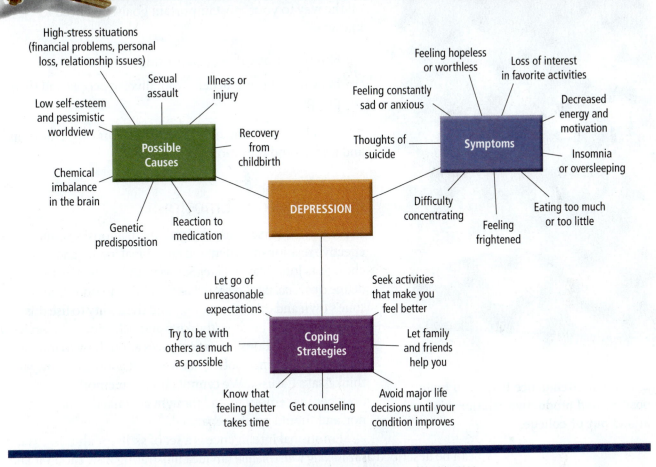

Possible Causes
- High-stress situations (financial problems, personal loss, relationship issues)
- Sexual assault
- Illness or injury
- Low self-esteem and pessimistic worldview
- Recovery from childbirth
- Chemical imbalance in the brain
- Genetic predisposition
- Reaction to medication

DEPRESSION

Symptoms
- Feeling hopeless or worthless
- Loss of interest in favorite activities
- Feeling constantly sad or anxious
- Decreased energy and motivation
- Thoughts of suicide
- Insomnia or oversleeping
- Difficulty concentrating
- Eating too much or too little
- Feeling frightened

Coping Strategies
- Let go of unreasonable expectations
- Seek activities that make you feel better
- Try to be with others as much as possible
- Let family and friends help you
- Know that feeling better takes time
- Get counseling
- Avoid major life decisions until your condition improves

Source: *Depression*, National Institutes of Health publications 02-3561, National Institutes of Health, 2002.

Nearly all goals seem more reachable and less stressful when you communicate and connect with others. With knowledge and skill, you can get the most out of your personal relationships.

How Can Learning to Work with Others Help You Reach Your Goals?
(shouldn't they be reachable without help?)

In college, being able to achieve your goals depends on your ability to relate effectively to others. Students may work on projects together, create and perform a presentation, or form a study group to prepare for an exam. Math and science instructors sometimes initiate student study groups, known as *peer-assisted study sessions* or *supplemental instruction*, to help students improve performance. Students in online courses may meet virtually for study group sessions or project work. All of this teamwork prepares you for the modern

© LifeBound, LLC

Emotional intelligence helps you build positive and productive relationships in and out of college.

workplace where working in teams is essential to success in almost every profession.

To communicate effectively and connect with purpose on the way to your most important goals, you need to know:

- How emotions affect relationships
- How to value and benefit from diverse people and their perspectives

Start by examining how to manage your own emotions and understand the emotions of others.

Focus on Your Emotions

Success in a diverse world depends on relationships, and effective relationships demand emotional intelligence. Psychologists John Mayer, Peter Salovey, and David Caruso define *emotional intelligence* (EI) as the ability to understand "one's own and others' emotions and the ability to use this information as a guide to thinking and behavior."[7] An understanding of emotions informs choices about how to interact. "Emotions influence both what we think about and how we think," says Caruso. "We cannot check our emotions at the door because emotions and thought are linked—they cannot, and should not, be separated."[8]

Emotional intelligence is a set of skills, or abilities, that can be described as *reasoning with emotion* (an idea illustrating how thought and emotion work together). Key 4.8 shows how you move through these skills when you reason with emotion.

Key 4.8 Take an emotionally intelligent approach.

PERCEIVING EMOTIONS	**THINKING ABOUT EMOTIONS**	**UNDERSTANDING EMOTIONS**	**MANAGING EMOTIONS**
Recognizing how you and others feel	Seeing what thoughts arise from the feelings you perceive, and how they affect your mindset	Determining what the emotions involved in a situation tell you, and considering how you can adjust your mindset or direct thinking in a productive way	Using what you learn from your emotions and those of others to choose behavior and actions that move you toward positive outcomes

Source: Adapted from Mayer, John D., Peter Salovey, and David R. Caruso, "Emotional Intelligence: New Ability or Eclectic Traits?" *American Psychologist*, vol. 63, no. 6, pp. 505–507. September 2008. Reprinted by Permission of the American Psychological Association.

The key is staying aware of what your goals demand from your relationships. For example, succeeding in class might require that you communicate in productive ways during class time and in communication with your instructor. Here are some examples of how emotional intelligence can help you set and pursue goals:

- You realize that you get bored quickly, and decide to create more short-term goals to keep you energized on the way to a long-term goal.
- You feel tension in your relationship with one of your instructors, and you request a conference during office hours, hoping that a productive discussion will help you feel more comfortable in the class and more motivated to do your best on assignments.
- You sense that your project partner is stressed out, so you offer to reschedule your work session and see if he wants to go for coffee after class and talk instead.

As you encounter references to emotional intelligence in this course and elsewhere, think of it as *thinking skills applied to relationships*. Putting emotional intelligence to work means taking in and analyzing how you and others feel, seeing the ideas those feelings create, and taking action in response—all with the purpose of achieving a goal. You are building your emotional intelligence throughout your work in this text, as you build Habits for Success as well as learn more about who you are through the self-assessments.

Often the people you work with have different values and cultural backgrounds. In an increasingly global world, learning to appreciate that diversity and to understand and accept those who differ from you will help you work with others more successfully.

Become Culturally Competent

Most academic goals that you set will require you to work with other students, teachers, and administrators. Work goals will require you to work with clients, colleagues, and employers. Chances are that you will work with others who differ from you in ways both visible (race, ethnicity, age) and invisible (family situation, sexual orientation, values). The goal of **cultural competence** is to interact successfully and productively with the people around you.

Building cultural competence means taking the following actions:[9]

1. **Value diversity**. Have a basic respect for the differences among people and an understanding of what is positive about those differences.
2. **Identify and evaluate personal perceptions and attitudes.** Examine whether you have any **prejudices** or judge based on **stereotypes**. Challenge yourself to set them aside as you get to know and work with others.
3. **Be aware of what tends to happen when cultures interact.** Work to notice, avoid, and combat discrimination and hate crimes.
4. **Build cultural knowledge.** Learn about people who are different from you, especially those you are likely to work with in college or on the job.

Cultural competence
the ability to understand and appreciate differences and to respond to people of all cultures in a way that values their worth, respects their beliefs and practices, and builds communication and relationships.

Prejudice
a preconceived judgment or opinion formed without just grounds or sufficient knowledge.

Stereotype
a standardized mental picture that represents an oversimplified opinion or uncritical judgment.

© Andres Rodriguez/Fotolia

5. **Adapt to diverse cultures**. Opening your mind will create opportunities. Look past external characteristics, put yourself in other people's shoes, and recognize what you have in common with people everywhere.

Some colleges have international exchange programs that can help you appreciate the world's cultural diversity. Engaging with students from other countries, whether they have come to your college or you have chosen to study abroad, can provide a two-way learning experience, helping each of you learn about the other's culture. Building knowledge also means exploring yourself. Talk with family, read, and seek experiences that educate you about your own cultural heritage; then share what you know with others.

Maximize Your Teamwork

Whether you aim to complete a project or study for an exam, what can you gain from working with others?

Increased knowledge.   When group members share knowledge, each member spends less time and energy learning the material. Another benefit: Reviewing concepts or teaching them to others helps solidify what you know.

More motivation.   Knowing that you are accountable to others and that they will see how prepared you are—or aren't—may encourage you to work hard.

Better teamwork skills.   Nothing teaches you how to communicate and work effectively in groups better than experience, both the positive and the problematic.

Strength from diversity.   The more diverse the group of people working together, the more ideas are generated, leading to more effective problem solving.

Strategies for Group Success

The way a group operates may depend on members' personalities, motivation, and knowledge; what you are studying; group size; and how you gather (in person or virtually). These general strategies will help all groups succeed:

- **Set long-term and short-term goals.** At your first meeting, decide what the group wants to accomplish. Having an *agenda* (a meeting plan) for each meeting—and sticking to it—helps people stay focused.

- **Set a schedule.** Determine how many meetings are needed and what team members can manage. If you are studying for a final, you might start a month before the test with a weekly meeting. As test day nears, you may decide to meet more frequently.

- **Choose a leader for each meeting.** Rotating the leadership among members willing to lead helps everyone take ownership of the group.

- **Be prepared and share the workload.** Make sure you have the materials you need, and pitch in. Your willingness to work is more important than how much you know.

- **Practice civility and respect.** Interact with others respectfully, even if the conversation gets heated. If you have an issue with someone, talk privately after the meeting. Set cell phones aside so that you can give your full attention to the meeting and your teammates.

For groups with a study focus, here are further tips:

- **Create materials for one another.** Give each group member one topic to compile, photocopy, and review for the others.
- **Help each other learn.** Have group members teach each other information, work on problems, give feedback on responses to essay questions, or go through flash cards together.
- **Pool your note-taking resources.** Compare notes and fill in any information you don't have.

Study groups and other teams need both leaders *and* participants to accomplish their goals[10](see Key 4.9).

Defuse Potential Problems

Issues can arise even with the most effective teams. Be prepared to address them if they happen:

- **People not fulfilling responsibilities.** If it's a one-time incident due to an illness or a personal problem, it's best to let it go. However, if it happens regularly, try reassigning tasks or having a group discussion and problem-solving session.
- **Trouble scheduling.** Finding a time—and location, if you are meeting in person—that works for a group can be challenging. Coordinate everything on a group e-mail or text first. If you find a time that works for all, schedule meetings consistently. If you can't, you may have to schedule each meeting as you go.

Key 4.9 **The group process needs leaders and participants.**

For Participant
- Do your share of the work.
- Stay organized and focused.
- Be open and willing to discuss.
- Perform your responsibilities on schedule.

For Leader
- Define projects, and focus everyone's efforts.
- Assign work tasks, and set a schedule and deadlines.
- Set meeting and project goals.
- Keep everyone on target and moving ahead.
- Set a fair, respectful, and encouraging tone.

- **Off-topic talking.** Even if group members are friends, you can set boundaries. Set up social time at the end as a reward for accomplishing a goal.

Identifying your core values, setting goals that reflect them, learning techniques to manage the stress that can keep you from reaching your goals, and connecting with purpose to team members will help you move toward what you most want to achieve in college and beyond.

HABIT IN ACTION WRAP-UP

© Courtesy of Elise Tran

What happened with Elise?

Elise earned admittance to the Colorado School of Mines and is currently studying mechanical engineering. She is an active member in her community and continues to help people around her. The Multicultural Engineering Program at Mines has become her second home, and the director of the program is a great resource when Elise has questions regarding college. Elise is also a part of Sigma Kappa sorority, which has helped her build lifelong friendships and provided opportunities to volunteer in her community. She continues to connect with purpose with her family and friends, who provide emotional and academic support for her on an ongoing basis.

Because of her previous experiences, she knows she wouldn't be where she is today without the help of a multitude of people in her life and wants to pay it forward. Her goal is to be the first person in her family to graduate from college and set a milestone for future generations, especially women in science, technology, engineering, or math (STEM) careers.

Connect this story to your life: What relationships of yours could use more effective communication and a purposeful connection? Identify one relationship to improve, and note specific ways in which you will improve how you communicate with this person. Describe the goal you seek with this connection, and keep that goal in the front of your mind so that you can connect with purpose.

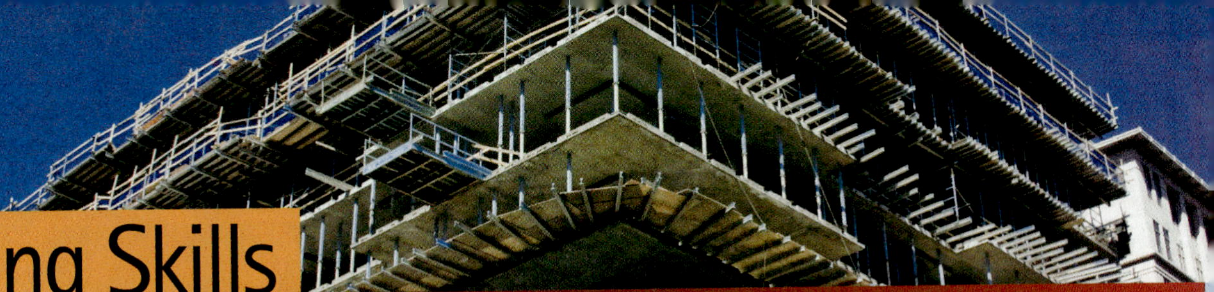

Building Skills
for successful learning

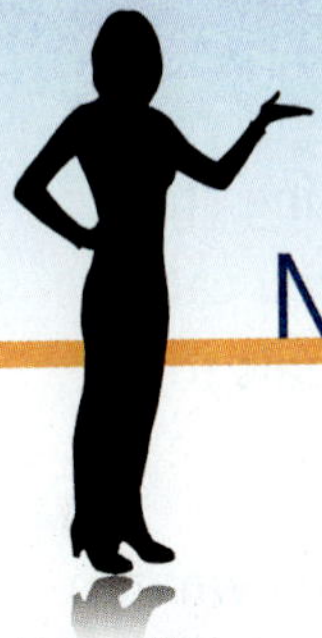

Note the Important Points

Describe one way that identifying your values can help you achieve college and life goals.

Explain what short-term and long-term goals are and how they relate.

Define what a S.M.A.R.T. goal is by naming what each letter stands for.

How do you define *stress*?

Name two stress-management strategies.

1. __________

2. __________

Define *emotional intelligence*.

What is the goal of cultural competence?

Critical Thinking

Use Short-Term Goals to Explore Majors

Declaring a major is a long-term goal made up of short-term goal steps. Although many entering students don't yet know what they want to study, it's smart to explore possibilities now so that you can match your talents, skills, and dreams with an academic path. Use the following short-term goals to get moving.

Short-term goal #1: Identify interests and talents. If you can choose a major that focuses on what interests you and what you do well, you are more likely to have a positive attitude and perform effectively. To pinpoint areas that may work for you, consider questions like the following:

- What are my favorite courses, topics to read about, activities?

- Am I a "natural" in any academic or skill area?

- How do I learn and work with others most effectively?

Based on your exploration, write down two majors that you think are worth considering.

- _____

- _____

Short-term goal #2: Explore general academic options. Use the course catalog, the school website, or other resources to explore the following:

- When do you have to declare a major? _____

- What majors are offered at your school? (No need to write here; just read through the list.)

- What are the options in majoring? (double majors, minors, "interdisciplinary" majors that combine more than one academic area) _____

  _____

- What is the process for changing a major once you have declared?

  _____

  _____

Short-term goal #3: Explore details of selected majors. Use the table to nail down specifics for each of the three majors that interest you. Check your course catalog and school website, talk to people currently majoring in this subject, and consult your academic advisor.

MAJORS	#1: _____	#2: _____
Minimum GPA for being accepted		
Minimum GPA required in coursework for the major		
Number of courses required		
Career areas that relate to this major		
Department head name		
Department administrator name and contact information		
How many students declare this major each year		
Where the department is located		
Courses you would have to take in the next year		

Finally, name the exact calendar date here when you will need to have declared your major:

_____ Put it in your planner and stick to it!

Team Building

collaborative solutions

Actively Dealing with Stress

First, look back at the college stress self-assessment you completed in All About Me. Note the items you marked as causing the most stress for you. As a class, discuss—in person or in a chat or discussion forum—which stressors seem to be most commonly experienced by students taking this course, and identify four stressors to focus on. Divide into four groups, and assign a stressor to each. Meet with your group virtually or in person to:

- Discuss your stressor and the effects it has on people.

- Generate coping strategies for this stressor, including ones that relate to health (eating, sleeping, exercise, substances, getting help).

- Come to consensus on the three most useful coping strategies.

- Present your conclusion, electronically or in person, to the class.

Test Prep   Start It Now

communicate

Work with Others to Prep for Tests

Take advantage of the benefits of teamwork by setting up a study group now for your next big test. Check your syllabi and note here the topic, date, and course for your closest upcoming test:

Test topic _____

_____

Test date and time _____

Course _____

Set up a study group with between one and four classmates. Write their names and contact information here:

_____   _____

_____   _____

_____   _____

_____   _____

How much time do you have from now until the test? _____

Plan at least two sessions during that time—one 2 days before the test and one a week or so earlier. For each, name the date, time, and location (put this information in your planner).

Session 1: _____

_____

Session 2: _____

_____

Finally, read over the strategies for group work success, and communicate with your group before you meet in order to set goals and decide who will serve as leader for both sessions.

5

critical and creative thinking

solving problems and making decisions

CLIFTON TAULBERT, *best-selling author and president and CEO of the Freemount Corporation and Roots Java Coffee*

Clifton Taulbert was born in 1945 in Glen Allan, a small Mississippi Delta cotton-producing community. Raised by extended family, in particular his great-aunt, he was "taught to be 'colored' more for others than ourselves," as he puts it, constantly reminded of the restrictions that his skin color imposed outside of his community. Despite being legally segregated, his community had a love of and emphasis on education that had a transformative impact on him. His great-aunt was up early each morning pulling the string of a 60-watt bulb on the porch to signal the bus driver, making sure he didn't miss a single bus ride to high school.

Having never seen evidence of racial equality, Clifton had no sense of the injustice of riding 100 miles round-trip to his all-black high school when the white high school was a stone's throw from his house. He worked hard, graduated as the valedictorian of his class, and dreamed of going to college. However, first he experienced a time of enormous transition—moving to St. Louis to meet his birth father, where he was met with race riots and took a low-paying job as a dishwasher. After moving up to a better job at Jefferson Bank and Trust, he received a low draft number and enlisted in the United States Air Force to avoid being drafted.

During his first permanent assignment in Maine, Clifton began studying at the University of Maine. Here, his lack of good grammar and writing skills caught up with him. His English professor gave him back a paper with so many red marks it looked bloody; more importantly, it had written on it a statement that would change his life: "Taulbert, you have so much to say, please learn how to say it." Upset and challenged, Clifton tried to imagine how he could extend his abilities to match his vision.

(to be continued . . .)

Some students, like Clifton, need to expand their abilities to reach their vision. Others need to expand their vision to understand what they can accomplish. You'll learn more about Clifton's experience at the end of the chapter.

Working through this chapter will help you to:

Text and photo used by permission of Clifton Taulbert

imagine

Every person has the power to imagine. Use this power to *expand* your thinking, creating new ideas and solutions to problems.

Why Is It Important to Ask and Answer Questions? *(what if you already know the answers?)*

What is thinking? According to experts, it is what happens when you ask questions and move toward the answers.[1] "To think through or rethink anything," says Richard Paul, director of research at the Center for Critical Thinking and Moral Critique, "one must ask questions that stimulate . . . thought. Questions define tasks, express problems and delineate issues. . . . Only students who have questions are really thinking and learning."[2] It's human to feel as though asking questions makes you look ignorant. However, questioning is what *combats* ignorance, inspiring imagination and expanding learning.

As you answer questions, you transform pieces of information into knowledge you can use. A computer programming student may ask how a certain code can make software perform a task. A pharmacy technology student may question which drug works best for a particular illness. An accounting student may ask how to set up a spreadsheet. All of these questioners seek information that they will use to achieve goals.

The questioning process may not be straightforward or quick. Sometimes the answer doesn't come right away. Often the answer leads to further, and more specific, questions. Effective questioning requires that you

- Define your purpose for questioning: "What am I trying to accomplish, and why?"

- Question in different ways: Analyze, compare, evaluate.

- Want to question. Having thinking skills is not enough—you also need to be willing to use them (which often requires that you understand how you will benefit from it).

As a college student, you are required to think in ways that go beyond the ability to memorize and retain what you learn. You are thinking *critically* and *creatively*, and you accomplish both through asking questions.

Critical thinking.   This can be defined as the process of gathering information, breaking it into parts, examining and evaluating those parts, and making

© Rusya M./Fotolia

connections for the purposes of gaining understanding, solving a problem, or making a decision.

Creative thinking. Some researchers define creativity as combining existing elements in an innovative way to create a new purpose or result. (Using a weak adhesive to mark pages in a book, a 3M scientist created Post-it Notes.) Others see creativity as the ability to generate new ideas from looking at how things are related. (Noting what ladybugs eat inspired organic farmers to bring them in to consume crop-destroying aphids.)[3] Psychologist Robert Sternberg notes that creative people tend to have ideas that go against the norm—ideas that at first are often rejected but later are widely accepted.[4]

This chapter describes critical and creative thinking in more detail and shows how the two work together to help you solve problems and make decisions more effectively. More developed thinking skills means better performance at school and at work. Critical and creative thinkers are in demand because of their ability to apply what they know, think through situations, imagine new ideas, and expand the selection of available options and solutions.

How Can You Improve Your Critical Thinking Skills? *(does it have anything to do with criticism?)*

Through the critical thinking process (which is different than criticizing something), you look for how pieces of information relate to one another, setting aside any pieces that are unclear, unrelated, unimportant, or biased. You may also form new questions that change your direction or even shift your purpose. Be open to them and to where they may lead you.

Gather Information

To start the thinking process, you gather information—the raw material for thinking. This requires analyzing how much information you need, how much time you should spend gathering it, and whether it is relevant. Say, for instance, that you have to write a paper on one aspect of the media (TV, radio, Internet) and its influence on a particular group. Here's how analyzing can help you gather information for that paper:

- Reviewing the assignment terms, you note two important items: The paper should be approximately 10 pages long and describe at least three significant points of influence.

- With an initial Google search, you find thousands of articles in this topic area. Analyzing how many articles treat certain aspects of the topic, you decide to focus your paper on how the Internet influences young teens (ages 13–15).

- Examining summaries of six comprehensive articles leads you to three in-depth sources.

In this way you achieve a subgoal—a selection of useful materials—on the way to your larger goal of writing a well-crafted paper.

Break Information into Parts

The next step is to search for the two most relevant parts of the information: The main idea(s) (also called the **argument** or viewpoint) and the evidence that supports them (also called reasons or supporting details).

Separate the ideas. Identify each of the ideas conveyed in what you are reading. You can use lists or a mind map to visually separate ideas from one another. For instance, if you are reading about how teens ages 13 to 15 use the Internet, you could identify the goal of each method of access they use (websites, YouTube, social media such as Snapchat and Instagram, and so on).

Identify the evidence. For each main idea, identify the evidence that supports it. For example, if an article claims that young teens rely on app-based messaging three times more than on e-mails, note the facts, studies, or other evidence cited to support the truth of the claim.

Examine and Evaluate

The third step lies at the heart of critical thinking. Examine the information to see if it will be useful for your purposes. Keep your mind open to all useful information, setting aside personal prejudices. Here are four different questions that will help you examine and evaluate effectively.

> **Argument**
> a set of connected ideas, supported by examples, that prove or disprove a point.

1. *Do examples support ideas?*

When you encounter an idea or a claim, examine how it is supported with examples or *evidence*—facts, expert opinion, research findings, personal experience, and so on. How useful an idea is to your work may depend on whether, or how well, it is backed up with solid evidence or made concrete with examples. Be critical of the information you gather; don't take it at face value.

For example, a v-blog by a 12-year-old may make statements about what kids do on the Internet. The word of one person, who may or may not be telling the truth, is not adequate support. However, a study of youth technology use by

© Juniart/Fotolia

Many types of work, such as the construction project these architects are discussing, involve analytical thinking.

the Department of Commerce under the provisions of the Children's Internet Protection Act may be more reliable.

2. Is the information factual and accurate, or is it opinion?

A *statement of fact* is information presented as objectively real and verifiable (e.g., "The Internet is a research tool"). In contrast, a *statement of opinion* is a belief, conclusion, or judgment that is inherently difficult, and sometimes impossible, to verify (e.g., "The Internet is always the best and most reliable research tool"). When you critically evaluate materials, one test of the evidence is whether it is fact or opinion. Key 5.1 defines important characteristics of fact and opinion.

3. Do causes and effects link logically?

Look at the reasons given for why something happened (causes) and the explanation of its consequences (effects, both positive and negative). For example, an article might detail what causes young teens to use the Internet after school and the effects that this has on their family life. The cause-and-effect chain in the article should make sense to you.

Key 5.1 Examine how fact and opinion differ.

FACTS INCLUDE STATEMENTS THAT . . .	OPINIONS INCLUDE STATEMENTS THAT . . .
. . . deal with actual people, places, objects, or events. Example: "In 2002, the European Union introduced the physical coins and banknotes of a new currency—the euro—that was designed to be used by its member nations."	**. . . show evaluation.** Any statement of value indicates an opinion. Words such as *bad, good, pointless*, and *beneficial* indicate value judgments. Example: "The use of the euro has been beneficial to all the states of the European Union."
. . . use concrete words or measurable statistics. Example: "The charity event raised $50,862."	**. . . use abstract words.** Complicated words like *misery* or *success* usually indicate a personal opinion. Example: "The charity event was a smashing success."
. . . describe current events in exact terms. Example: "Mr. Barrett's course has 378 students enrolled this semester."	**. . . predict future events.** Statements about future occurrences are often opinions. Example: "Mr. Barrett's course is going to set a new enrollment record this year."
. . . avoid emotional words and focus on the verifiable. Example: "Citing dissatisfaction with the instruction, 7 out of the 25 students in that class withdrew in September."	**. . . use emotional words.** Emotions are unverifiable. Words such as *delightful* or *miserable* express an opinion. Example: "That class is a miserable experience."
. . . avoid absolutes. Example: "Some students need to have a job while in school."	**. . . use absolutes.** Absolute qualifiers, such as *all, none, never*, and *always*, often express an opinion. Example: "All students need to have a job while in school."

Source: Adapted from Ben E. Johnson, *Stirring Up Thinking*. New York: Houghton Mifflin, 1998, pp. 268–270.

Bias

a preference or inclination, especially one that prevents even-handed judgment.

Perspective

a characteristic way of thinking about people, situations, events, and ideas.

Assumption

a judgment, generalization, or bias influenced by experience and values.

An important caution: Analyze carefully to seek out key or "root" causes—the true and significant causes of a problem or situation. For example, many factors may be involved in why young teens spend large amounts of time on the Internet, including availability of service, previous experience, and education level of parents, but on careful examination one or two factors seem to be more significant than others.

4. Is the evidence biased?

Evidence with a **bias** is evidence that is slanted in a particular direction. Searching for a bias involves looking for hidden perspectives or assumptions that lie within the material.

A **perspective** can be broad (such as a generally optimistic or pessimistic view of life) or more focused (such as an attitude about whether students should commute or live on campus). Perspectives are associated with **assumptions**. For example, the perspective that people can maintain control over technology leads to assumptions such as "Parents can control children's exposure to the Internet." Having a particular experience with children and the Internet can build or reinforce a perspective.

Assumptions often hide within questions and statements, blocking you from considering information in different ways. Take this classic puzzler as an example: "Which came first, the chicken or the egg?" Thinking about this question, most people assume that the egg is a chicken egg. If you think past that assumption and come up with a new idea—such as the egg is a dinosaur egg—then the obvious answer is that the egg came first. Different sources may make different assumptions about the same topic. In researching how teens' grades are affected by Internet use, for example, you may find that a teaching organization has a much different view than a company that sells Internet advertising on search engines.

Examining perspectives and assumptions helps you judge whether material is *reliable*. The less bias you can identify, the more reliable the information.

After the questions: What information is most useful to you?

You've examined your information, looking at its evidence, its validity, its perspective, and any underlying assumptions. Now, based on that examination, you evaluate whether an idea or piece of information is important or unimportant, relevant or not, strong or weak, and why. You then set aside what is not useful and use the rest to form an opinion, possible solution, or decision.

In preparing your paper on young teens and the Internet, for example, you've analyzed a selection of information and materials to see how they applied to the goal of your paper. You then selected what you believe will be most useful, in preparation for drafting.

How do you perceive yourself as a critical thinker? For each statement, circle the number that feels right to you, from 1 for "not at all true for me" to 5 for "very true for me."

1.	I recognize and define problems effectively.	1 2 3 4 5
2.	I see myself as "a thinker," "analytical," "studious."	1 2 3 4 5
3.	I need to see convincing evidence before accepting information as fact.	1 2 3 4 5
4.	In a group setting, I like to break down a problem into parts and evaluate them.	1 2 3 4 5
5.	I notice when ideas are not backed up by solid evidence.	1 2 3 4 5
6.	I focus on whether ideas are logically connected.	1 2 3 4 5
7.	I read everything carefully–even e-mails–to make sure that I understand what the writer intends to say.	1 2 3 4 5

Total your answers here: _____

If your total ranges from 7 to 14, you consider your critical thinking skills to be *weak.*

If your total ranges from 15 to 24, you consider your critical thinking skills to be *average.*

If your total ranges from 25 to 35, you consider your critical-thinking skills to be *strong.*

TAKE ACTION
Analyze a Statement

Consider the statement below. Use your critical thinking skills to answer the questions that follow:

"The Internet is the best place to find information about any topic."

Is this statement fact or opinion? Why?

_____

What assumption(s) underlie the statement, and how might these assumptions affect how you complete research assignments?

_____

What examples can you think of that support or disprove this statement?

_____

As a result of your critical thinking, what is your evaluation of this statement?

_____

_____

Make Connections

The last part of critical thinking takes place when, after you have broken information apart, you find new and logical ways to connect pieces together. This step is crucial for research papers and essays because it is where original ideas are born and creative skills come into play (more on that in the next section). When you begin to write, you focus on your new ideas, supporting them with information you've learned from your analysis. Following are some ways to make connections.

Key 5.2   Ask questions like these to think critically.

To gather information, ask:	▪ What kinds of information do I need to meet my goal? ▪ What information is available? Where and when can I get to it? ▪ Of the sources I found, which ones will best help me achieve my goal?
To analyze, ask:	▪ What are the parts of this information? ▪ What is similar to this information? What is different? ▪ What are the reasons for this? Why did this happen? ▪ What ideas, themes, or conclusions emerge from this material? ▪ How would you categorize this information?
To see if evidence or examples support an idea, ask:	▪ Does the evidence make sense? ▪ How do the examples support the idea/claim? ▪ Are there examples that might disprove the idea/claim?
To distinguish fact from opinion, ask:	▪ Do the words in this information signal fact or opinion? ▪ What is the source of this information? Is the source reliable? ▪ If this is an opinion, is it supported by facts?
To examine perspectives and assumptions, ask:	▪ What perspectives might the author have, and what may be emphasized or deemphasized as a result? ▪ What assumptions might lie behind this statement or material? ▪ How could I prove, or disprove, an assumption? ▪ How might my perspective affect the way I see this material?
To evaluate, ask:	▪ What information will support what I'm trying to prove or accomplish? ▪ Is this information true or false, and why? ▪ How important is this information?

Source: Adapted from www-ed.fnal.gov/trc/tutorial/taxonomy.html (Richard Paul, *Critical Thinking: How to Prepare Students for a Rapidly Changing World*, 1993) and from www.kcmetro.edu/longview/ctac/blooms.htm (Barbara Fowler, Longview Community College "Bloom's Taxonomy and Critical Thinking").

Compare and contrast. Look at how ideas are similar to, or different from, each other. You might explore how different young teen subgroups (boys vs. girls, for example) have different purposes for setting up Tumblr accounts or creating Twitter handles.

Look for themes, patterns, and categories. Note connections that form as you look at how bits of information relate to one another. For example, you might see patterns of Internet use that link young teens from particular cultures or areas of the country together into categories.

Come to new information ready to hear and read new ideas, think about them, and make informed decisions about what you believe. The process will expand your perspectives, sharpen your thinking skills, and give you more information to work with as you encounter life's problems. See Key 5.2 for some questions you can ask to build and use critical thinking skills.

Pursuing your goals, both in school and in the workplace, requires not just analyzing information but also thinking creatively about how to use what your thinking has uncovered.

How Can You Improve Your Creative Thinking Skills? *(doesn't creativity require artistic talent?)*

Although creativity is often equated with visual and performing arts, it goes far beyond, into areas like auto innovations, business ideas, and teaching techniques. In a general sense, to think creatively is to expand the mind in ways that generate change-promoting ideas, whether the change consists of world-altering communication technology or a tooth brushing technique that more effectively prevents cavities. Set the stage for developing creative thinking skills by gathering five ingredients of creativity:

1. **Belief that you can develop creativity.** Creative thinking is a skill that can be developed. Says creativity expert Roger von Oech, "Like race-car drivers who shift in and out of different gears depending on where they are on the course," you can learn to "shift in and out of different types of thinking depending on the needs of the situation at hand."[5]

2. **Curiosity and exploration.** Seeking out new information and experiences will broaden your knowledge, giving you more raw materials with which to build creative ideas.[6] Think about what sparks your curiosity, and expand your knowledge about it.

3. **Time alone.** Research indicates that creativity demands time and independent thinking.[7] Along with the time you may spend generating ideas with others, find time alone to imagine, letting your mind toss those ideas around.

© 123RF

4. **Risk-taking and hard work.** Creativity demands time, ideas, and enormous effort. "All creative geniuses work passionately hard and produce incredible numbers of ideas, most of which are bad," reports creativity expert Michael Michalko, recounting, among other examples, the fact that Picasso created more than 20,000 pieces of art.[8]

5. **Acceptance of mistakes as part of the process.** Mistakes can reveal ideas and promote productivity. Says Michalko, "Whenever you try to do something and do not succeed, you do not fail. You have learned something that does not work."[9]

Now, explore actions that will help you build your creative thinking skill: Brainstorming, shifting your perspective, and taking risks.

Brainstorm

Brainstorming is also referred to as *divergent thinking*: You start with a question and then let your mind diverge—that is, go in many different directions—in search of solutions. Brainstorming is *deliberate* creative thinking. When you brainstorm, generate ideas without thinking about how useful they are; evaluate their quality later. Brainstorming works well in groups because group members can become inspired by, and make creative use of, one another's ideas.[10]

One way to inspire ideas when brainstorming is to think of similar situations—in other words, to make *analogies* (comparisons based on a resemblance of things otherwise unlike). For example, Velcro is a product of analogy: When imagining how two pieces of fabric could stick to each other, the inventor thought of a burr sticking to clothing. Strategies that promote effective brainstorming include:

- **Avoid looking for one right answer.** Questions may have many "right answers"—or many answers that have degrees of usefulness. The more possibilities you generate, the better your chance of finding the best one.

- **Mix collaboration with private time.** Consider having individuals generate ideas on their own before bringing them to the group.

- **Keep recording tools at the ready.** Creative ideas can pop up randomly; keep a pen and notebook with you, or use a smartphone, to record them before they fade.

- **Don't stop when you think you have the best answer**—expand the list until you are out of steam. You never know what may come up in those last gasps of creative energy.[11]

Shift Your Perspective

If no one ever questioned established opinion, people would still think the sun revolved around the earth. Here are some ways to change how you look at a situation or problem:

> **Brainstorming**
> letting your mind free-associate to come up with different ideas.

Challenge assumptions. Don't assume something has to be done a certain way because it *always* has been done that way. In the late 1960s, conventional wisdom said that school provided education and television provided entertainment. Jim Henson, a pioneer in children's television, asked, "Why can't we use TV to educate young children?" From that question, the characters of *Sesame Street*, and eventually a host of other educational programs, were born.

Try on another point of view. Ask others for their perspectives, read about new ways to approach situations, or deliberately go against your first instinct.[12] Then use what you learn to inspire creativity. For a fun example of how looking at something in a new way can unearth a totally different idea, look at the perception puzzles in Key 5.3.

With you think through something with others in a group, the variety of ideas gives you a better chance of finding a workable solution to a problem.

Ask "what if" questions. Set up imaginary environments in which new ideas can grow, such as "What if I had unlimited money or time?" For example,

Key 5.3 Use perception puzzles to experience a shift in perspective.

There are two possibilities for each image. What do you see?
(See page 143 for answers.)

imagine

POWERFUL QUESTIONS

STUDENT TO STUDENT

Grace Murray Hopper, a Navy admiral and mathematician, said, "A ship in port is safe, but that's not what ships are built for." Pair up with a fellow student. Take turns asking each other:

What does this quote say to you? How does it relate to the habit of imagining and expanding? Think of goals you believe your "ship"—your mind—is built to pursue. Choose one to consider. What kinds of risks are you willing to take to accomplish that goal?

the founders of Seeds of Peace, faced with long-term conflict in the Middle East, imagined: What if Israeli and Palestinian teens met at a summer camp in Maine to build mutual understanding and respect? Based on the ideas that came up, they created an organization that helps teenagers from the Middle East to develop leadership and communication skills.

Take Risks

Creative breakthroughs can come from targeted risk taking.

Go against established ideas. The founders of Etsy.com went against the idea that the American consumer prefers cheap, conventional, mass-produced items. In 2005, they took the risk of creating an online company that allows artisans to offer one-of-a-kind, handmade products to the consumer, and were rewarded with a thriving site.

Risk leaving your comfort zone. Rewards can come when you expand your experiences and seek out new environments. Go somewhere you've never been. Listen to mp3s of music you've never heard of. Seek out interesting people with whom you would not normally connect. Check out a website or Netflix documentary that is completely outside of your experience. Even small risks like these can create ideas that generate big changes.

As with critical thinking, asking questions powers creative thinking. See Key 5.4 for examples of the kinds of questions you can ask to get your creative juices flowing.

To brainstorm, ask:	■ What do I want to accomplish?
	■ What are the craziest ideas I can think of?
	■ What are 10 ways that I can reach my goal?
	■ What ideas have worked before, and how can I apply them?
To shift your perspective, ask:	■ How has this always been done—and what would be a different way?
	■ How can I approach this task or situation from a new angle?
	■ How would someone else do this or view this?
	■ What if . . . ?
To set the stage for creativity, ask:	■ Where, and with whom, do I feel relaxed and inspired?
	■ What music helps me think out of the box?
	■ When am I most likely to have creative ideas?
	■ What do I think would be new and interesting to try, to see, to read?
To take risks, ask:	■ What is a totally different way to do this?
	■ What would be a risky approach to this problem or question?
	■ What is the worst that can happen if I take this risk? What is the best?
	■ What have I learned from this mistake?

TAKE ACTION
Gather Evidence of Your Creativity

First, think about the past month; then list three creative acts you performed.

1. While I studied, I _____

2. In my personal life, I _____

3. In class, I _____

Now, think of a problem or situation that is on your mind. Brainstorm one new creative idea for how to deal with it.

_____

Let the question sit for *at least* 24 hours. Come back to this page, and write one more idea.

_____

How do you perceive yourself as a creative thinker? For each statement, circle the number that feels right to you, from 1 for "least like me" to 5 for "most like me."

1.	I tend to question rules and regulations.	1 2 3 4 5
2.	I see myself as "unique," "full of ideas," "innovative."	1 2 3 4 5
3.	Too much routine in my work or schedule drains my energy.	1 2 3 4 5
4.	When working with a group, I generate a lot of ideas.	1 2 3 4 5
5.	If you say something is too risky, I'm ready to give it a shot.	1 2 3 4 5
6.	I feel comfortable allowing myself to make mistakes as I test out ideas.	1 2 3 4 5
7.	I often wonder if there is a different way to get something done.	1 2 3 4 5

Total your answers here: _____

If your total ranges from 7 to 14, you consider your creative thinking skills to be *weak.*

If your total ranges from 15 to 24, you consider your creative thinking skills to be *average.*

If your total ranges from 25 to 35, you consider your creative thinking skills to be *strong.*

When you combine critical thinking, creativity, and emotional intelligence, you have a powerful set of skills. Put them into action together to solve problems and make decisions.

How Can You Solve Problems and Make Decisions Effectively?
(and more independently?)

Problem solving and decision making follow similar paths. Both require you to identify and analyze a situation, generate possible solutions, choose one, follow through, and evaluate its success. Key 5.5 gives an overview of the paths, indicating how you think at each step. Keys 5.7 and 5.8 on pages 133 and 135 will show you how to use this path, through a visual organizer, to map out problems and decisions.

Understanding the differences between problem solving and decision making will help you know how to proceed. See Key 5.6 for more information. Whereas all problem solving involves decision making, only some decision making requires you to solve a problem.

Key 5.5   Solve problems and make decisions using a plan of action.

PROBLEM SOLVING	THINKING SKILL	DECISION MAKING
Define the problem—recognize that something needs to change, identify what's happening, look for true causes.	STEP 1 DEFINE	**Define the decision**—identify your goal (your need) and then construct a decision that will help you get it.
Analyze the problem—gather information, break it down into pieces, verify facts, look at perspectives and assumptions, evaluate information.	STEP 2 ANALYZE	**Examine needs and motives**—consider the layers of needs carefully, and be honest about what you really want.
Generate possible solutions—use creative strategies to think of ways you could address the causes of this problem.	STEP 3 CREATE	**Name and/or generate different options**—use creative questions to come up with choices that would fulfill your needs.
Evaluate solutions—look carefully at potential pros and cons of each, and choose what seems best.	STEP 4 ANALYZE (EVALUATE)	**Evaluate options**—look carefully at potential pros and cons of each, and choose what seems best.
Put the solution to work—persevere, focus on results, and believe in yourself as you go for your goal.	STEP 5 TAKE PRACTICAL ACTION	**Act on your decision**—go down the path and use practical strategies to stay on target.
Evaluate how well the solution worked—look at the effects of what you did.	STEP 6 ANALYZE (REEVALUATE)	**Evaluate the success of your decision**—look at whether it accomplished what you had hoped.
In the future, apply what you've learned—use this solution, or a better one, when a similar situation comes up again.	STEP 7 TAKE PRACTICAL ACTION	**In the future, apply what you've learned**—make this choice, or a better one, when a similar decision comes up again.

Key 5.6   Examine how problems and decisions differ.

SITUATION	YOU HAVE A PROBLEM IF . . .	YOU NEED TO MAKE A DECISION IF . . .
PLANNING SUMMER ACTIVITIES	Your low GPA means you need to attend summer school—and you've already accepted a summer job.	You've been accepted into two summer abroad internship programs.
DECLARING A MAJOR	It's time to declare, but you don't have all the prerequisites for the major you want.	There are three majors that appeal to you and you qualify for them all.
HANDLING COMMUNICATIONS WITH INSTRUCTORS	You are having trouble following the lecture style of a particular instructor.	Your psychology survey course has seven sections taught by different instructors; you have to choose one.

Solving a Problem

Use these strategies as you move through the problem-solving process outlined in Key 5.7.

Use probing questions to define problems.   Ask: What is the problem? And what is *causing* the problem? Imagine possibilities and engage your emotional intelligence. If you determine that you are not motivated to do work for a class, for example, ask questions like these:

- Do my feelings come from interactions with instructor or classmates?
- Is the subject matter difficult? Uninteresting? Too much work?

Your answers may help define the problem and ultimately solve it.

Analyze carefully.   Gather information that will help you examine the problem. Consider how the problem is similar to, or different from, other problems. Clarify facts. Note your own perspective, and look for assumptions.

Generate possible solutions based on causes, not effects.   Addressing a cause provides a lasting solution, whereas trying to address the effect cannot. Say, for example, that your shoulder hurts when you type. Getting a massage is a temporary solution because the pain returns whenever you go back to work. Changing your keyboard height is a lasting solution to the problem because it eliminates the cause of your pain.

Consider how possible solutions affect you and others.   Which would suit you best? Which considers other people's needs?

Inside Tips from Carol, Career Coach

Throughout your career, people will evaluate you based on how you solve problems, make decisions, and create new options and opportunities. Your brain and your capacity to challenge it and grow it will determine much of your success in college and throughout your career.

Ask yourself: Where do you most need to grow your brain? In the area of critical thinking, creative thinking, problem solving? Choose one area. Find someone in a job that interests you, and ask that person how your chosen area affects success in that job. Determine an action you can take each week to improve in this area. Through this action, work consistently to improve, and keep tabs on your results either on your own or by reporting to a friend.

Evaluate your solution and act on it in the future.   Once you put a solution into action, ask: What worked that you would do again? What didn't work that you would avoid or change in the future?

What happens if you don't work through a problem comprehensively? Take, for example, a student having an issue with an instructor. He may get into an argument with the instructor, stop attending class, or do halfhearted work on assignments. These choices have negative consequences. Now look at how he might use critical and creative thinking to work through the problem. Key 5.7 shows how his effort can pay off.

DEFINE PROBLEM HERE:

I don't like my Sociology instructor

ANALYZE THE PROBLEM

We have different styles and personality types—I am not comfortable working in groups and being vocal.

I'm not interested in being there, and my grades are suffering from my lack of motivation.

Use boxes below to list possible solutions:

POTENTIAL POSITIVE EFFECTS	SOLUTION #1	POTENTIAL NEGATIVE EFFECTS
List for each solution: Don't have to deal with that instructor Less stress	Drop the course	*List for each solution:* Grade gets entered on my transcript I'll have to take the course eventually; it's required for my major
Getting credit for the course Feeling like I've honored a commitment	**SOLUTION #2** Put up with it until the end of the semester	Stress every time I'm there Lowered motivation Probably not such a good final grade
A chance to express myself Could get good advice An opportunity to ask direct questions of the instructor	**SOLUTION #3** Schedule meetings with advisor and instructor	Have to face instructor one-on-one Might just make things worse

Now choose the solution you think is best—circle it and make it happen.

ACTUAL POSITIVE EFFECTS	PRACTICAL ACTION	ACTUAL NEGATIVE EFFECTS
List for chosen solution: Got some helpful advice from advisor Talking in person with the instructor actually promoted a fairly honest discussion I won't have to take the course again	I scheduled and attended meetings with both advisor and instructor and opted to stick with the course.	*List for chosen solution:* Still have to put up with some group work I still don't know how much learning I'll retain from this course

FINAL EVALUATION: Was it a good or bad solution?

The solution has improved things. I'll finish the course, and I got the chance to fulfill some class responsibilities on my own or with one partner. I feel more understood and more willing to put my time into the course.

Source: Based on heuristic created by Frank T. Lyman Jr. and George Eley, 1985.

Making a Decision

As you use the steps in Key 5.5 to make a decision, remember these strategies.

Look at the given options—then try to expand your thinking to generate more.   Some decisions have a given set of options. For example, your school may allow you to major, double major, or major and minor. However, you may be able to work with your advisor to come up with another option such as an interdisciplinary major. Consider similar situations you've been in or heard about, what decisions were made, and what resulted from those decisions. Talk with others who made similar decisions.

Look at the long-term effects.   As with problem solving, it's key to examine what happened after you put a decision into action. For important decisions, do a short-term evaluation and another evaluation after a period of time. Consider whether your decision sent you in the right direction or whether you should rethink your choice.

Think about how your decision affects others.   What you choose might have an impact on friends, family, and others around you.

What happens when you make important decisions too quickly? Consider a student trying to decide whether to transfer schools. If she makes her decision based on a reason that ultimately is not the most important one for her (for example, a close friend attends the other school), she may regret her choice later.

Now look at how this student might make an effective decision. Key 5.8 shows how she used her critical and creative thinking in the process.

Stay in Touch with Yourself and Others

Remember that emotional intelligence and cultural competence are key tools for problem solving and decision making. Success in a sociology course, for example, may depend as much, if not more, on finding a way to get along with your instructor than on answering multiple-choice questions on a test. Your emotional intelligence can help you to:

- Define a problem effectively by understanding the negative effects a situation has on you.
- Brainstorm potential solutions that take your abilities and level of motivation into account.
- Persist through a problem-solving or decision-making process.
- Consider how potential solutions and choices may affect others.
- Behave in social situations in a way that motivates people to work with you.

  Your cultural competence can help you to:

- Value the diverse perspectives people bring to the discussion.
- Gather different ideas from others who may have been in similar situations.
- Be aware of, and try to avoid, problematic stereotypes and assumptions.
- Focus on the needs of others involved in the problem or decision.

Key 5.8 Make a decision about whether to transfer schools.

DEFINE PROBLEM HERE:

Whether or not to transfer schools

EXAMINE NEEDS AND MOTIVES

My father has changed jobs and can no longer afford my tuition.
My goal is to become a physical therapist, so I need a school with a
full physical therapy program.
My family needs to cut costs. I need to transfer credits.

Use boxes below to list possible solutions:

POTENTIAL POSITIVE EFFECTS	SOLUTION #1	POTENTIAL NEGATIVE EFFECTS
List for each solution:	Continue at the current college	*List for each solution:*
No need to adjust to a new place or new people		Need to finance most of my tuition and costs on my own
Ability to continue course work as planned		Difficult to find time for a job
		Might not qualify for aid
	SOLUTION #2	
Some coursework available that would apply toward physical therapy degree	Transfer to less expensive school	No personal contacts there that I know of
Reasonable tuition		Will have to investigate whether credits will transfer
Parents have a friend who works in advising there		No full physical therapy program
	SOLUTION #3	
Opportunity to earn tuition money	Stop out for a year	Could forget so much that it's hard to go back
Could live at home		Could lose motivation
Status should be intact		A year might turn into more

Now choose the solution you think is best—circle it and make it happen.

ACTUAL POSITIVE EFFECTS	PRACTICAL ACTION	ACTUAL NEGATIVE EFFECTS
List for chosen solution:	Go to less expensive school for two years; then transfer to a school that offers complete physical therapy coursework in connection with a B.A.	*List for chosen solution:*
Money saved		Less contact with friends
Opportunity to spend time on studies rather than on working to earn tuition money		Will need to transfer again at some point
Availability of classes I need		Additional time and effort required to map out new academic plan

FINAL EVALUATION: Was it a good or bad solution?

I'm satisfied with the decision. It can be hard adjusting to a new place and making new friends, but with fewer social distractions I'm getting more work done. And the reduced cost suits my needs perfectly right now.

Source: Based on heuristic created by Frank T. Lyman Jr. and George Eley, 1985.

MULTIPLE INTELLIGENCE STRATEGIES

For Team Problem Solving

Name a situation that will require problem solving with one or more other people:

_____

In the right-hand column, record specific ideas for how MI strategies can help you work with others to generate effective solutions.

Intelligence	Use MI Strategies to Come Up with Solutions	Identify MI Strategies that Can Help You Problem Solve Together
Verbal–Linguistic	• Find opportunities to express your thoughts and feelings to others—either in writing or in person. • Listen actively to understand the other person's point of view.	
Logical–Mathematical	• Think through a problem before discussing it. Clarify your thoughts by writing them out. • When communicating with others who are not as logic-focused, ask specific questions to learn the facts you need.	
Bodily–Kinesthetic	• Pay attention to your own body language. Make sure it supports what you want to communicate. • Hone in on the signals from other people's body language.	
Visual–Spatial	• Make a drawing or diagram of points you want to communicate during an important discussion. • If you are in a formal classroom or work setting, use visual aids to explain your main points.	
Interpersonal	• Consider how you tend to operate in a group. If you tend to dominate, focus on listening; if you prioritize others' opinions, try to express your opinion more assertively. • Stay aware of what others need to hear from you and respond accordingly.	
Intrapersonal	• Spend time thinking about what you want to say so that it comes out exactly right. • Use your understanding of yourself to tune into what others feel and think.	
Musical	• Before communicating difficult thoughts or feelings, listen to music that relates to what you are thinking. • Be sensitive to the rhythms of a conversation. Sense when to voice your opinion and when to hang back.	
Naturalistic	• Use your ability to recognize patterns to evaluate communication situations. Employ patterns that work well and avoid those that do not. • When appropriate, make an analogy from the natural world to clarify a point in a conversation.	

Keep Your Balance

No one has equal strengths in critical and creative thinking. Effective problem solvers and decision makers assess their abilities, develop creative ideas that maximize their strengths and support their weaknesses, and take action. Staying as balanced as possible requires that you:

- Use what you've learned in this chapter and the rest of the text to maximize your critical and creative thinking skills.
- Reflect on what you do well and focus on strengthening weaker skills.
- Engage emotional intelligence as you solve problems and make decisions.
- Believe in your skills as a critical and creative thinker.

In school, in your personal life, and at work, you will face obstacles of all kinds. Use what you learned here about questioning and thinking to face those obstacles with imagination, expand your options for how to move through them, and keep moving toward your goals.

HABIT IN ACTION WRAP-UP

© Courtesy of Clifton Taulbert

What happened with Clifton?

Despite his challenges, Clifton was determined to, as his Glen Allan community would say, "go all the way." After four years of service in the military with coursework at both the University of Maine and the University of Maryland, he enrolled in Oral Roberts University (ORU) in Tulsa and majored in history and sociology. Racism still showed up even on ORU's campus, but in the military Clifton had learned to embrace his strengths and hang out with those people who thought as he did.

After graduation he continued to show he had what his community called "gumption," building trust in himself through studies, faith, and hard work. Determined to be successful so that he could help others, Clifton began his entrepreneurial career working in retirement home development and expanded from there into several business ventures. "If someone was doing something new and exciting, I wanted to see how I could become involved," says Clifton. "I made many mistakes, but knew I could add value if given the opportunity."

The better life that Clifton has always imagined for himself and for others has led him to write 14 books, with one nominated for a Pulitzer Prize. He continues to write, consult, and speak, as well as work as president and CEO of the Freemount Corporation and Roots Java Coffee; "I understand rest," he says, "but not retirement." Every day he tries to think of ways that he can expand— "go all the way"—and in so doing help others along. "In all that I do, I include the transformative power that comes from building community within all the places of our lives. People matter. If we start from this simple but powerful premise, we set in place the possibility that others can go all the way."

Connect this story to your life: Think about what you imagine is possible for you to do and achieve in your life. Expand your vision to include how you can make a difference for others using your strengths and gifts. Describe the expanded vision you imagine, including a detail or two about how you can begin moving toward it now.

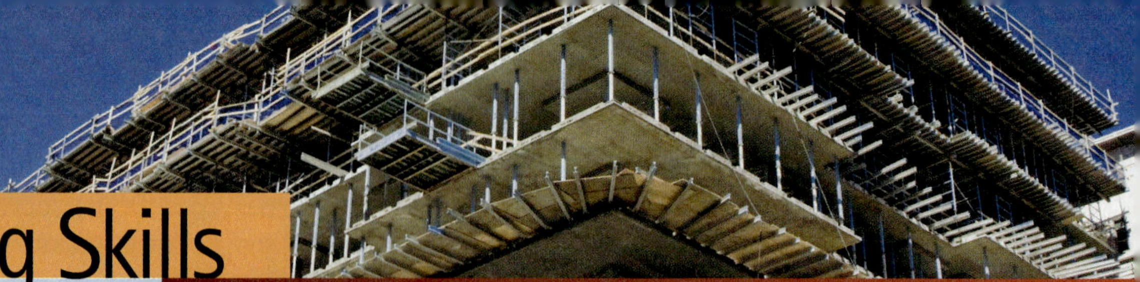

Building Skills
for successful learning

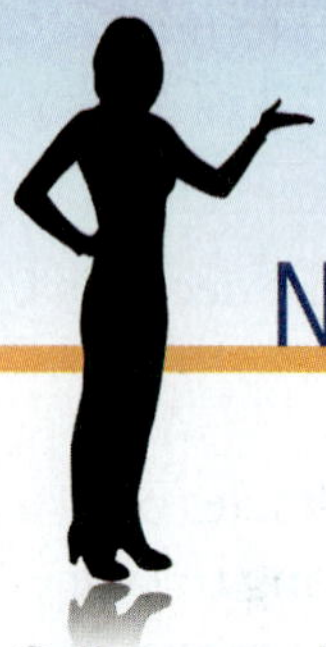

Note the Important Points

College requires you to go beyond information retention by thinking in what two ways?

____

____

Name the four stages of the critical thinking process.

1. ____________________ 2. ____________________

3. ____________________ 4. ____________________

What is the difference between a fact and an opinion?

____

____

Identify the five ingredients of creativity.

____

____

Define brainstorming, and name one brainstorming strategy.

____

____

Name the steps of the problem-solving and decision-making path.

____

____

____

Critical Thinking

applying learning to life

Make an Important Decision

Put the decision-making process to work on something that matters to you. Use paper or create an electronic document if you need more space.

Step 1: Define the decision.   First, describe an important decision that you need to make soon. (Example: Should you take a part-time job?)

_____

_____

Describe the goal you are working toward with this decision. (Example: Paying your tuition bill.)

_____

_____

Step 2: Examine needs.   Who and what will be affected by your decision? How will they be affected? (Example: How might your work schedule and your increased income have a positive or negative effect on your family and friends?)

_____

_____

_____

_____

Step 3: Generate options.   Expand your thinking to imagine different options, even if they seem impossible or unlikely; you can evaluate them later. Some decisions only have two options (such as to look for a new apartment mate or not); others have more. List two possible options for your decision. (Example: Take fewer courses to make room in my schedule for a job.)

Option 1: _____

Option 2: _____

Step 4: Evaluate potential effects.   What might result from choosing each option?

Option 1: _____

Positive effects: _____

Negative effects: _____

Option 2: _____

Positive effects: _____

Negative effects: _____

Consider whether you or someone else you know ever made a similar decision. If so, what can you learn from that decision?

_____

_____

Step 5: Decide on a plan and take action.   Taking your entire analysis into account, decide what to do. Write your decision here.

_____

_____

Next is perhaps the most important part of the process: Act on your decision.

Step 6: Evaluate the result.   After you take action, evaluate: What were the effects on you? On others? List two effects here, noting whether you find them positive or negative.

Effect: _____

Effect: _____

Final evaluation: Think about the entire process and indicate whether you think you made the right decision and why. List any adjustments you could have made to improve the outcome.

_____

_____

_____

_____

Team Building

Solve a Problem

On a 3-by-5 card or a posting area online, each student writes an academic problem, either specific to one class or general to all classes. Problems could involve a fear, a challenge, or a roadblock. Students post or hand these in without names. The instructor collects them and shares the list either on the board or the website.

Divide into groups of two to four. Each group chooses a different problem to work on in person or in an online chat or discussion forum. Use the empty problem-solving flowchart (see Key 5.9) to fill in your work.

1. **Define the problem.** State your specific problem. Explore what is causing the problem and what negative effects come from it.

2. **Examine the problem.** Pick it apart to see what's happening. Gather information from all group members, verify facts, and go beyond assumptions.

3. **Generate possible solutions.** From the most likely causes, derive possible solutions. Record all the ideas that group members offer. Each group member should choose one possible solution to evaluate.

4. **Evaluate each solution.** Independently, each group member should weigh the potential positive and negative effects of this solution and think about how the solution addresses the causes of the problem. Is it a good one? Will it work?

5. **Choose a solution.** Group members then share observations and recommendations, and take a vote: Which solution is the best? Try to find the solution that most people agree on, or consider combining elements of different solutions to create a new one. Then, together, come up with a plan for putting your solution to work.

6. **Evaluate your solution.** As a group, discuss whether you think the chosen solution can be successful. List the positive and negative effects you think it may have.

Key 5.9 Work through a problem using this flowchart.

DEFINE PROBLEM/DECISION:

ANALYZE PROBLEM/DECISION

Use center boxes to list possible options:

POTENTIAL POSITIVE EFFECTS

List for each:

OPTION #1

POTENTIAL NEGATIVE EFFECTS

List for each:

OPTION #2

OPTION #3

Now choose the one you think is best—circle it and make it happen.

ACTUAL POSITIVE EFFECTS

List for chosen option:

PRACTICAL ACTION

ACTUAL NEGATIVE EFFECTS

List for chosen option:

FINAL EVALUATION: Did your action, overall, have a positive or negative result?

Source: Based on heuristic created by Frank T. Lyman Jr. and George Eley, 1985.

imagine

Use Your Critical Thinking Skills to Broaden Your Knowledge

Many essay tests require you to take your thinking beyond recall and into the realm of critical thinking. Name a course you are currently taking that will have at least one essay test:

_____

Now, name an important topic in the course that you need to understand comprehensively.

_____

On a separate sheet of paper or on a computer file, use what you learned about critical thinking to prepare yourself for the test. Create notes on

- Themes and patterns that define the topic

- Facts and opinions about this topic and evidence that supports them

- How parts of this topic are similar to or different from one another as well as other topics

- Causes and effects that are part of this topic

- Arguments you might make to support your point of view

- Assumptions that people tend to make about this topic

When you are done, you will be more prepared to handle an essay question on this topic.

Answers to perception puzzles on p. 127

First puzzle: A duck or a rabbit
Second puzzle: Lines or the letter E

6

active reading

learning from print and online materials

CHANDA HINTON, *executive director of the Chanda Plan Foundation*

Chanda Hinton was just 9 years old when her life path was forever altered. While visiting with family friends, Chanda and two 14-year-old boys were playfully arguing over popsicles. One of the boys picked up a gun, not knowing it was loaded. The gun discharged, the bullet struck Chanda in the back of her neck. The impact of the blow resulted in a spinal cord injury in the C5–C6 vertebrae, rendering Chanda a quadriplegic, unable to move or feel from the neck down.

Perhaps because she was so young, Chanda dealt with the transition. She was able to inquire in a way that brought meaning and fulfillment, asking herself questions about how she could stay active and continue to thrive. "Elementary and high school were really great," Chanda recalls. "My outlook was super-positive." Buoyed by a large network of friends, she was a role model, and was chosen as Homecoming Queen.

Things changed when Chanda moved into adulthood. Her spinal cord injury had compromised her health, as her weight dropped to 59 pounds. The pain was chronic, the emergency 911 calls and doctor visits more frequent. Mentally, she struggled too, especially when college took her away from her comfort zone, the close-knit rural Nebraska town where everyone cherished her.

Going to college was immensely difficult. "At the University of Denver it was tough for me because they were looking upon me as a woman in a wheelchair as opposed to, 'Oh hey, there's Chanda.' " Worried about her health and career prospects, she dropped out of college and stopped asking productive questions about how to cope. At age 21 she was bedbound, dependent on medicine and painkillers, and inactive, wondering what kind of life was left for her to live.

(to be continued . . .)

Being willing to inquire and to excavate for knowledge, in written materials as well as in conversation with others, leads to lifelong learning and growth. You'll learn more about Chanda's experience at the end of the chapter.

Working through this chapter will help you to:

- Improve reading comprehension. p. 146
- Understand and use the SQ3R reading technique. p. 150
- Effectively highlight and annotate reading. p. 156
- Choose what is important to remember. p. 157
- Read online materials productively. p. 162

Text and photo used by permission from Chanda Hinton

inquire

Inquiry is the foundation of learning. Questions help you see what you do—and don't— understand. Asking questions as you read print and online materials will *excavate* and anchor new knowledge.

What Improves Reading Comprehension?
(and makes reading time feel productive in some way?)

> **Reading comprehension**
>
> understanding concepts and being able to show your knowledge on exams and use it to solve problems.

Reading comprehension is the gateway to success in school and beyond. Why? Because if you can read and *understand* something, you can learn it and *use* it. Effective reading earns you a broad and deep range of knowledge that will help you perform in advanced coursework as well as use information effectively on the job.

Don't be fooled by the fact that the modern workplace relies heavily on delivering content electronically. No matter the format in which content comes to you, deep and focused reading is necessary to excavate knowledge and meaning from it. The more effectively you can learn from a college textbook, the more you will build skill that will allow you to analyze a legal brief, understand a marketing report, identify key points in a journal article on an improved respiratory therapy technique, or perform any other work task that relies on your reading skill.

College reading assignments are often challenging, requiring more focus and new strategies on your part. During any given week you may have a variety of assignments, such as:

- A textbook chapter on the history of South African apartheid (world history)
- A research study linking sleep deprivation and memory problems (psychology)
- A journal article on police in society (criminal justice)
- A technical manual on the design of antivirus programs (computer software design)

To face reading challenges like these, use specific techniques. Here's how to prepare for making the most of your reading, even before you open a book or log onto a computer.

Define Your Reading Purpose

To define your purpose, complete this sentence: "In reading this material, I intend to define/learn/answer/achieve…" Write down your goal before you begin, and look at it whenever you lose focus or get bogged down in details. With a clear purpose in mind, you can decide how much time and effort to spend. Key 6.1 shows four common reading purposes. Depending on what your instructor expects, you may have as many as three reading purposes for one assignment, such as understanding, critical evaluation, and practical application.

Use the class syllabus to help define your purpose for each assignment. For example, if your syllabus shows that inflation is the topic of your next economics class lecture, read the assigned chapter with that focus in mind: mastering the definition of inflation, evaluating historical economic events that caused inflation, and so on. In addition, remain open to the possibility that any reading assignment with purpose 1, 2, or 3 may also bring you enjoyment (purpose 4).

Take an Active and Positive Approach

Instructors expect you to complete most reading assignments on your own. How can you approach difficult reading material actively and positively so that you can excavate the knowledge you need?

Start with an attitude of inquiry. Before reading, ask questions, such as "How can I connect the reading to what I already know?" Look at chapter headings and question what the material might mean and why it is being presented in this way.

Look for order. Use reading strategies (explained later in the chapter) to discover patterns, logic, and relationships. Text cues—how the material is organized, outlines, bolded terms, and more—help you anticipate what's coming next.

Have an open mind. Be careful not to prejudge assignments as impossible, boring, or a waste of time before you even begin.

Key 6.1 **Establish why you are reading a given piece of material.**

WHAT'S MY PURPOSE?	EXPLANATION
1. To understand	Read to comprehend concepts and details, and to explain them in your own words. Concepts provide a framework for details, and details help explain or support general concepts.
2. To evaluate analytically	Read with an open mind as you examine causes and effects, evaluate ideas, and ask questions that test arguments and assumptions. Develop a level of understanding beyond basic information recall.
3. For practical application	Read to find information to help reach a specific goal. For instance, when you read a lab manual for chemistry, your goal is to successfully perform the lab experiment.
4. For pleasure	Read for entertainment, such as reading *Sports Illustrated* magazine or a science fiction, mystery, or romance novel.

You may be more able to concentrate in some locations than in others. Try many, at different times of day, and see what works best for you. This student enjoys reading in her room in the daytime.

© LifeBound, LLC

Plan for multiple readings. Knowledge excavation is not a speedy operation. Don't expect to master challenging material on the first pass. Get an overview of key concepts and basic organization during your first reading. Use later readings to build understanding, relate information to what you already know, and apply information. Commit to spending as much time as it takes to get what you need out of the material.

Get help. If material is tough to understand, consult resources including instructors, study-group partners, tutors, related texts, and websites. Build a library of texts in your major and minor areas of study and refer to them whenever necessary.

Learn to Concentrate

Primary sources
original documents, including academic journal articles and scientific studies.

Even well-written college textbooks may require a lot of focus, especially when you encounter complex concepts and new terms. That kind of focus is also useful when assignments are from **primary sources** rather than from **secondary sources**.

When you focus your attention on one thing and one thing alone, you are engaged in the act of *concentration*. As you study, try the following strategies to remain focused.

- **Deal with internal distractions.** When worries come up, such as to-do list items for other projects, write them down and deal with them later. Sometimes you may want to take a break to deal with what's bothering you. For example, if you are hungry, get a snack; if you lose focus, an exercise break may energize you and help you concentrate.

- **Take control of technology.** Web surfing, texting, Snapchatting, and messaging can distract you. In addition, forcing your brain to switch back and forth between tasks can increase work time and errors. Instead, save technology for breaks or after you finish your work.

Secondary sources
other writers' interpretations of primary source documents.

- **Choose time and location carefully.** As much as you can, read in locations that offer minimal distractions and at times of day when you have the energy to stay focused.

- **Structure your work session.** Set realistic goals and a specific plan for dividing your time. Tell yourself, "I'm going to read 30 pages and then go online for 30 minutes."

- **Have a break planned.** Think of something you would look forward to doing during your break. You deserve it!

The strongest motivation to concentrate comes from within. When you see the connection between what you study and your short- and long-term goals, you will be better able to focus, to remember, to learn, and to apply what you have learned.

Expand Your Vocabulary

As reading materials become more complex, your vocabulary influences how much and how easily you understand. The more you read, the more words you are exposed to, and the greater your word comprehension becomes. When reading a textbook, the first "dictionary" to search is the end-of-book glossary explaining technical words and concepts (if applicable). The definitions there are usually limited to the meanings used in the text. Standard dictionaries provide broader information such as word origin, pronunciation, part of speech, synonyms, antonyms, and multiple meanings. Refer to websites like www.dictionary.com, use a dictionary app on your smartphone or tablet, or consider buying a hard-copy dictionary. The suggestions in Key 6.2 will help you use a dictionary effectively.

Key 6.2 Make the most of your dictionary.

Use the word in the next 24 hours.

Not only does this demonstrate that you know how to use the word, but it also helps you memorize the word.

Analyze word parts.

Many English words combine prefixes, roots, and suffixes. Prefixes are word parts that are added to the beginning of a root. The root is the central part or basis of a word around which prefixes and suffixes are added to produce different words. Suffixes are added to the end of the root. Recognizing the root of a word and the meaning of its suffixes can boost comprehension.

Read beyond the first definition.

Think critically about which meaning suits the context of the word in question and choose the one that makes the most sense.

dic·tio·nary

Pronunciation; \'dik-shə-,ner-ē, -,ne-rē\

Function: *noun*

Inflected Form(s): *plural* **dic·tio·nar·ies**

Etymology: Medieval Latin *dictionarium*, from Late Latin *diction-*, *dictio* word, from Latin, speaking

Date: 1526

1. A reference source in print or electronic form containing words usually alphabetically arranged along with information about their forms, pronunciations, functions, etymologies, meanings, and syntactical and idiomatic uses.

2. A book giving information on particular subjects or on a particular class of words, names, or facts, usually arranged alphabetically: *a biographical dictionary; a dictionary of mathematics.*

3. (*computing*) An associative array, a data structure where each value is referenced by a particular key, analogous to words and definitions in a physical dictionary.

Say and spell new words to boost recall.

Listen to the pronunciation on a handheld electronic or online dictionary and repeat it out loud. Then, practice writing the word to verify that you know the spelling. This is a good way to "learn by doing."

Restate the definition in your own words.

When you can do this with ease (and maybe even explain it clearly to someone else), you know you understand the meaning and are not merely parroting a dictionary definition.

How Can SQ3R Help
You Own What You Read?
(does anyone need a specific technique to read?)

Skimming

rapid, superficial reading of material to determine central ideas and main elements.

Scanning

reading material in an investigative way to search for specific information.

Begin with the SQ3R study system, which was developed decades ago by Francis Robinson.[1] SQ3R is an acronym for *survey, question, read, recite,* and *review*. This technique requires that you interact with reading material by asking questions, marking ideas, discovering connections, and more. Your efforts earn you greater ability to understand and remember what you read.

As you move through the stages of SQ3R, you will skim and scan your text. **Skimming** involves the rapid reading of such chapter elements as section introductions and conclusions, boldfaced or italicized terms, pictures, tables, charts, and chapter summaries. The goal of skimming is a quick construction of the main ideas. In contrast, **scanning** involves a careful search for particular information.

SQ3R works best if you adapt it to your needs. For example, you and another classmate may focus on elements in a different order when you survey, write different questions, or favor different review strategies. Explore strategies, evaluate what works, and then make the system your own. See the Multiple Intelligences grid in this chapter for ideas about how to apply your MI strengths to different choices in the SQ3R process.

Keep in mind that SQ3R works best with textbook-based courses like science, math, social sciences, and humanities. SQ3R is *not* recommended for reading literature.

Survey

Surveying, the first stage in **S**Q3R, is the process of previewing, or pre-reading a book before you study it. Compare surveying to looking at a map before a road trip; determining the route in advance will save time and trouble while you travel. Survey tools provided by most textbooks (both hard copy and electronic) include the following:

Front matter. Skim the *table of contents* for the chapter titles, the main topics in each chapter, and the order in which they will be covered, as well as special features. Then skim the *preface* in which the author tells you what the book will cover and her point of view. For example, the preface for the American history text *Out of Many* states that it highlights "the experiences of diverse communities of Americans in the unfolding story of our country."[2] This tells you that cultural diversity is a central theme.

For Reading

Name an upcoming reading assignment (material, course, date due): _____.
In the right-hand column, record specific ideas for how MI strategies can help you complete it.

Intelligence	Use MI Strategies to Become a Better Reader	Identify MI Reading Strategies that Can Help You Improve Comprehension
Verbal-Linguistic	• Use the steps in SQ3R, focusing especially on writing Q-stage questions, summaries, and so on. • Make marginal text notes as you read.	
Logical-Mathematical	• Logically connect what you are reading with what you already know. Consider similarities, differences, and cause-and-effect relationships. • Draw charts showing relationships and analyze trends.	
Bodily-Kinesthetic	• Use text highlighting to take a hands-on approach to reading. • Take a hands-on approach to learning experiments by trying to re-create them yourself.	
Visual-Spatial	• Make charts, diagrams, or think links illustrating difficult ideas you encounter as you read. • Take note of photos, tables, and other visual aids in the text.	
Interpersonal	• Discuss reading material and clarify concepts in a study group. • Talk to people who know about the topic you are studying.	
Intrapersonal	• Apply concepts to your own life; think about your personal responses to them. • Consider personal strengths and weaknesses when preparing to lead a study group.	
Musical	• Recite text concepts to rhythms or write a song to depict them. • Explore relevant musical links to the material.	
Naturalistic	• Tap into your ability to notice similarities and differences in objects and concepts by organizing reading materials into relevant groupings.	

Chapter elements. Text chapters generally use different devices to structure their information and highlight content. Here are some typical devices and how they help the reader.

- Chapter titles establish the topic and often the author's perspective.
- Chapter introductions or outlines generally list objectives or key topics.
- Level headings (first, second, third) break down material into bite-size chunks.
- Margin materials can include definitions, quotes, questions, and exercises.
- Tables, charts, photographs, and captions illustrate important concepts visually.
- Sidebars or boxed features are connected to text themes and introduce information that supplements the text.
- Different styles or arrangements of *type* (**boldface**, *italics*, <u>underlining</u>, larger fonts, • bullet points, boxed text) can flag vocabulary or important ideas.
- End-of-chapter summaries review chapter content and main ideas.
- Review questions and exercises help you understand and apply content.

Back matter. Some texts include a *glossary* that defines text terms, an *index* to help you locate topics, and a *bibliography* that lists additional readings.

Key 6.3 shows a typical page from the college textbook *Psychology: An Introduction,* by Charles G. Morris and Albert A. Maisto. How many elements do you recognize in it? How do these elements help you grasp the subject even before reading it?

Question

The next step in S**Q**3R is to *ask questions* about your assignment. Inquiry leads you to excavate knowledge, become more invested in the material, and remember it more effectively. Here's the process.

© Intellistudies/Shutterstoc

Step 1: Ask yourself what you know about the topic. Before you begin reading, think about, and summarize in writing if you can, what you already know about the topic. When your brain has some existing knowledge about a topic, new knowledge related to that topic is more likely to stick. This principle is especially important in the coursework for your major, where the concepts you learn in introductory courses prepare you for higher-level courses.

Step 2: Write questions linked to chapter headings. Next, examine chapter headings and, on a separate page or in the text margins, write questions linked to them. When you encounter a reading without headings, divide the material into logical sections, and then develop questions based on what you think is the main idea of each section. There is no "correct" set of questions. Given the same headings, you

Key 6.3   Various survey elements are included on this text page.

186   **Chapter 5** • Learning

Classical (or Pavlovian) conditioning The type of learning in which a response naturally elicited by one stimulus comes to be elicited by a different, formerly neutral stimulus.

Unconditioned stimulus (US) A stimulus that invariably causes an organism to respond in a specific way.

Unconditioned response (UR) A response that takes place in an organism whenever an unconditioned stimulus occurs.

Conditioned stimulus (CS) An originally neutral stimulus that is paired with an unconditioned stimulus and eventually produces the desired response in an organism when presented alone.

Conditioned response (CR) After conditioning, the response an organism produces when only a conditioned stimulus is presented.

you are experiencing insight. When you imitate the steps of professional dancers you saw last night on television, you are demonstrating observational learning. Like conditioning, cognitive learning is one of our survival strategies. Through cognitive processes, we learn which events are safe and which are dangerous without having to experience those events directly. Cognitive learning also gives us access to the wisdom of people who lived hundreds of years ago, and it will give people living hundreds of years from now some insight into our experiences and way of life.

Our discussion begins with *classical conditioning*. This simple kind of learning serves as a convenient starting point for examining what learning is and how it can be observed.

Classical Conditioning

How did Pavlov's discovery of classical conditioning help to shed light on learning?

Ivan Pavlov (1849–1936), a Russian physiologist who was studying digestive processes, discovered classical conditioning almost by accident. Because animals salivate when food is placed in their mouths, Pavlov inserted tubes into the salivary glands of dogs to measure how much saliva they produced when they were given food. He noticed, however, that the dogs salivated before the food was in their mouths: The mere sight of food made them drool. In fact, they even drooled at the sound of the experimenter's footsteps. This aroused Pavlov's curiosity. What was making the dogs salivate even before they had the food in their mouths? How had they learned to salivate in response to the sound of the experimenter's approach?

To answer these questions, Pavlov set out to teach the dogs to salivate when food was not present. He devised an experiment in which he sounded a bell just before the food was brought into the room. A ringing bell does not usually make a dog's mouth water but, after hearing the bell many times just before getting fed, Pavlov's dogs began to salivate as soon as the bell rang. It was as if they had learned that the bell signaled the appearance of food, and their mouths watered on cue even if no food followed. The dogs had been conditioned to salivate in response to a new stimulus—the bell—that would not normally have prompted that response (Pavlov, 1927). Figure 5–1, shows one of Pavlov's procedures in which the bell has been replaced by a touch to the dog's leg just before food is given.

Elements of Classical Conditioning

Generally speaking, **classical (or Pavlovian) conditioning** involves pairing an *involuntary* response (for example, salivation) that is usually evoked by one stimulus with a different, formerly neutral stimulus (such as a bell or a touch on the leg). Pavlov's experiment illustrates the four basic elements of classical conditioning. The first is an **unconditioned stimulus (US)**, such as food, which invariably prompts a certain reaction—salivation, in this case. That reaction—the **unconditioned response (UR)**—is the second element and always results from the unconditioned stimulus: Whenever the dog is given food (US), its mouth waters (UR). The third element is the neutral stimulus—the ringing bell—which is called the **conditioned stimulus (CS)**. At first, the conditioned stimulus is said to be "neutral" with respect to the desired response (salivation), because dogs do not salivate at the sound of a bell unless they have been conditioned to react in this way by repeatedly presenting the CS and US together. Frequent pairing of the CS and US produces the fourth element in the classical conditioning process: the **conditioned response (CR)**. The conditioned response is the behavior that the animal has learned in response to the conditioned stimulus. Usually, the unconditioned response and the conditioned

Source: Charles G. Morris and Albert A. Maisto, *Psychology: An Introduction*, 12th ed., © 2005. Printed and electronically reproduced by permission of Pearson Education, Inc.

could create different questions. Your goal is to engage the material and begin to think critically about it. As with Step 1, this primes your brain to more effectively retain new information when it comes along.

Key 6.4 shows how this works. The column on the left contains primary- and secondary-level headings from a section of *Out of Many.* The column on the right rephrases these headings in question form.

Use Bloom's Taxonomy to Formulate Questions

Educational psychologist Benjamin Bloom developed *Bloom's taxonomy* because he believed that different questions promote different levels of learning.[3] Key 6.5 shows the six levels of learning identified by Bloom: knowledge, understanding, application, analysis, synthesis, and evaluation. Beneath the illustration of the levels, the table explains what each level is (column 1), lists common verbs associated with each level (column 2), and provides an example question for that level of learning (column 3, showing questions on topics from *Out of Many*). When you read, use these verbs to create specific questions that will help you learn.

Read

Your text survey and questions give you a starting point for reading, the first R in SQ**3R**. Remembering what you read requires an active approach.

- **Focus on the key points of your survey.** Pay attention to information in the headings, boldface type, chapter objectives, the summary, and other emphasized text.

Key 6.4   Create questions from headings.

HEADINGS	QUESTIONS
The Meaning of Freedom	What did freedom mean for both slaves and citizens in the United States?
Moving About	Where did African Americans go after they were freed from slavery?
The African American Family	How did freedom change the structure of the African American family?
African American Churches and Schools	What effect did freedom have on the formation of African American churches and schools?
Land and Labor After Slavery	How was land farmed and maintained after slaves were freed?
The Origins of African American Politics	How did the end of slavery bring about the beginning of African American political life?

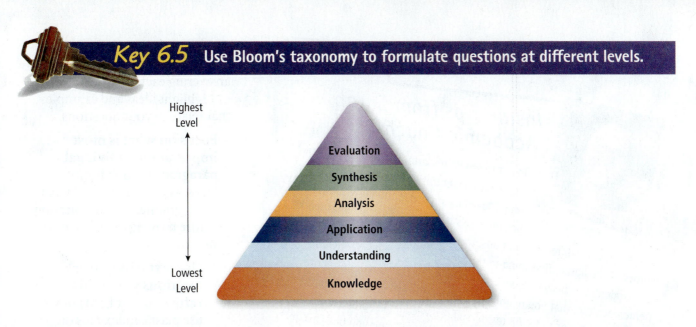

The table below explains each level in the taxonomy illustration, provides common verbs to help you recognize each level, and provides a sample question you might ask at that level. The questions are based on the headings from *Out of Many*.

LEVEL OF LEARNING	COMMON VERBS THAT INDICATE THE LEVEL	SAMPLE QUESTIONS DEMONSTRATING THE LEVEL OF LEARNING
KNOWLEDGE. Memorize words and ideas.	average, define, duplicate, label, list, memorize, name, order, recognize, relate, recall, repeat, reproduce, state	*List* three main characters of the early African American political scene.
UNDERSTANDING. Explain ideas in your own words.	classify, describe, discuss, explain, express, identify, indicate, locate, recognize, report, restate, review, select, translate	*Explain* the struggles faced by African American politicians.
APPLICATION. Apply what you learn.	apply, choose, demonstrate, dramatize, employ, illustrate, interpret, operate, practice, schedule, sketch, solve, use, write	*Interpret* the impact of slavery on the early African American politicians.
ANALYSIS. Analyze information and look at similarities and differences.	analyze, appraise, calculate, categorize, compare, contrast, criticize, differentiate, discriminate, distinguish, examine, experiment, question, test	*Compare and contrast* the Caucasian political environment of the time with that of the emerging African American politicians.
SYNTHESIS. Put together information "from scratch."	arrange, assemble, collect, compose, construct, create, design, develop, formulate, manage, organize, plan, prepare, propose, set up, write	*Arrange* the major events of the era as they corresponded with the emerging political movement.
EVALUATION. Examine different ideas and make decisions about their merit.	appraise, argue, assess, attach, choose, compare, defend, estimate, evaluate, judge, predict, rate, score, select, support, value	*Rate* the effectiveness of the first African American political campaign and note any changes since.

Inside Tips from Sarah, Academic Coach

One of the most important ingredients in your recipe for concentration is the right study setting. Move beyond conventional wisdom or anyone else's habit as you define what works best for you. Try different locations, times, and atmospheres. A quiet corner of the library first thing in the morning can be as effective for one student as a busy outdoor cafe in the afternoon can be for another. Remember, too, that you might prefer different settings for different academic materials or tasks. All of this self-knowledge will prove critical in the job hunt as you look for not just work that will suit you but also an environment in which you can be productive.

- **Focus on Q-stage questions.** Read with the purpose of answering each question. Write or highlight ideas and examples that relate to your questions.

- **Focus on what is most important in individual paragraphs.** Look for main ideas. Try to understand what a paragraph is communicating before moving on to the next one.

- **Use text tabs to mark locations you need to return to.** For hard copy, use plastic index tabs or adhesive notes. For electronic copy, use any tabbing tool your e-reader may provide.

Mark Up Your Text

Getting what you need out of textbook reading demands that you interact with the material. Marking up your text through annotation and highlighting, in whatever style feels natural to you, reminds you what each passage is about and what is important to remember. This combination turns the text into an effective, personalized study tool.

Annotate your text.   Annotating refers to taking notes in the margins of your textbook pages. If the book is yours, write notes in the margins, circle main ideas, or underline supporting details. If you are reading an e-book, use the "insert comments" feature or other annotating tools. These cues will boost memory and help you study for exams. Here's how to annotate:

Topic sentence
a statement describing the main idea of a paragraph.

- Use pencil so you can erase comments or questions that are answered later.

- Write your Q-questions in the margins next to text headings.

- Mark critical sections with marginal notations such as "def." for definition, "e.g." for a helpful example, "concept" for an important concept, and so on.

- Write notes at the bottom of the page connecting the text to what you learned in class or in research. You can also attach adhesive notes with your comments.

- Circle the **topic sentence** in a paragraph to focus on the most important information.

Highlight your text.   The goal of *highlighting* is to call out important concepts and information so that they get your attention. Use these tips to make highlighting work for you:

- **Develop a system and stick to it.** Decide if you will use different colors to highlight different elements, bracket long passages, or underline. When working with e-books, use the highlighting function to color over important text.

- **Consider using a regular pencil or pen instead of a highlighter pen.** The copy will be cleaner and look less like a coloring book than a textbook.

- **Mark text carefully if you are using a rented book or a book to be re-sold.** Use pencil and erase your marks at the end of the course. Write on sticky notes. Make copies of important chapters or sections and mark up the pages. If renting, check with the rental service to see what it permits.

- **Read an entire paragraph before you begin to highlight it.** Only when you have a sense of what's important should you highlight main ideas, key terms, and crucial supporting details and examples.

- **Avoid overmarking.** Underlining or highlighting everything makes it impossible to tell what's important. If you decide that a whole passage is important to call out, try marking it with brackets.

- **Know that highlighting is just the beginning of learning the material.** To learn the information you've highlighted, interact with it through surveying, questioning, reciting, and review.

Key 6.6 shows a page from an introduction to business textbook that describes the concepts of target marketing and market segmentation. The page illustrates how to underline and take marginal notes. Then, the Take Action exercise gives you a chance to do some more reading and practice marking up the text.

Yes, marking up your textbook means you may not be able to sell it back. However, students who interact with material stand to gain greater depth of learning than those who don't. If learning is your goal, the cost may be worth it. Your marked-up text is uniquely yours; no one else has your exact combination of knowledge, learning preferences, and study habits. Keep this in mind if you consider buying used texts that are heavily highlighted or filled with notes. Even if the previous owner was a good student, he or she is not you—and the added element of someone else's responses may make it more challenging for you to take in the material.

Create a Full-Text Summary

One more way to remember materials and deepen your understanding as you read is to create a full-text summary. Focus on the main ideas and supporting examples, and don't include any of your own ideas or evaluations at this

Chapter 10: Understanding Marketing Processes and Consumer Behavior   **297**

How do target marketing and market segmentation help companies sell product?

TARGET MARKETING AND MARKET SEGMENTATION

Marketers have long known that products cannot be all things to all people. Buyers have different tastes, goals, lifestyles, and so on. The emergence of the marketing concept and the recognition of consumer needs and wants led marketers to think in terms of **target markets**—groups of people with similar wants and needs. Selecting target markets is usually the first step in the marketing strategy.

Definitions

target market
Group of people that has similar wants and needs and that can be expected to show interest in the same products

Target marketing requires **market segmentation**—dividing a market into categories of customer types or "segments." Once they have identified segments, companies may adopt a variety of strategies. Some firms market products to more than one segment. General Motors (*www.gm.com*), for example, offers compact cars, vans, trucks, luxury cars, and sports cars with various features and at various price levels. GM's strategy is to provide an automobile for nearly every segment of the market.

GM eg

market segmentation
Process of dividing a market into categories of customer types

In contrast, some businesses offer a narrower range of products, each aimed toward a specific segment. Note that segmentation is a strategy for analyzing consumers, not products. The process of fixing, adapting, and communicating the nature of the product itself is called *product positioning*.

GM makes cars for diff. market segments

How do companies identify market segments?

Identifying Market Segments

By definition, members of a market segment must share some common traits that affect their purchasing decisions. In identifying segments, researchers look at several different influences on consumer behavior. Three of the most important are *geographic, demographic,* and *psychographic variables.*

What effect does geography have on segmentation strategies?

Geographic Variables Many buying decisions are affected by the places people call home. The heavy rainfall in Washington State, for instance, means that people there buy more umbrellas than people in the Sun Belt. Urban residents don't need agricultural equipment, and sailboats sell better along the coasts than on the Great Plains. **Geographic variables** are the geographical units, from countries to neighborhoods, that may be considered in a segmentation strategy.

Buying decisions influenced by where people live

geographic variables
Geographical units that may be considered in developing a segmentation strategy

These patterns affect decisions about marketing mixes for a huge range of products. For example, consider a plan to market down-filled parkas in rural Minnesota. Demand will be high and price competition intense. Local newspaper ads may be

— good eg — selling parkas in Minnesota

Thought
Geographical variables change with the seasons

Source: Ronald J. Ebert and Ricky W. Griffin, *Business Essentials,* 5th ed., © 2005. Printed and electronically reproduced by permission of Pearson Education, Inc.

Below, the text material in Key 6.6 continues. Put pencil to paper as you highlight concepts and take marginal notes. Compare your efforts to those of your classmates (use your interpersonal intelligence) to see how each of you approached the task and what you can learn from others.

298

Part IV: Understanding Principles of Marketing

effective, and the best retail location may be one that is easily reached from several small towns.

Although the marketability of some products is geographically sensitive, others enjoy nearly universal acceptance. Coke, for example, gets more than 70 percent of its sales from international markets. It is the market leader in Great Britain, China, Germany, Japan, Brazil, and Spain. Pepsi's international sales are about 15 percent of Coke's. In fact, Coke's chief competitor in most countries is some local soft drink, not Pepsi, which earns 78 percent of its income at home.

demographic variables
Characteristics of populations that may be considered in developing a segmentation strategy

Demographic Variables Demographic variables describe populations by identifying such traits as age, income, gender, ethnic background, marital status, race, religion, and social class. For example, several general consumption characteristics can be attributed to certain age groups (18–25, 26–35, 36–45, and so on). A marketer can, thus, divide markets into age groups. Table 10.1 lists some possible demographic breakdowns. Depending on the marketer's purpose, a segment can be a single classification (aged 20–34) or a combination of categories (aged 20–34, married with children, earning $25,000–$34,999). Foreign competitors, for example, are gaining market share in U.S. auto sales by appealing to young buyers (under age 30) with limited incomes (under $30,000). Whereas companies such as Hyundai (*www.hyundai.net*), Kia (*www.kia.com*), and Daewoo (*www.daewoos.com*) are winning entry-level customers with high quality and generous warranties, Volkswagen (*www.vw.com*) targets under-35 buyers with its entertainment-styled VW Jetta.[4]

psychographic variables
Consumer characteristics, such as lifestyles, opinions, interests, and attitudes, that may be considered in developing a segmentation strategy

Psychographic Variables Markets can also be segmented according to such psychographic variables as lifestyles, interests, and attitudes. Take, for example, Burberry (*www.burberry.com*), whose raincoats have been a symbol of British tradition since 1856. Burberry has repositioned itself as a global luxury brand, like Gucci (*www.gucci.com*) and Louis Vuitton (*www.vuitton.com*). The strategy, which recently resulted in a 31-percent sales increase, calls for attracting a different type of customer—the top-of-the-line, fashion-conscious individual—who shops at such stores as Neiman Marcus and Bergdorf Goodman.[5]

Psychographics are particularly important to marketers because, unlike demographics and geographics, they can be changed by marketing efforts. For example, Polish companies have overcome consumer resistance by promoting the safety and desirability of using credit rather than depending solely on cash. One product of changing attitudes is a booming economy and the emergence of a robust middle class.

TABLE 10.1
Demographic Variables

Age	Under 5, 5–11, 12–19, 20–34, 35–49, 50–64, 65+
Education	Grade school or less, some high school, graduated high school, some college, college degree, advanced degree
Family life cycle	Young single, young married without children, young married with children, older married with children under 18, older married without children under 18, older single, other
Family size	1, 2–3, 4–5, 6+
Income	Under $9,000, $9,000–$14,999, $15,000–$24,999, $25,000–$34,999, $35,000–$45,000, over $45,000
Nationality	African, American, Asian, British, Eastern European, French, German, Irish, Italian, Latin American, Middle Eastern, Scandinavian
Race	Native American, Asian, Black, White
Religion	Buddhist, Catholic, Hindu, Jewish, Muslim, Protestant
Sex	Male, female

Ronald J. Ebert and Ricky W. Griffin, *Business Essentials*, 5th ed., © 2005. Printed and electronically reproduced by permission of Pearson Education, Inc.

point. A summary simply condenses the material, making it easier to focus on concepts and their relationships. Here are some suggestions:

- Use your own words. Include technical vocabulary specific to the material.

- Be as simple, clear, and brief as you can. Leave out less important details.

- Consider outlining the text so you can see how ideas relate to one another.

- Include information from tables, charts, and visuals (either in words or with your own charts and drawings).

- Use shorthand symbols.

- Use a color-coding system to indicate levels of importance of different ideas.

Recite

Once you finish reading a section of text, recite answers to the questions you raised in the Q stage—say them aloud, silently speak them to yourself, "teach" them to someone, or write them in note form. The action of speaking or writing anchors material in your brain. This is the second R in SQ**3R**. Repeat the question–read–recite cycle until you complete the chapter you are reading.

Writing is often the most effective way to learn new material. Write responses to your Q-stage questions and use your own words to explain new concepts. Save your writing as a study tool for review. Writing gives you immediate feedback. When your writing agrees with the material you are studying, you know the information. When it doesn't, you still need work.

Keep your learning preferences in mind when you explore different strategies. For example, an intrapersonal learner may prefer writing, while an

© Pearson Education, Inc.

interpersonal learner may choose to recite answers aloud to a classmate. A logical-mathematical learner may benefit from making detailed outlines or using an app to organize notes, while a musical learner might want to chant information aloud to a rhythm and record it on a voice memo to play back.

When do you stop to recite? Waiting until the end of a chapter is too late, but stopping at the end of one paragraph is too soon. The best plan is to recite at the end of each text section, right before a new heading. Repeat the question–read–recite cycle until you complete the chapter. If you fumble for thoughts, reread the section until you are on solid ground.

Review

Reviewing is the third R in SQ**3R**. When you review early and often in the days and weeks after you read, you will better memorize, understand, and learn material. *Reviewing is your key to learning.* Reviewing the same material over several short sessions will also help you identify knowledge gaps. It's natural to forget material between study sessions, especially if it's complex. When you come back after a break, you can focus on where you need the most help.

Try some or all of the following reviewing techniques and use the ones that work best for you. Using more than one strategy, and switching among strategies, can strengthen learning and memory.

- Reread your notes, then summarize them from memory.
- Review and summarize in writing the text sections you highlighted or bracketed.
- Rewrite key points and main concepts in your own words. Create written examples that will help solidify the content in your mind.
- Answer the end-of-chapter review, discussion, and application questions.
- Reread the preface, headings, tables, and summary.
- Recite important concepts to yourself (although you may risk looking silly, this technique's high effectiveness may be a worthwhile reward).
- Record information and play it back.
- Listen to audio recordings of your text and other reading materials on an iPod.

ALL ABOUT YOU

On a scale of 1 to 10, with 1 being the lowest and 10 being the highest, rate yourself on your ability to complete each SQ3R stage at this moment in time. Circle the stage that you feel most needs focus and development in order for you to use SQ3R effectively.

Stage	Description	Rating
Survey	Pre-reading a book before studying it—skimming and scanning front matter, chapter elements, and back matter for clues about content and organization	_____
Question	Developing questions linked to chapter headings and to what you already know	_____
Read	Reading to answer Q-stage questions and find main ideas; taking notes as you read or highlighting your text	_____
Recite	Answering, perhaps for a second time, your Q-stage questions; reciting the answers aloud or silently to yourself, teaching them to a study partner, or recording them in writing	_____
Review	Learning the material through summarizing notes; answering study questions; writing outlines or think links; reciting concepts, using flash cards, thinking critically, and so on	_____

- Make hard-copy or electronic flash cards with a word or concept on one side and a definition, examples, or other related information on the other. Test yourself daily.

- Quiz yourself, using the questions you raised in the Q stage.

- Discuss the concepts with a classmate or in a study group. Answer one another's Q-stage questions.

- Ask your instructor for help with difficult material.

Refreshing your knowledge is easier and faster than excavating it for the first time. Make a weekly review schedule and stick to it. A combination of short daily reviews in the morning, between classes, or in the evening is far more effective than an all-night cramming session before a test.

How Can You Read Online Materials Effectively?
(and somehow avoid being distracted?)

Students have more choices than ever before about how they access reading materials. Digital tools for reading include desktop or laptop computers, touch screen smartphones, and tablets such as the iPad. Many, though not all, reading materials are available in formats and applications that work on these devices. Although college students are more likely to use digital devices for research and studying than for reading, a recent survey of students who own digital devices indicated that over 60% had used them to read an electronic textbook at least once, and almost half did so regularly.[4]

If you grew up using the Internet and computers, you may be a "digital native"[5] who is:

- Frequently interacting with others all over the globe.

- Online, using one device or another, for hours a day.

- Comfortable with the culture of sharing; willing to speak up and to disclose personal data.

- A creator rather than a passive user.

© LifeBound, LLC

- A grazer who takes in small segments of information and moves quickly, often spending very little time on any one information source or task.

- Convinced of your ability to do several things at once and comfortable with many different digital tasks occurring simultaneously.

- Likely to have several online and offline "identities," many of which overlap and blur, and to understand that choosing how you represent yourself online is the same as deciding how you dress and act in person.

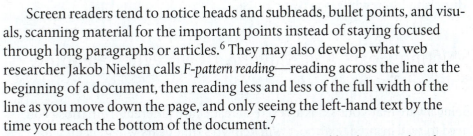

POWERFUL QUESTIONS

inquire

STUDENT TO STUDENT

Powerful questions are at the heart of this chapter's Habit for Success—inquiring so that you can excavate knowledge. Pair up with a fellow student and ask each other these questions:

In what ways do you read print and online materials differently? Which do you feel you learn more effectively from? If you identify issues that interfere with your ability to learn from either print or online materials, define an action you can take to address the problem and commit to taking that action in the next week.

Screen readers tend to notice heads and subheads, bullet points, and visuals, scanning material for the important points instead of staying focused through long paragraphs or articles.[6] They may also develop what web researcher Jakob Nielsen calls *F-pattern reading*—reading across the line at the beginning of a document, then reading less and less of the full width of the line as you move down the page, and only seeing the left-hand text by the time you reach the bottom of the document.[7]

Your college success depends on being able to read both printed and on-screen material effectively. Whether you prefer printed materials you can hold and write on or convenient electronic materials, you are likely to have to read some material online. You have two goals: to improve your screen reading skills so that you learn the material, and to be able to shift to a slower gear when you read a printed text.

Reading and Studying Online Material

When you are reading on-screen articles that you need for class, you need to capture important ideas so that you can come back to them. Jacob Nielsen suggests a step-by-step process, which includes aspects of SQ3R:

1. **Skim through the article.** See whether it contains important ideas.

2. **Before reading in depth, save the article on your computer or device.** This gives you the ability to highlight and add notes, either on the electronic copy or on a hard copy that you can print out.

3. **Survey the article.** Read the title, subtitle, headings, figures, charts, and tables.

4. **Come up with questions to guide your reading**. Ask yourself what general and specific information you want to learn from the article.

5. **Read the article in depth.** You have already judged that the material is important, so take it much slower than you would normally.

6. **Highlight and take notes.** Use the program or app's highlighter and comment functions.

7. **Print out articles you would rather study on paper.** Make sure the printouts include any electronic highlighting and comments you've created.

8. **Review your notes.** Combine them with your class and text notes.

Screen reading for extended periods can cause eye strain, so position the monitor to minimize glare, and give your eyes a short break every half hour. If you can change the typeface, choose one that minimizes strain such as Verdana, Trebuchet, or Georgia.

Finally, knowing your learning preferences will help you read more effectively on the computer. If you are a visual learner, you may want to print out materials on a regular basis. If you are a bodily-kinesthetic learner, you might want to surround yourself with your printouts in idea stacks. If you are a musical learner, you may want to open a music app like Spotify or Apple Music and listen while you read.

Shifting Gears and Slowing Down When Reading Printed Texts

Being aware that your skills as a screen reader are different from those you need to read printed textbooks will help you shift gears when picking up a book. Textbooks require close, slow reading that may seem like walking through mud after spending hours a day on the Internet.

Textbooks provide a comprehensive framework on a topic that goes beyond the just-in-time information nuggets that the Internet tends to deliver. Often, textbooks need greater concentration than Internet pages and an undistracted focus when material is difficult. They require what developmental psychologist Maryanne Wolf calls *deep reading*—reading that goes beyond scanning words and involves comprehension and interaction with the material.[8]

Reading challenging college-level material demands significant effort, but only through that effort and inquiry will learning happen. Remember that "it is not so much about the tool and what it can do, but more about the purpose for using the tool," says educator Mary Beth Hertz.[9] Whether you read a printed page or an electronic document on a screen, what counts is that you are excavating knowledge you can use.

© Courtesy of Chanda Hinton

What happened with Chanda?

"One of my healing mantras," says Chanda, "is that everything happens for a purpose."

First, her sister inquired about Chanda's willingness to try integrative therapies, specifically physical therapy, massage therapy, adaptive yoga, and acupuncture. As she excavated increased understanding of those treatments and gave them a try, Chanda began to thrive once again. She also got a service dog, Flint, who performs tasks for her and knows her so well that he can sense if something is wrong. As her health improved, she returned to college, joined activities, and rediscovered her outgoing nature.

Chanda's renewed energy inspired her to inquire how she could live her life's mission. In answer to this question, she created her own foundation—The Chanda Plan Foundation—which provides extensive support for persons with physical disabilities, working to improve quality of life through education and programs to access integrative therapies. Since 2006, The Chanda Plan Foundation has provided the opportunity for increased health and hope by covering 11,600 integrative therapies for participants in the Quality of Life program. In addition to running her foundation, Chanda is actively pushing legislation for federal funding of integrative therapies. Her willingness to inquire has excavated knowledge and meaning that continue to improve the lives of all who benefit from The Chanda Plan's services.

Connect this story to your life: Although your problems are most likely different than Chanda's, you too can use inquiry to excavate meaning and benefit from a challenging situation. Consider a problem you face right now that is draining your energy. Inquire: Whom can you turn to for help in untangling this problem? Chanda's sister made a difference for her—find a person who can help you ask productive questions in a similar way. Get in contact with this person and see what can result from asking for help.

Building Skills

for successful learning

Note the Important Points

Name and describe three strategies that improve reading comprehension.

1. _____

2. _____

3. _____

List and define the five parts of SQ3R.

1. _____

2. _____

3. _____

4. _____

5. _____

Compare and contrast *skimming* and *scanning*.

_____

_____

Describe three useful ways to mark up a text.

1. _____

2. _____

3. _____

Name two characteristics of a "digital native."

_____

_____

List two actions you can take to improve screen reading skills.

1. _____

2. _____

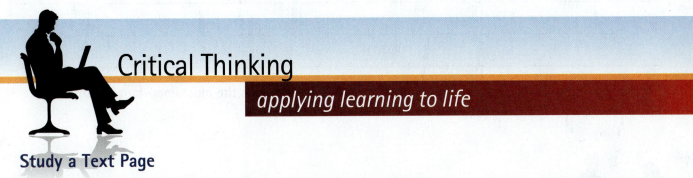

Critical Thinking

applying learning to life

Study a Text Page

Choose a textbook (hard copy or e-text) that you are reading for a course this term. Apply SQ3R as you read one chapter that has been assigned to you. Use what you learned in this chapter to complete the questions that follow (some questions ask you to mark the page itself).

Step 1: Survey. First gather: Skim the chapter. Identify the headings on the page and the relationships among them. Mark primary-level headings with a #1, secondary headings with a #2, and third-level headings with a #3.

Then analyze: What do the headings tell you about the chapter content?

_____

_____

Step 2: Question. Identify three key concepts, and then write three study questions that will help you learn them.

1. _____

_____

2. _____

_____

3. _____

_____

Step 3: Read.   Put SQ3R to work as you read. Highlight key phrases and ideas. Write marginal notes for later review. Identify where you might write "e.g." to flag an example. Keep in mind the study questions you created.

Step 4: Recite.   Check your understanding by answering your study questions.

1. _____

_____

2. _____

_____

3. _____

_____

Step 5: Review.   Write a brief summary of the chapter, focusing on the most important information.

Team Building
collaborative solutions

Improve Your Highlighting Skills

1. Photocopy (if hard copy) or block (if e-text) a three- to four-page textbook section, and have everyone in the group highlight what's important. Compare versions in person or by sharing documents electronically. Ask group members to explain why they highlighted certain material and not others and to describe how they made their choices.

2. Each group member should then pledge to use, over a period of a week, one highlighting technique that is new to him or her.

3. At the end of the week, discuss the results. Have each person answer this question: "Am I a better highlighter as a result of this exercise, and am I learning more content?" Based on your experience, explain here how your highlighting has changed (or not), and how you believe any changes you've put into place will help you.

_____

_____

_____

Start It Now

inquire

Make Inquiry Part of Your Study Routine

Do you have a test or midterm coming up in the next few weeks? Now is the time to start studying. Ask yourself these questions to excavate the knowledge you need from your reading materials:

- Have I checked my syllabus to identify exactly what will be on the test?

- Am I using SQ3R to study the material?

- What steps will I take to maximize my learning preferences as I study?

- Are the highlighting and notes I've taken on the text or other materials helping me study? If not, how can I improve them?

- Do I read online materials as carefully as printed materials? If not, what steps am I taking to become a better screen reader?

- When I finish studying, am I able to summarize the material in writing or teach it to another student? If not, have I asked for help?

Looking at your answers, describe at least two ways in which you will adjust your studying to improve results.

_____

_____

After the exam, assess whether these adjustments helped you learn. Write your thoughts about the experience below.

_____

_____

7

reading and information literacy

targeted and critical strategies

GARRETT MINTZ, *student,* **Indiana University**

Born with a natural talent for entrepreneurship, Garrett Mintz did not immediately find the most positive and productive way to put it to work. When he was 15, his family moved to a new town. Trying to fit in, Garrett joined the tennis team, but the friends he made there used drugs. To afford the drugs and keep those friends he ended up working as a drug dealer, selling various drugs but mostly marijuana. He continued this work into college, where it ended abruptly when an undercover police operation led to his arrest and multiple felony charges.

Although Garrett thought this was the worst thing that could happen, crisis shifted his thinking. The arrest forced him to realize that in his exclusive focus on himself, he had not noticed the impact that his actions were having on people who mattered to him. His thoughts turned to his family, his college, his friends, and even his country. He knew he wanted to contribute to others, not create obstacles for them.

Garrett's first impulse was to move away because everyone he knew at that point was affiliated with the drug trade. He landed in Utah where he started a nonprofit organization that helped young adults with substance abuse issues and helped them get hired and keep jobs. He was strongly motivated to help people improve their position in life, but knew he needed to develop his own education and workplace readiness so that he could give others his best.

(to be continued . . .)

If you work to understand and build your strengths, you can contribute in ways that add value to the lives of others. You'll learn more about Garrett's experience at the end of the chapter.

Working through this chapter will help you to:

- Use targeted strategies for specific subjects. p. 172
- Know a basic search strategy for library and electronic research. p. 182
- Critically evaluate reading materials. p. 186
- Use strategies to assess the quality of materials found online. p. 188

Text and photo used by permission from Garrett Mintz

contribute

When you contribute what you already know, you move further along toward your goals. Your contribution will *add value* to any learning or problem-solving process.

What Will Help with Specific Subjects and Formats?

(when some materials are so different than others?)

Getting a college education involves studying a variety of subjects. If your college has **general education requirements**, you may have to take a wide variety of courses in order to graduate. Knowing how to approach reading materials in different academic areas can make learning easier.

> **General education requirements**
>
> courses in a variety of academic fields, including the humanities, social sciences, math, and science, that are required for graduation.

Math and Science

Math and science courses relate closely to one another, since almost all science courses require basic math knowledge. Mathematical and scientific strategies help you develop thinking and problem-solving skills. They also help you create monthly budgets, choose auto insurance, understand illnesses, and more.

In a world that is being transformed by new discoveries and technologies, having a strong math and science background prepares you for tomorrow's jobs. Key 7.1 lists just some of the math and science courses you may take, along with related careers.

Working with Textbooks

Math and science textbooks move *sequentially*. That is, your understanding of later material depends on how well you learned material in earlier chapters because the topics build upon one another. Try the following strategies to get the most from your textbooks, and if you are confused about something, get extra help right away so you don't fall behind.

Interact with math material actively through writing. Math textbooks are made up of problems and solutions. As you read, highlight important information and take notes of examples. Work out any missing problem

© Nomad Soul/Fotolia

steps on book pages or scrap paper. Draw sketches to help visualize the material. Try not to move on until you understand example problems and how they relate to the central ideas. Write down questions to ask your instructor or fellow students.

Pay attention to formulas. Math and science texts are filled with **formulas**. Try to learn the ideas behind each formula so that if you forget one, you can re-create it (this is called "deriving" a formula). Always do the practice problems, using the formulas to make sure your understanding sticks.

Use memory strategies to learn science. Science textbooks are packed with field-specific vocabulary (for example, an environmental science text may refer to the *greenhouse effect*). Use mnemonic devices, test yourself with flash cards, and rehearse aloud or silently. Selective highlighting and writing summaries, perhaps in table form, will also help.

Formulas
general facts, rules, or principles usually expressed in mathematical symbols.

Key 7.1 Math and science courses prepare you for different careers.

COLLEGE COURSES	ASSOCIATED CAREERS IN DIFFERENT FIELDS
MATH	
- Pre-calculus - Calculus - Geometry - Algebra - Statistics - Symmetry - Differential equations	- Hospital insurance manager - Pharmacist and pharmacy technician - Network systems analyst - Data communication analyst - Real estate appraiser - Auto insurance claims adjuster - Marketing research analyst - Personal financial advisor - Government tax agent - Credit counselor
SCIENCE	
- Anatomy and physiology - Biology and microbiology - Chemistry - Environmental sciences - Geology and oceanography - Kinesiology - Nutrition - Physics - Astronomy - Computer science - Horticulture	- Medical doctor - Dental hygienist - Physician's assistant - Nurse or nurse practitioner - Nutritionist - Physical or occupational therapist - Veterinarian and veterinary technician - Software designer and programmer - Medical case manager - Pharmaceutical sales representative - Sports physiologist - Jet engine repair specialist - Landscaper and arborist - Skin care specialist - Emergency medical technician

Most college students need to fill a wide-ranging set of general education requirements before specializing in a major or concentration. Each student approaches coursework with a unique set of strengths and challenges, likes and dislikes. What are yours?

The list below represents a selection of academic disciplines that are often included in general education requirements. For each subject area, choose a reaction rating:

1 = *significant dislike and challenge*
2 = *mild dislike and challenge*
3 = *neutral reaction*
4 = *mild preference and strength*
5 = *significant preference and strength*

1. History _____
2. Literature _____
3. Writing _____
4. Communications _____
5. Arts _____
6. Philosophy/Religion _____
7. Computer science _____
8. Math and Statistics _____

9. Biology _____
10. Chemistry _____
11. History _____
12. Sociology _____
13. Economics _____
14. World cultures _____
15. World languages _____
16. Physical Education _____

Take a look at your responses, keeping in mind that areas that challenge you are likely to require more focus, study time, and targeted efforts. Consider your current coursework: Which courses are in your areas of dislike and challenge? Plan now to step up and diversify your efforts in those courses to increase your chances of success.

Studying and Homework

Doing homework in math and science requires perseverance and action.

Review materials.   Review your class notes as soon as possible after each class; reinforcing your previous knowledge will add value to the work you are doing. Fill in missing steps in the instructor's examples before you forget them. Compare notes to the textbook.

Do problems, problems, and more problems.   Working through problems helps you understand concepts and formulas. In addition, becoming familiar with a group of problems and related formulas will help you apply what you know to similar problems on other assignments and tests.

?

STUDENT TO STUDENT

You may have used your math knowledge to calculate your GPA or to analyze student loan refinancing options. If you don't feel capable of handling practical math problems like these, think about what you *can* contribute that will provide a foundation for learning more. Pair up with a fellow student and ask each other:

What math can you do comfortably and with confidence? What numbers work causes struggle or anxiety for you? The next time you face an academic math problem or practical math task, how can you use your existing skills to add value and reduce anxiety? Identify other resources that can provide support if you need it.

contribute

Fight frustration with action. If you get stuck on a problem, try another one. If you repeatedly get a wrong answer, examine the steps you've taken. If you hit a wall, try taking a break, asking a friend or an instructor for help, or consulting a Khan Academy video or other online resource.

Work with others. Do as much of your homework as you can on your own, and then meet in person or communicate online with others to discuss it and work through additional problems.

Engage learning preferences. Use strategies that activate your strengths. A visual learner might draw pictures to illustrate problems, and an interpersonal learner might organize a study group. Musical learners might create songs describing math concepts (see Key 7.2 for one of 40 math concept songs instructor Barbara Aaker wrote for her students).

Strive for accuracy. Complete a step of an algebra problem or biology lab project inaccurately, and your answer will be incorrect. In class, the consequences of inaccuracy are reflected in low grades. In life, the consequences could show in a patient's health or in the strength of a bridge. Check over the details of your work, and strive to get it exactly right.

For Working With Numbers

Name an upcoming math or science assignment (material, course, date due):

_____

In the right-hand column, record specific ideas for how MI strategies can help you complete it.

Intelligence	Use MI Strategies to Improve Quantitative Work	Identify MI Strategies that Can Help You Work More Effectively with Numbers
Verbal–Linguistic	• Whenever possible, convert numerical problems and formulas to word problems. • Convert word problems into numbers to solidify the relationship between words and the numbers they signify.	
Logical–Mathematical	• Use math games and puzzles. • Make sure you understand every formula; then, carefully work through each step of the problem-solving process.	
Bodily–Kinesthetic	• Find physical representations of problems. Use pennies; cut up an apple; drive distances. • For hands-on experience, take science classes that have a lab component.	
Visual–Spatial	• Draw visual representations of problems—geometrical shapes, grids, charts, matrices—and use plenty of space. • Circle important items in the description of the problem.	
Interpersonal	• Go over homework problems with a study partner or study-group member. Discuss different approaches. • Schedule a time to communicate with your instructor about difficult concepts.	
Intrapersonal	• Find a solitary spot to read or do homework. • Take quiet breaks when you hit a roadblock. Take a walk or a nap; it may help you think of a new approach.	
Musical	• Listen to music whenever possible. The rhythms and notes of music are based in mathematics.	
Naturalistic	• When you need science credits, look for courses in biological sciences and/or botany. • Find patterns and categorize the information whenever possible.	

"HOW MUCH IS THAT *X* IN THE EQUATION?"
(to the tune of "How Much Is That Doggie in the Window?")

How much is that *x* in the equation?
What value will make it be true?
To find the *x* and get the solution
The numbers attached we **undo.**

The **connector** is plus or minus seven,
To find *x* we have to **undo.**
Just write below both sides—make it even.
We **undo** to find the *x* value.

If multiply or divide is showing,
The **connector** tells what has been done.
To **undo** is where we still are going—
We're trying to get *x* alone.

Source: "Take a Musical Approach to Math" from Mathematics: The Musical by Barbara Aaker Copyright © 1999. Used by permission of Barbara Aaker.

Social Sciences and Humanities

Courses in the social sciences and humanities prepare you to be a well-rounded person, able and ready to fulfill your responsibilities to yourself, your family, and a free democracy. They also prepare you for 21st-century jobs by focusing on critical thinking, civic and historic knowledge, and ethical reasoning. Key 7.3 lists just some of the social science and humanities courses you may take in college and some related careers.

As you study these disciplines, look for themes and use critical thinking as the foundation for your work. Build knowledge by using what you know to learn new material.

Inside Tips from Carol, Career Coach

Teamwork is at the heart of how nearly every modern workplace operates. The process of finding and solving problems, a heavy focus for information age businesses, is often far more successful when team members bring a variety of different approaches and ideas to the table. However, many college students prefer to work independently and hesitate to trust others to do their part.

Consider an area of academic work where you would like to improve your performance. Would you be willing to try this work in a pair or group? Choose one item—a writing assignment, a math problem, a research task—and join forces with one or two other students to work through it. Afterward, evaluate the result. Remember to include "teamwork experience" as one of the benefits.

Key 7.3 Courses in the social sciences and humanities prepare you for different careers.

COLLEGE COURSES	ASSOCIATED CAREERS IN DIFFERENT FIELDS

SOCIAL SCIENCES

COLLEGE COURSES	ASSOCIATED CAREERS IN DIFFERENT FIELDS
- Anthropology - Criminal justice - Business - Information science - Sociology - Social work - Political science - Psychology - Archaeology - Economics - Geography - International relations - Education - Linguistics	- Lawyer - Paralegal - Mental health and substance abuse social worker - Geriatric care social worker - Elementary and high school teacher - Online instructor - Human resources manager - Advertising copy writer - Web-based journalist - Nonprofit foundation fund-raiser - Government staff worker - College admissions manager - Police officer - Publishing sales representative - Labor union official - Retirement counselor

HUMANITIES

COLLEGE COURSES	ASSOCIATED CAREERS IN DIFFERENT FIELDS
- Art history - English literature - Film and theater - Music appreciation - World languages - Communications - Religion - Philosophy - History - African American studies - Latino studies - Women's and gender studies	- Museum curator - Architect - Graphic designer - Actor/director - Musician - Writer/content developer - College professor - Government official - International business

Look for Themes

The National Council for the Social Studies (www.socialstudies.org) organized the study of the social sciences and humanities into 10 themes:[1]

- Culture
- Time, continuity, and change
- People, places, and environment
- Individual development and identity
- Individuals, groups, and institutions
- Power, authority, and governance
- Production, distribution, and consumption

- Science, technology, and society
- Global connections
- Ideals and practices of citizenship

Look for these themes as you read, even if they are not spelled out. For example, as you read a chapter in a political science text on presidential politics, you might think of the history of presidential elections or how the Internet is changing electoral politics.

Learn Through Critical Thinking

Courses in the social sciences ask hard questions about what it means to be an individual, a family member, a citizen of a local community, a nation, and the world. They focus on ethics, human rights and freedoms, and personal and community responsibility, both over time and in different cultures. Critical thinking skills will help you maximize social sciences learning:

- Use SQ3R to question new material.
- Think of social sciences topics (affordable housing, stock market behavior, health care policy, and so on) in terms of problems and solutions.
- Look for strong evidence and logic, and evaluate whether arguments hold up or fall apart.
- Look for bias both in materials and in your own views; set aside assumptions as you read.
- Examine overarching statements for sound cause-and-effect logic.

Your personal beliefs—your definition of a family, your view of history, your understanding of how others influence how you think—may be tested in your social science courses, but the payoff of greater knowledge and broader perspective is worth the effort.

Visual Aids

Many textbooks on many subjects use visual aids—tables, charts, drawings, maps, and photographs, for example—to show, clarify, or summarize information. Pay attention to these visuals as you read; they often contain important information not found elsewhere. Visual learners may especially benefit from information delivered in a format other than text.

Certain types of visual aids, such as word and data tables, as well as charts and graphs, are designed to compare information and statistics that show the following information:

- **Trends over time.** For example, the number of computers with Internet connections per household in 2015 as compared to the number in 2005.
- **Relative rankings.** For example, the sizes of the advertising budgets of four major companies.
- **Distributions.** For example, student performance on standardized tests by geographic area.

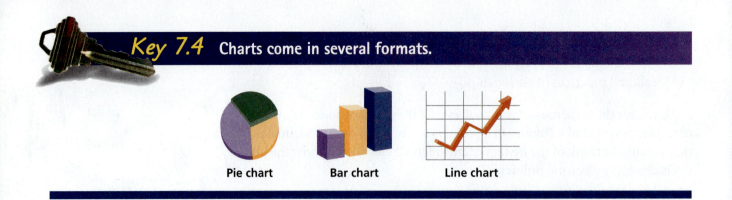

Pie chart   Bar chart   Line chart

- **Cycles.** For example, the regular upward and downward movement of the nation's economy as defined by periods of prosperity and recession.

Key 7.4 demonstrates the appearance of common types of charts: pie, bar, and line.

Literature

Even if you're not an English major, you will probably take one or more literature courses because they are required or out of interest. Studying literature can:

- allow you to experience other times and cultures.
- expose you to a variety of writing approaches and styles.
- help you understand how others react to the problems of daily life.
- provide insight into your own thinking and worldview.

Key 7.5 lists just some of the literature courses you may take in college and related careers. Although some careers may have nothing to do with literature on the surface, they are listed because studying literature requires careful critical thinking, essential for success in many fields.

Key 7.5   Literature courses prepare you for different careers.

COLLEGE COURSES	ASSOCIATED CAREERS IN DIFFERENT FIELDS	
▪ 20th-century American literature	▪ Editor in web-based publishing	▪ Paralegal
▪ Modern European literature	▪ Human resource manager	▪ Teacher
▪ 19th-century Romantic poetry	▪ Sales representative	▪ Government official
▪ Greek and Roman drama	▪ Public relations account manager	▪ Writer/journalist
▪ African myth and literature	▪ Internet-based librarian	▪ Community organizer
	▪ Actor/director/producer	▪ Filmmaker

Connect Courses in Different Disciplines to Your Own Success

Identify a major you are considering or a career area that interests you:

_____

_____

Now, list three required general education courses that are *unrelated* to your potential major or career:

Course #1: _____

Course #2: _____

Course #3: _____

Talk to someone—an instructor, a fellow student, an advisor—about how these courses may help you with your major and in your career. List three ways that you came up with together:

1. _____

2. _____

3. _____

Literature courses ask you to look at different literary elements—plot, setting, and so on—to find meaning. As you read, consider critical thinking questions that focus on these literary elements:

- **Character.** How do characters reveal who they are? How are the main characters similar or different? How do a character's actions change the course of the story?

- **Plot.** How would you evaluate the power of the story? Did it hold your interest?

- **Setting.** How does the setting relate to the actions of the major and minor characters?

- **Point of view.** How are the author's views expressed through characters' actions?

- **Style.** How would you describe the writing style? How does it compare to other works you have read?

- **Imagery.** How does the author use imagery as part of the theme?

After you read the work completely, use critical thinking skills to consider larger questions:

- What is the goal of the work? What are its themes? What do they mean to you?

- Has the work changed your thoughts, attitudes, or feelings in any way?

- Did you personally identify with any of the characters?

- Did the work give you greater understanding of a different time or culture?

This analysis will help you appreciate literature on many levels. Every time you analyze a work, you peel away layers of meaning to reveal artistry you may not see in a casual reading.

How Can You Build Information Literacy?
(is it necessary for both reading and research?)

When it comes to research, most students' first instinct is to power up a Google search or consult Wikipedia. However, the Internet is only one resource available to you. Library materials, having been evaluated by librarians and researchers, can be trusted to be reliable—whereas many Internet sources can turn out to be conjecture, opinion, and rants. With so much information available, and with a workplace focused on knowledge and technology rather than labor, **information literacy** has become an essential skill. Time and effort, combined with information literacy, will help you find the most accurate and reliable information.

Information literacy
the ability to know when information is needed, evaluate the quality of information, and select and use the information best suited to a task or goal.

Map Out the Possibilities

To select the most useful information for your research, get an overview of what is available. For a library you visit in person, sign up for an orientation or tour to learn where resources are located; for an online library, complete a virtual tour of the website. Get to know a librarian who can help you locate sources, navigate catalogs and databases, and uncover research shortcuts. At most schools, you can query a librarian by e-mail or text. Know what you want to accomplish before asking a question.

Conduct an Information Search

To avoid being overwhelmed, use a practical, step-by-step search method. Key 7.6 shows how to start wide and then narrow your search for a closer look at specific sources.

Searching library databases requires a *keyword search*—an exploration that uses a topic-related, natural-language word or phrase as a starting point to locate other information. To narrow your search and reduce the number of *hits* (results returned by your search), add more keywords to your search criteria. For example, instead of searching through the broad category "art," focus on "French art" or, more specifically, "nineteenth-century French art." Key 7.7 shows how to use the key-word system to narrow your search with what is called *Boolean logic.*

© LifeBound, LLC

Much, although not all, research can be done using online databases. Get to know the databases and other resources your school makes available to students.

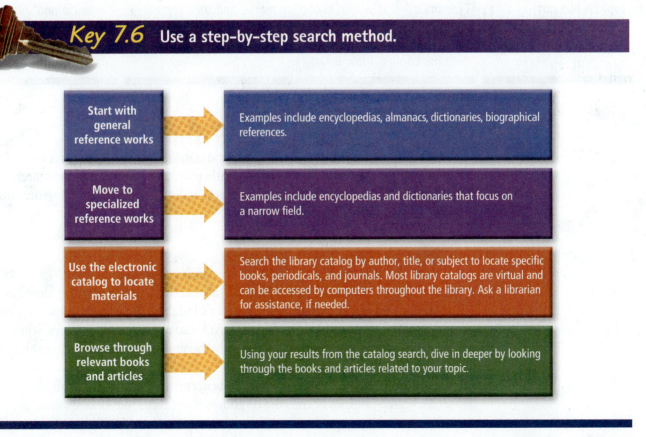

Key 7.6 Use a step-by-step search method.

Start with general reference works	Examples include encyclopedias, almanacs, dictionaries, biographical references.
Move to specialized reference works	Examples include encyclopedias and dictionaries that focus on a narrow field.
Use the electronic catalog to locate materials	Search the library catalog by author, title, or subject to locate specific books, periodicals, and journals. Most library catalogs are virtual and can be accessed by computers throughout the library. Ask a librarian for assistance, if needed.
Browse through relevant books and articles	Using your results from the catalog search, dive in deeper by looking through the books and articles related to your topic.

IF YOU ARE SEARCHING FOR . . .	DO THIS	EXAMPLE
A word	Type the word normally.	Aid
A phrase	Type the phrase in its normal word order (use regular word spacing) or surround the phrase with quotation marks ("x"). Quotation marks ensure the search engine finds the words together in the same phrase, rather than the individual words on the same page.	financial aid, "financial aid"
Two or more keywords without regard to order	Type the words in any order, surrounding the words with quotation marks. Use *and* to separate the words.	"financial aid" and "scholarships"
Topic A <u>and</u> topic B	Type the words in any order, surrounding the words with quotation marks. Use *and* to separate the words. The search engine will list a result only if it contains BOTH topics A and B.	"financial aid" and "scholarships"
Topic A <u>or</u> topic B	Type the words in any order, surrounding the words with quotation marks. Use *or* to separate the words. The search engine will list a result if it contains EITHER A or B.	"financial aid" or "scholarships"
Topic A <u>but not</u> topic B	Type topic A first within quotation marks, and then topic B within quotation marks. Use *not* to separate the words. The search engine will list a result if it contains only Topic A and does not contain Topic B.	"financial aid" not "scholarships"

Be a Critical Internet Searcher

Unlike your college library collection or databases, Internet resources are not always evaluated by trustworthy authorities. As a result, your research depends on critical thinking to sort out the valid, credible materials from the invalid, not-so-credible ones.

Start with Search Engines

Among the most popular and effective search engines are Google (www.google.com) and Yahoo! (www.yahoo.com). Search engines aimed at academic audiences include the Librarian's Index to the Internet (www.lii.org) and INFOMINE (www.infomine.com). At these academic directories, someone has screened the sites and listed only those sources that are reputable and regularly updated.

In addition, your school may include access to certain nonpublic academic search engines in the cost of your tuition. Sites like LexusNexus, InfoTrac, GaleGroup, and OneFile are known for their credibility. Ask a librarian if you have access to these sites.

Use a Search Strategy

The World Wide Web has been called "the world's greatest library, with all its books on the floor." With no librarian in sight, you need to master a practical Internet search strategy.

1. *Use natural language phrases or keywords to identify what you are looking for.* University of Michigan professor Eliot Soloway recommends first phrasing your search in the form of a question. Then he advises identifying the important words in the question, as well as related words. This will give you a collection of terms to use in different combinations as you search (see example below).[2]

   Initial question: What vaccines are given to children before age 5?

   Important words: vaccines, children, before age 5

   Related words: polio, shot, pediatrics

   Final search criteria (important + related words):   vaccines children "before age 5" "polio shot" pediatrics

   Note: Some of the terms in the final search criteria above are enclosed in quotes and others are not. By putting terms in quotes, you tell the search engine that the words *must* appear next to one another, rather than at different locations on the same web page.

2. *Use a search engine to isolate valuable sites.*   Enter your questions, phrases, and keywords in various combinations to generate lists of hits. Vary word order to see what you can generate. If you get too many hits, try using more specific keywords.

3. *Evaluate the list of results.*   The first links in the list of search results are not always the most relevant. Often, the top hits belong to individuals or companies that have paid money to have their sites show up first. Scan through the list of results. You may need to look further down the list of hits to find what you need.

4. *Skim sites to evaluate what seems most useful.*   Once you identify a potentially useful link, go to the site and evaluate it. Does the site seem relevant and reputable? What is its purpose? For example, a blog is apt to focus on opinion; a company's site is likely to promote its products; an article in a scholarly journal may focus on research findings.

5. *Save, or bookmark, the sites you want to focus on.*   Make sure you can access them again. You may want to copy URLs and paste them into a separate document. Consider printing Internet materials that you know you will need to reference over and over again.

6. *When you think you are done, start over.*   Choose another search engine and search again. Different systems access different sites.

The limitations of Internet-only research make it smart to combine Internet and library research. Search engines cannot find everything for several reasons:

- Not all sources are in digital format.
- The Internet prioritizes current information and may not find older information.

- Some digital sources may not be part of your library's subscription offerings.
- Internet searches require electricity or battery power and an online connection.

Use the Internet as a starting point to get an idea of the various documents you may want to locate in the library and read in print. When you find a blog or website that provides only a short extract of important information and then references the rest, find that original article or book and read the information in its entirety. Often, the time and effort that extra searching takes will produce more accurate, in-depth, and useful information.

Your need to be an effective researcher doesn't stop at graduation, especially in a workplace dominated by information and media. The skills you develop as you research school projects will add value in any kind of job that requires use of the Internet and other resources to find and evaluate information.

How Can You Respond Critically to What You Read?
(can everything be questioned?)

Question everything you read—books, articles, online documents, and even textbooks (which are supposed to be as accurate as possible). Think of the critical reading process as an archaeological dig. First, you excavate a site and uncover the artifacts. Then you sort what you've found, make connections among items, and judge their importance. This process of questioning, analysis, and evaluation rewards you with the ability to focus on the most important materials.

Different reading purposes engage different types of critical reading. When you read to learn and retain information, you focus on important ideas (analyzing and evaluating how they are structured, how they connect, and what is most crucial to remember). When you read to search for truth, you ask questions to evaluate arguments (analyzing and evaluating the author's point of view as well as the credibility, accuracy, reliability, and relevancy of the material).

© S_l/Fotolia

Focus on Important Information

Before determining how to respond to something you've read, ask yourself what is important and what you need to remember. According to Adam Robinson, co-founder of *The Princeton Review*, "The only way you can effectively absorb the relevant information is to ignore the irrelevant information."[3] The following questions should help you determine what is relevant (if you answer "yes," it's probably relevant):

- Does it contain headings, charts, tables, and captions; key terms and definitions; or an introduction or summary?

- Does it offer definitions, crucial concepts, examples, an explanation of a variety or type, critical relationships, or comparisons?
- Does it spark questions and reactions as you read?
- Does it surprise or confuse you?
- Does it mirror what your instructor emphasizes during class or in assignments?

When trying to figure out what to study and what to skim, ask yourself whether your instructor would expect you to know the material. If you are unsure and the topic is not on your syllabus, e-mail your instructor and ask for clarification.

Ask Questions to Evaluate Arguments

An *argument* refers to a persuasive case that a writer makes to prove or disprove a point. Many scholarly books and articles are organized around particular arguments. However, other online materials offer *claims* instead—arguments that appear to be factual but don't have adequate evidence to support them.

Critical readers know that just because you read it online or in print doesn't mean it's true. Ask questions to determine whether arguments and claims are accurate and logical. Evaluating an argument involves questioning:

- The quality of the *evidence* (facts, statistics, and other materials supporting an argument)
- Whether the evidence fits the idea concept
- The logical connections

Key 7.8 shows specific questions to ask about an argument.

Key 7.8 Ask questions like these to evaluate arguments.

EVALUATE THE VALIDITY OF THE EVIDENCE	DETERMINE WHETHER THE EVIDENCE SUPPORTS THE CONCEPT
Is the source reliable and free of bias?	Is there enough evidence?
Who wrote this and with that intent?	Do examples and ideas logically connect?
What assumptions underlie this material?	Is the evidence convincing?
Is this argument based on opinion?	Do the examples build a strong case?
How does this evidence compare with evidence from other sources?	What different and perhaps opposing arguments seem equally valid?

Evaluate Every Source

Because the reliability of Internet content varies widely, your Internet research is only as strong as your critical thinking. Robert Harris, professor and web expert, has developed a system for evaluating Internet information called the CARS test for information quality (**C**redibility, **A**ccuracy, **R**easonableness, **S**upport). Use the information in Key 7.9 to question sources as you conduct research. You can also use it to test the reliability of non-Internet sources.

Your future demands that you be able to read, understand, and critically evaluate information on a daily basis in school, on the job, and in life (your 401[k] retirement plan, local and world news, the fine print in a cell phone contract). Develop the ability to read with focus, purpose, and follow-through, adding value to your reading by contributing what you already know, and you will never stop enjoying the benefits.

 **Key 7.9** Use the CARS test to determine information quality on the Internet.

CREDIBILITY	ACCURACY	REASONABLENESS	SUPPORT
Examine whether a source is believable and trustworthy.	Examine whether information is correct—that is, factual, comprehensive, detailed, and up to date (if necessary).	Examine whether material is fair, objective, moderate, and consistent.	Examine whether a source is adequately supported with citations.
What are the author's credentials?	*Is it up to date and is that important?*	*Does the source seem fair?*	*Where does the information come from?*
Look for education and experience, title or position of employment, membership in any known and respected organization, reliable contact information, biographical information, and reputation.	If you are searching for a work of literature, such as Shakespeare's play *Macbeth*, there is no "updated" version. However, you may want reviews of its latest productions. For most scientific research, you will need to rely on the most updated information you can find.	Look for a balanced argument, accurate claims, and a reasoned tone that does not appeal primarily to your emotions.	Look at the site, the sources used by the person or group who compiled the information, and the contact information. Make sure that the cited sources seem reliable and that statistics are documented.

CREDIBILITY	ACCURACY	REASONABLENESS	SUPPORT
Is there quality control?	*Is it comprehensive?*	*Does the source seem objective?*	*Is the information corroborated?*
Look for ways in which the source may have been screened. For example, materials on an organization's website have most likely been approved by several members; information coming from an academic journal has to be screened by several people before it is published.	Does the material leave out any important facts or information? Does it neglect to consider alternative views or crucial consequences? Although no one source can contain all of the available information on a topic, it should still be as comprehensive as is possible within its scope.	While there is a range of objectivity in writing, you want to favor authors and organizations who can control their bias. An author with a strong political or religious agenda or an intent to sell a product may not be a source of the most truthful material.	Test information by looking for other sources that confirm the facts in this information—or, if the information is opinion, sources that share that opinion and back it up with their own citations. One good strategy is to find at least three sources that corroborate each other.
Is there any posted summary or evaluation of the source?	*For whom is the source written, and for what purpose?*	*Does the source seem moderate?*	*Is the source externally consistent?*
You may find abstracts of sources (summary) or a recommendation, rating, or review from a person or organization (evaluation). Either of these—or, ideally, both—can give you an idea of credibility before you decide to examine a source in depth.	Looking at what the author wants to accomplish will help you assess whether it has a bias. Sometimes biased information will not be useful for your purpose; sometimes your research will require that you note and evaluate bias (such as if you were to compare Civil War diaries from Union soldiers with those from Confederate soldiers).	Do claims seem possible, or does the information seem hard to believe? Does what you read make sense when compared to what you already know? While wild claims may turn out to be truthful, you are safest to check everything out.	Most material is a mix of both current and old information. External consistency refers to whether the old information agrees with what you already know. If a source contradicts something you know to be true, chances are higher that the information new to you may be inconsistent as well.
Signals of a potential lack of credibility:	*Signals of a potential lack of accuracy:*	*Signals of a potential lack of reasonableness:*	*Signals of a potential lack of support:*
Anonymous materials, negative evaluations, little or no evidence of quality control, bad grammar or misspelled words	Lack of date or old date, generalizations, one-sided views that do not acknowledge opposing arguments	Extreme or emotional language, sweeping statements, conflict of interest, inconsistencies or contradictions	Statistics without sources, lack of documentation, lack of corroboration using other reliable sources

Source: Harris, Robert. "Evaluating Internet Research Sources." *VirtualSalt*, November 22, 2010.

© Courtesy of Garrett Mintz

What happened with Garrett?

Refocusing on his goal to earn a degree and engage his talents, Garrett returned to Indiana University, was accepted to the Kelley School of Business, and his felony charges were downgraded to a misdemeanor. His desire to add value to student life led him to start an organization called CLEAR (College Lifestyles Excluding Alcohol and Recreational drugs) that provides alternatives to using and abusing drugs and alcohol. CLEAR hosts fun, free events like ultimate Frisbee and scavenger hunts.

Thinking more specifically about his motivation to help students enter the workforce and thrive, Garrett then founded AIM (Ambition In Motion), an organization that prepares college students for postgraduation life. AIM helps students understand their strengths and weaknesses through feedback from their peers, develop emotional intelligence and interpersonal skills through workshops and mentorship, and connect with career opportunities at companies where the work culture and environment aligns with a student's strengths. After students who go through this process are hired, AIM helps integrate these students into the companies that hired them by providing software that helps them develop and improve communication with their supervisors. With AIM, Garrett contributes to a better world every day, striving to add value to the student experience in a way that lasts long after graduation.

Connect this story to your life: Garrett's personal experiences led him to a specific way of contributing to others that adds value to the world as well as adding meaning to his life. Your own experiences can do the same, and you too have the potential to contribute. What about your life up until this point motivates you to contribute to the world and the lives of others? Describe how you want to contribute, and be specific about how your actions will add value.

Building Skills

for successful learning

Note the Important Points

Name two strategies that will help you read and comprehend math and science texts.

1. _____

2. _____

Name three themes that characterize social science texts.

1. _____

2. _____

3. _____

Name and describe three of the elements that help you understand a literary work.

1. _____

2. _____

3. _____

Compare and contrast the Internet and the library as research resources.

_____

Identify and briefly describe the four concepts in the CARS test for information quality.

1. _____

2. _____

3. _____

4. _____

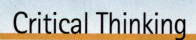

Critical Thinking

Get the Most from Your Coursework

At least once if not several times, usually when taking required general education courses, college students find themselves asking the question: "What will I ever do with this?" True, one or more courses will seem unrelated to your interests and goals, especially during your first year. However, such courses can still offer a variety of benefits. Some examples:

- An art history course can reinforce your understanding of historical times, places, and events.

- A political science course may help you understand why it's important to vote.

- A literature course may help you think about important ideas and explore human nature.

- An earth science course can increase your understanding of alternative energy sources.

- A statistics course may help you determine your risk of developing a disease that runs in your family.

From a textbook for a course you are currently taking that doesn't seem relevant to you, choose a chapter that you are about to cover in class. Do the following to maximize your understanding:

1. Read the chapter now, before its material is covered in class. Take notes. Check this box when you have read it through: ☐

2. Identify and work through one challenging concept or formula. Develop a plan to learn it. Base your plan on what will help most—memory techniques, study groups, practice with problems, asking your instructor for help, and so forth.

Note the concept or formula here:

_____

_____

_____

Briefly describe your plan:

_____

_____

_____

_____

_____

Check the box when you have put your plan into action. Work done? ☐

Finally, evaluate the difference your efforts made in your ability to retain the challenging information you were focusing on. How did your plan help?

_____

_____

_____

Team Building

Build Information Literacy by Sharing Perspectives

With the amount of information available on search engines and databases, and the wide range of things to evaluate on any one source or site, being a careful, information literate researcher can present challenges. One way to make the evaluation process more effective is to work with a group so that you can discuss different perspectives and come to agreement on whether a source is valuable.

Gather in person or online with a group of three to five students. If you can, form your group with students who are all taking the same course. It's even better if this course requires Internet research for one or more assignments or projects.

Choose a topic to research together (if you all are in the same course, select a topic that will be useful for an assignment or project; if you are not in the same course, find a topic that interests the group). Decide on a specific set of keywords (no more than 4) you will use to research the topic.

Conduct an initial search by putting those keywords into a popular search engine. From the top 10 hits, each group member should choose one source to investigate more fully (only one group member per source). After each group member has made their choice, select one more source that ALL group members will evaluate. This means that each group member will be looking at two sources—one that everyone will evaluate, and one that only he or she will examine.

Each group member will evaluate the two sources on their own time, using the CARS test (review the material in the chapter for more details), looking carefully at:

- Credibility
- Accuracy
- Reasonableness
- Support

After each student has finished, the group should gather again in person or online and share evaluations. First, take turns presenting opinions about the shared evaluation, inviting discussion in case opinions differ about the value of the source. Then, share impressions about the individually-researched sources.

After talking through each source that was researched, come to group agreement on the three most valuable sources from the original list of hits. Keep them handy if they are on a topic that will prove useful to you for a course.

Test Prep   Start It Now

contribute

Add Value to Study Time

Studying is challenging enough without feeling like you are starting from
scratch every time you begin a study session. Make an effort to add value to your
study time by bringing what you already know into the forefront of your mind before you begin.

Name the next quiz or test you have to study for:

_____

1. Create a list of topics you need to know for this quiz or test.
2. Before you begin studying, take your topic list and do a "brain dump" of what you know on each
   topic. You can freewrite on a pad, speak into a recording app, or type on a computer or device.
3. Then begin studying your notes, textbook, and other materials. As you move through each topic, compare and contrast your materials with what you wrote or recorded before: Are you missing knowledge
   that you need to spend extra study time on? Do you have knowledge on which you are solid and don't
   need much work? Is there something you thought you knew but remembered incorrectly?
4. Let what you learn from this comparison add value to your study plan. Adjust time and focus
   according to where you most and least need reinforcement.

8

listening and note taking
taking in and recording information

MASTER SERGEANT JOHANCHARLES VAN BOERS,
U.S. Army, Ret., graduate of Summit University, Barstow Community College, and Palomar Community College

Johancharles Van Boers, known as Chuck, comes from a long line of warriors. Growing up as a Lipan Apache in a family with a strong tradition of service, he perceived the military as his greatest area of opportunity. With the help of his mother, an Army recruiter, he enlisted in the U.S. Army—following the path of his parents, uncles, and tribe leaders—shortly before the start of his senior year of high school. He also had a passion for photography, but was unsure how that would translate to a career.

From listening to advice from his mother, Chuck found that the Army provided opportunities to both hone his photography skills (as a combat photographer) and preserve his traditions as an Apache Warrior. After Chuck graduated from basic training, his uncle gave him two eagle feathers that had been carried first by family during their time as Apache Scouts, then by relatives in World War I, World War II, Korea, and Vietnam. Chuck continued the tradition by carrying the feathers inside his combat vest on every one of his deployments including Grenada, Saudi Arabia, Iraq, Kuwait, Haiti, Sarajevo, Bosnia, and Kosovo.

After years of distinguished service, two Bronze Star medals, and three Purple Hearts, Chuck returned to civilian life, but found it nearly impossible to readjust. As a result of the traumatic brain injury (TBI) he had sustained due to mortar and rocket blasts, he suffered from memory loss, confusion, poor balance, daily migraines, and emotional turmoil. He enrolled in college, but experienced incidents such as waking up confused and ready for combat and trying to dress in a uniform when he had put all his uniforms away. Chuck had not yet come to understand how he could apply the skills he had learned in the military to life as a civilian.

(to be continued . . .)

Listening for understanding can mean paying close attention to your own values and goals as well as taking in the perspectives of others. You'll learn more about Chuck's experience at the end of the chapter.

Working through this chapter will help you to:

- Actively listen for meaning and important information. p. 198

- Record effective notes in class. p. 203

- Understand outline, Cornell, and mind-map note-taking formats. p. 205

- Identify which note-taking format will work best for different situations. p. 205

- Determine which note-taking format feels most comfortable to you. p. 205

Text and photo used by permission from Johancharles Van Boers

listen

Consider what others say as you work to *understand* different perspectives and new ideas. Listen for ideas that diverge from your own thinking so that you can increase understanding of different perspectives.

How Can You Become a Better Listener?

(isn't listening just something you do automatically when you can hear?)

Listening
a process that involves sensing, interpreting, evaluating, and reacting to spoken messages.

The act of hearing isn't the same as the act of listening. *Hearing* refers to sensing spoken messages from their source. You can hear things but not comprehend or remember them. **Listening** starts with hearing, but then continues with focused thinking about what you hear, leading to greater understanding.

Listening is a learnable skill that brings increased ability to relate to work and school colleagues, friends, and family. For online students, listening is valuable for taking in recorded lectures and materials, real-time virtual interactions, and future work relationships. Listening has value that extends far beyond your academic experience.

Key 8.1   **The listening process.**

SPEAKER DELIVERS MESSAGE TO LISTENER

REACTION
Listener provides feedback to speaker through questions and comments

EVALUATION
Listener judges message against personal needs and values

INTERPRETATION
Listener attaches meaning to message

SENSATION
Listener hears message when ears pick up sound waves

© (l) Imagedb.com/Fotolia; (r) Lisa F. Young/Fotolia

Know the Stages of Listening

Listening is made up of four stages that take the message from the speaker to the listener and back to the speaker: sensation, interpretation, evaluation, and reaction. These stages take the message from the speaker to the listener and back again to the speaker (see Key 8.1). You can become a better listener by managing listening challenges (maximizing the sensation stage) and becoming actively involved with the material (maximizing the interpretation and evaluation stages).

Manage Listening Challenges

When students do things that interfere with listening—texting, surfing the Internet, talking, sleeping, daydreaming—they tend to absorb less information and learn less. Read on to learn how to address this challenge and others as you turn listening into a tool for understanding.

Issue #1: Distractions that Divide Your Attention

Common distractions that interfere with listening include *internal distractions* (worry, anticipation, hunger, feeling too hot or too cold) and *external distractions* (chatting, texting, computer use, any kind of movement or noise). These distractions prevent you from paying full attention to what is said. As a result, you can easily miss or misunderstand things.

Fix #1: Focus, Focus, Focus

Find practical ways to minimize distractions, such as the following:

- Sit where you can focus (if you take a class online, find a quiet environment; if you take a class in person, move away from talkative classmates and sit close enough to hear well).

- Unless class requires you to use it, put away your cell phone.

- Consider writing your notes by hand rather than using a laptop.

- If you do take notes on a computer, use it for class-related tasks only during class time.

- Get enough sleep to stay alert.

- Eat enough so that you're not hungry—or bring small snacks if allowed.

Although it can be hard, try to put nonacademic thoughts and worries aside during class time. "Switch-tasking"—switching back and forth between tasks—reduces focus and increases the chance of making

Listening to other students can be as important as listening to instructors. These students may learn something useful from their fellow student's perspective.

mistakes. In a study at Stanford, people switching between fewer tasks (low multitaskers) actually outperformed people switching between more tasks (high multitaskers) on all tasks.[1]

Issue #2: Listening Lapses

Even the most fantastic instructor cannot *make* you listen. Whether or not to listen actively is your decision. If you find a subject difficult or uninteresting, you may tune out completely. Or you may focus on only certain points and shut out everything else. Either type of listening lapse can cause you to miss valuable information.

Fix #2: An I-Can-Do-It Attitude

- *Start with a productive mindset.* If the class is hard, being determined to pay attention will help you learn more effectively.

- *Refocus.* If you stop listening, try to get back into the presentation instead of worrying about what you missed. Later, consider looking at a classmate's notes to fill in the gaps.

- *Be aware.* Pay attention to **verbal signposts**. These are words or phrases that call attention to what comes next, help organize information, connect ideas, and indicate what is important and what is not. See Key 8.2 for examples.

Issue #3: Rushing to Judgment

It's common to stop listening when you hear something you don't like, don't agree with, or don't understand. Judgments also involve reactions to speakers.

Verbal signposts
spoken words or phrases that connect ideas and signal what is important.

listen

POWERFUL QUESTIONS

STUDENT TO STUDENT

Consider any instructors you don't like or with whom you disagree—either now or from previous coursework. Pair up with a fellow student and ask each other:

What happens when you don't get along with or agree with an instructor—do you stop paying attention, engage in an internal argument, think of a response, or something else? What does your response cost you, if anything, in terms of your learning goals? Come up with actions you are willing to take so that you can listen and learn the next time you are in this type of situation.

Key 8.2 Pay attention to verbal signposts.

SIGNALS THAT POINT TO KEY CONCEPTS	SIGNALS THAT SUPPORT
A key point to remember . . .	A perfect example . . .
Point 1, point 2, etc. . . .	Specifically, . . .
The impact of this was . . .	For instance, . . .
The critical stages in the process are . . .	Similarly, . . .

SIGNALS THAT POINT TO DIFFERENCES	SIGNALS THAT SUMMARIZE
On the contrary, . . .	From this you have learned . . .
On the other hand, . . .	In conclusion, . . .
In contrast, . . .	As a result, . . .
However, . . .	Finally, . . .

If you do not like your instructors or have preconceived notions about race, ethnicity, gender, physical characteristics, or disability, you may hamper your ability to learn from them. Judgmental reactions may cause students to miss important information, which can hurt at test time.

Fix #3: Recognize and Adjust Your Patterns

College provides an opportunity to broaden your horizons and consider what diverse people can teach you. How can you address an emotional reaction to a speaker or a message?

- **Observe your patterns.** When you feel yourself reacting to something, stop and take a deep breath. Count to 10. Ask yourself: What assumptions or biases are causing this?

- **Shift your perspective.** You cannot hear or learn from others if you are filled with preconceived notions about them and their ideas. Put yourself in their shoes and be open to their ideas as you would want others to be open to yours.

- **Be determined.** Even when you disagree or have a negative reaction about an instructor, keep listening. Being open to the new and different, even when it makes you a bit uncomfortable, can bring learning and understanding that changes you for the better.

Issue #4: Partial Hearing Loss and Learning Disabilities

If you have a hearing loss or a learning disability, listening to a lecture may prove challenging. Learning disabilities come in a variety of forms affecting different parts of cognition.

Fix #4: Get Help

If you have a hearing loss and attend class in person, find out if there is amplification equipment you can use during class time. If recordings are available for download to a computer or iPod, listen to them to pick up what you missed the first time. Meet with your instructor outside of class to clarify your notes or sit near the front of the room. If you take an online class that features video or audio recordings, you can turn the volume up or listen to them more than once.

If you have, or think you have, a learning disability, learn what services are available. Seek connections with people who can reward you with productive help. Talk to your advisor and instructor about your problem, seek out a tutor, visit academic centers that can help (such as the writing center, if you have a writing issue), scan the college website, and connect with the office of students with disabilities.

ALL ABOUT YOU

On a scale of 1 to 10—10 being the most effective and 1 being the least—rate yourself in each category.

Characteristics of an effective listener (10)	Characteristics of an ineffective listener (1)	How do you rate?
I make a conscious decision to work at listening and consider difficult material a challenge.	I don't think that listening requires any particular process. I tune out difficult material.	
I fight distractions by concentrating harder.	I get pulled away by distractions and stop listening.	
I continue to listen to difficult or dry material, hoping to learn something interesting.	I give up when I lose interest.	
I withhold judgment until I hear everything.	I focus on my own thoughts as soon as a speaker says something controversial.	
I keep focused by listening for organizational patterns, transitional language, and summary statements.	I get sidetracked by random comments. If the material is worth listening to, I shouldn't have to use strategies.	
I adapt my note-taking style to the style and organization of the speaker.	I always take notes in the same way, no matter the speaker's style.	
I set aside any initial negative reactions I may have and continue to listen actively.	If I have a negative emotional response, I stop listening.	
During any spare moments I evaluate, summarize, and question what I heard and anticipate what comes next.	During any spare time my mind wanders to other topics and often I miss a lot.	

Issue #5: Comprehension Difficulties for Non-native English Speakers

If English is not your first language, it may be challenging to listen and understand material. Specialized vocabulary, informal language, and the rate of speech can add to the challenge. Succeeding in class will require concentration, dedication, and patience.

Fix #5: Take a Proactive Approach to Understanding

Talk to your instructor early in the course. In some cases, your instructor will give you a list of key terms to review before class. During class, keep a running list of unfamiliar words and phrases to look up later. Focus on the main points of the lecture and meet with classmates after class to fill in the gaps in your understanding. If after several weeks you're still having difficulties, consider enrolling in an English refresher course, getting a tutor, or visiting the campus advising center for more assistance. Be proactive about your education.

Effective listening skills are the basis for effective note taking—an essential and powerful study tool.

How Can You Improve Your Note-Taking Skills?
(will it matter once college is done?)

Note taking makes you an active class participant, even when you don't say a word. Because it is virtually impossible to write or type every word you hear, note taking encourages you to critically evaluate what is worth remembering. Note taking involves you in the learning process and sets the stage for deeper understanding, providing you with thinking skills and knowledge necessary for success in both academic and workplace settings.

Taking Notes in Class

Class notes serve two primary purposes: (1) they record what happened in class, and (2) they provide study materials. Exploring the strategies outlined next helps you prepare for class, take notes in class, and review notes after class.

Prepare

Showing up for class on time is just the start. Here's more about preparing to take notes:

- **Preview your reading material.** Reading assigned materials before class will give you the background to take effective notes and is one of the most rewarding possible study strategies. Check your class syllabi daily for assignment due dates, and plan your reading time with these deadlines in mind.

- **Review what you know.** Taking 15 minutes before class to review previous notes and reading will help you to follow the lecture from the start.
- **Set up your environment.** Find a spot where you can concentrate. Set up your notebook or computer and find the right page or electronic file. Be ready to write or type as soon as class begins.
- **Gather support.** In each class, set up a support plan with one or two students so you can discuss questions you have or look at their notes after being absent. Find students who seem dedicated and hard-working.

Record Information Effectively during Class

The following practical suggestions will help you record information to review later:

© WavebreakmediaMicro/Fotolia

In the classroom or when watching a video lecture, good listening powers note taking. When taking notes during class time, stop to listen to the information before deciding what to write down.

- Write down all key terms and definitions.
- For difficult concepts, note relevant examples, applications, and links to other material.
- If questions are welcome during class, ask them. If you prefer to ask questions after class, jot down questions as you think of them through the class period.
- Write down every question your instructor raises, since these questions may be on a test.
- Be organized but not fussy. Remember that you can always improve your notes later.
- Draw pictures and diagrams to illustrate ideas.
- Be consistent. Use the same system to show importance—such as indenting, spacing, or underlining—on each page.
- If you have trouble with a concept, leave space for an explanation and flag it with a question mark. After class, consult your text or ask a classmate or instructor for help.
- Go beyond the PowerPoint. When instructors use electronic resources, expand on the main points listed there with details from the lecture.
- Consider learning preferences. The Multiple Intelligences table in this chapter suggests MI-related note-taking strategies.

Finally, don't stop taking notes when your class engages in a discussion. Even though it isn't part of the instructor's planned presentation, it often includes important information. Key 8.3 has suggestions for how to take notes during class discussions (equally useful during work meetings).

Review and Revise Your Notes

The process of note taking doesn't end when you put your pen down or close your browser at the end of the class period. Notes are only useful to you if you review and revise them and within as short a time period as you

- Listen to everyone; you never know when something important will be said.

- Listen for threads that weave through comments. They may signal an important point.

- Listen for ideas the instructor likes and for encouraging comments, such as "You make a great point" or "I like your idea."

- Take notes when the instructor rephrases and clarifies a point.

can manage. The sooner you review notes, the more likely you are to understand them.

Class notes often have sections that are incomplete, confusing, or illegible. Review and revise your notes as soon as possible after class to fill in gaps, clarify sloppy handwriting, and raise questions while the material is still fresh in your mind. Rewriting or retyping notes is a great way to reinforce what you heard in class, review ideas, and create easy-to-read study aids.

One way to improve your chances of taking clear and useful notes is to know several note-taking formats. The following formats will help you create notes that will reinforce your learning each time you turn to them throughout the term.

What Note–Taking Formats Can You Use? (is there one best format?)

Now that you have gathered some useful strategies for what goes into your notes and how to study that material, take a look at different note-taking formats. As you read, keep some questions in mind:

- How could I make use of this format?
- What class or type of instruction is each format best suited for? Why?

- Which format seems most comfortable to me?
- What format might be most compatible with my learning preferences? Why?

This section discusses different note-taking formats. Different formats may suit different courses, so don't assume that the format that seems most comfortable to you will be the best choice for every academic subject. Take instructor style, course format and material, and learning preferences into account as you select a format to use in any class.

Look at examples of various note-taking formats and how they work.

Outlines

Outlines use a standard structure to show how ideas interrelate. *Formal outlines* indicate idea dominance and subordination with Roman numerals, upper-case and lowercase letters, and numbers. In contrast, *informal outlines* show the same associations but replace the formality with a format of consistent indenting and dashes.

When a lecture seems well organized, an informal outline can show how ideas and supporting details relate and can indicate levels of importance. Key 8.4 shows how the structure of an informal outline could help a student take notes on the topic of tropical rain forests. During class time, it is usually easier and faster to use an informal outline than to carefully construct a formal outline using letters and numbers to identify pieces of information.

When an instructor's presentation is disorganized, it may be difficult to use an outline. Focus instead on taking down whatever information you can as you try to connect key topics. Other note-taking methods can be beneficial in such situations.

Guided Notes

Sometimes instructors distribute guided notes, usually in the form of an outline, to help you follow the lecture. Guided notes do *not* replace your own notes. Designed to be sketchy and limited, they require you to fill in the details during class, which helps you to pay attention. In addition, the act of writing helps anchor information in memory and build understanding.

When you get guided notes on paper, fill in additional information during class. When guided notes are written or projected on the board, copy them into your notebook or computer file, leaving space for what you will add. When you receive these notes as an electronic file, save the document and annotate it during class.

Cornell T-Note Format

The Cornell note-taking format, also known as the *T-note format,* consists of three sections on ordinary notepaper:[2]

- *Notes,* the largest section, is on the right. Record your notes here in what-ever form you choose. Skip lines between topics so you can clearly see where a section begins and ends.

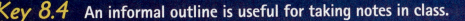

Key 8.4   An informal outline is useful for taking notes in class.

Tropical Rain Forests

What are tropical rain forests?
- — Areas in South America and Africa, along the equator
- — Average temperatures between 25° and 30° C (77°–86° F)
- — Average annual rainfalls range between 250 and 400 centimeters (100–160 inches)

Rain forests are the Earth's richest, most biodiverse ecosystem.
- — A biodiverse ecosystem has a great number of organisms coexisting within a defined area.
- — Examples of rain forest biodiversity
  - — 2½ acres in the Amazon rain forest has 283 species of trees
  - — a 3-square-mile section of a Peruvian rain forest has more than 1,300 butterfly species and 600 bird species
- — Compare this biodiversity to what is found in the entire United States.
  - — only 400 butterfly species and 700 bird species

How are humans changing the rain forest?
- — Humans destroy an estimated 50,000 square miles of rain forest a year (10 times the area of Connecticut).
  - — Cutting down trees for lumber
  - — Clearing the land for ranching or agriculture
- — Rain forest removal is also linked to the increase in atmospheric carbon dioxide, which worsens the greenhouse effect (where gases such as carbon dioxide trap the sun's energy in the Earth's atmosphere as heat resulting in global warning).

Source: Audesirk, Teresa, Gerald Audesirk, and Bruce E. Byers. *Life on Earth,* 9th ed. Upper Saddle River, NJ: Prentice Hall, 2011, pp. 559–561.

- The *cues* column goes on the left side of your notes. Leave it blank while you read or listen, and then fill it in later while you review. You might insert keywords or comments that highlight ideas, clarify meaning, add examples, link ideas, or draw diagrams. Many students use this column to raise questions, which they answer when they study.

- The *summary* goes at the bottom. Here you reduce notes to critical points, a process that helps you learn the material. Fill in this area when reviewing after class.

Create this note-taking structure *before* class begins by following these directions:

- Start with a sheet of 8.5-by-11-inch lined paper. Label it with the date and lecture title.

- To create the cues column, draw a vertical line about 2.5 inches from the left side of the paper. End the line about 2 inches from the bottom of the sheet.

- To create the summary area, start at the point where the vertical line ends (about 2 inches from the bottom of the page) and draw a horizontal line that spans the entire paper.

Cues	Notes

Summary

Label a sheet of paper with the date and title of the lecture.

Create the **cue column** by drawing a vertical line about 2-½ inches from the left side of the paper. End the line about 2 inches from the bottom of the sheet.

Create the **summary area** by starting where the vertical line ends (about 2 inches from the bottom of the page) and drawing a horizontal line across the paper.

October 3, 2014, p. 1

Understanding Employee Motivation

Why do some workers have a better attitude toward their work than others?

Some managers view workers as lazy; others view them as motivated and productive.

Maslow's Hierarchy

self-actualization needs (challenging job)
esteem needs (job title)
social needs (friends at work)
security needs (health plan)
physiological needs (pay)

Purpose of motivational theories
— To explain role of human relations in motivating employee performance
— Theories translate into how managers actually treat workers

2 specific theories
— Human resources model, developed by Douglas McGregor, shows that managers have radically different beliefs about motivation.
— Theory X holds that people are naturally irresponsible and uncooperative
— Theory Y holds that people are naturally responsible and self-motivated
— Maslow's Hierarchy of Needs says that people have needs in 5 different areas, which they attempt to satisfy in their work.
— Physiological need: need for survival, including food and shelter
— Security need: need for stability and protection
— Social need: need for friendship and companionship
— Esteem need: need for status and recognition
— Self-actualization need: need for self-fulfillment
Needs at lower levels must be met before a person tries to satisfy needs at higher levels.
— Developed by psychologist Abraham Maslow

Two motivational theories try to explain worker motivation. The human resources model includes Theory X and Theory Y. Maslow's Hierarchy of Needs suggests that people have needs in 5 different areas: physiological, security, social, esteem, and self-actualization.

Both the cue column and the summary area help you build understanding of what you've recorded in the notes section. Key 8.5 shows how the Cornell format was used to take notes in a business course.

Mind Maps

A mind map, also known as a *think link* or *word web,* is a visual form of note taking that encourages flexible thinking and making connections. When you draw a mind map, you use shapes and lines to connect ideas with supporting details and examples. The visual design makes the connections easy to see, and shapes and pictures extend the material beyond words.

To create a mind map, start by circling or boxing your topic in the middle of the paper. Next, draw a line from the topic and write the name of one major idea at the end of the line. Circle that idea. Then, jot down specific facts related to the idea, linking them to the idea with more lines. Continue the process, identifying thoughts with words and circles, and connecting them to one another with lines. Key 8.6 shows a mind map illustrating the sociological concept called stratification.

A mind map does not have to include circles and lines; it can take on a number of different forms, such as a "jellyfish" (main idea at the top with examples dangling down below) or a series of stairs with examples building to the idea at the top. Engage your creativity to develop a shape that works for you. If you take notes on a computer, explore mind-map creation apps like mindmapfree.com or mindmup.com. If a mind map is difficult to construct in class, consider transforming your notes into a mind-map format later when you review.

Key 8.6 Use a mind map to connect ideas visually.

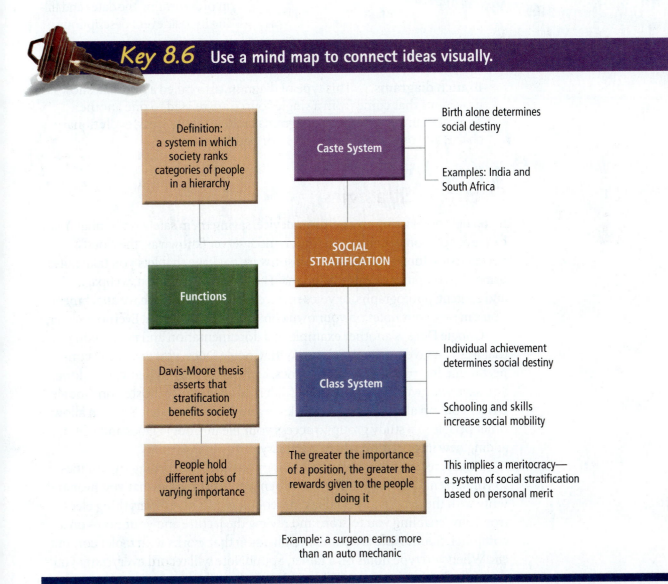

Inside Tips from Carol, Career Coach

Your ability to take good notes is directly related to your ability to follow up action items after a business meeting. Without careful notes, you can forget what was said, which often leads to mistakes regarding what you have to do next. Note taking in the world of work is associated with being conscientious and with effective follow-through on action plans. Consider: What is it worth to you to build a skill that employers value and reward, separate from how you may value the skill? Keep in mind: The higher you rise in an organization, the more important this skill becomes.

Other Visual Note-Taking Strategies

Several other note-taking strategies will help you organize information and are especially useful to visual learners. These strategies may be too involved to complete in class, so save them for when you take text notes or combine class and text notes.

- **Timelines.** Use a timeline to organize information in chronological order. Draw a vertical or horizontal line on the page and place tic marks on the line in order, noting the dates and filling in basic event descriptions.

- **Tables.** Use the columns and rows of a table to organize information as you condense and summarize your class and text notes.

- **Branch diagrams.** This type of diagram, also called a *tree chart,* shows how items that come from a single source are related to one another. Typical examples of branch diagrams include family trees, evolutionary charts, and organizational charts (for people or files).

Electronic Strategies

If you take notes using an electronic device, saving them safely is essential. You can save notes on your device or on a remote server (known as "the cloud") connected to the Internet. Evernote is a software package that lets you take notes using any computer or Android phone. These notes include text, webpage URLs and content, photographs, or voice memos—all of which can have attachments. You can save your notes on your own computer or on a special Evernote server.

Google Docs is another example of a documentation and note-taking tool that lets you save text to the cloud. With Google Docs, you need only connect to the Internet, open Google Docs, and start typing. When you're done, you save your work to a collection (folder) of your choice, hosted on Google Drive. You can also download the file to your own computer. You can allow other people in a study group to access your file in Google Docs and edit it, adding new information where necessary.

Finally, recent note-taking technology has added recording capabilities to your arsenal. The Livescribe "smartpen" records exactly what you hear and write with the pen on a specialized notebook which saves everything electronically, enabling you to store and review the lecture and your notes on a computer. SoundNote is a similar application that works with tablet computers. When you type notes on a tablet, SoundNote will record everything you type as well as what you are hearing during the class.[3]

No matter whether your notes are electronic or on paper, combining class and text notes will provide you with a comprehensive review of the material you need to know.

TAKE ACTION

Prepare to Listen and Take Notes in Your Hardest Class

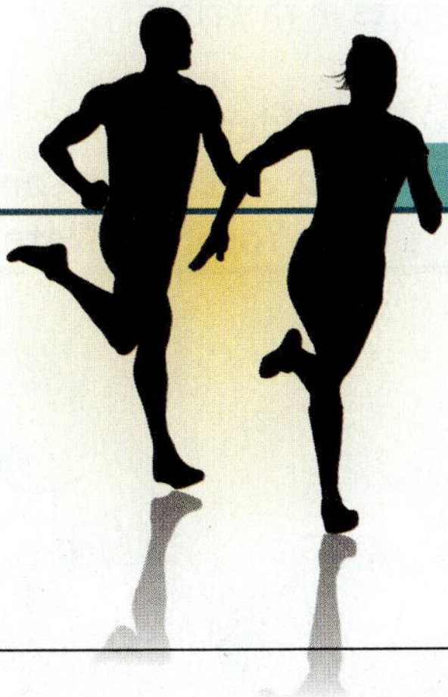

Get set to take in and record information in your most difficult class.

Course name and date of next class:

____

Consult your syllabus, and then list everything you have to read before the next class (include pages from text and supplemental sources):

____

____

List two strategies you can use to minimize distractions during the class:

1. ______________________________

2. ______________________________

Which note-taking format is best suited for the class? Why?

____

____

Write the names and contact information of two classmates whose notes you can borrow if you miss a class or are confused about material:

1. ______________________________

2. ______________________________

MULTIPLE INTELLIGENCE
STRATEGIES

For Note Taking

Name an upcoming class meeting (date, time, course): . _____

In the right-hand column, record specific ideas for how MI strategies can help you take notes in this class.

Intelligence	Use MI Strategies to Improve Your Notes	Identify MI Strategies that Can Help You Take Notes
Verbal–Linguistic	• Rewrite your class notes in an alternate note-taking style to see connections more clearly. • Combine class and textbook notes to get a complete picture.	
Logical–Mathematical	• When reviewing or rewriting notes, put information into a logical sequence. • Create tables that show relationships.	
Bodily–Kinesthetic	• Think of your notes as a crafts project with "knowledge layers" of different colors. Use colored pens to texture your notes. • Study with your notes spread in sequence around you so that you can see knowledge building from left to right.	
Visual–Spatial	• Take notes using colored markers or pens. • Rewrite lecture notes as a mind map, focusing on the most important points.	
Interpersonal	• Try to schedule a study group right after class to discuss class notes. • Review class notes with a study buddy and compare notes to see what each of you missed.	
Intrapersonal	• Schedule some quiet time soon after class to review and think about your notes. • As you review your notes, decide whether you grasp the material or need help.	
Musical	• To improve recall, recite concepts in your notes to rhythms. • Write a song that includes material from your class and text notes. Use the refrain to emphasize what is important.	
Naturalistic	• Notice similarities and differences in concepts by organizing material into natural groupings.	

How Do You Combine Class and Text Notes to Create a Master Set?

(what is the benefit of all that work?)

Studying from either text or class notes alone is not enough, since your instructor may present material in class that is not in your text or may gloss over topics that your text covers in depth. The process of combining class and text notes enables you to see patterns and relationships among ideas, find examples for difficult concepts, and build understanding. It strengthens memory and offers a cohesive and comprehensive study tool, which is especially useful at midterm or finals time.

To create a **master note set**, first identify the topics you need to know, and then choose the class notes and text notes (or text sections, if you haven't taken notes on them) that deal with these topics. With both class notes and text notes (or text) in front of you, create a new document. Combine, reduce, and summarize material from both sources so that your document covers all the bases but contains only the most important ideas and key supporting details (terms, dates, formulas, and examples). Key 8.7 shows a comprehensive outline and a reduced key term outline of the same material.

Use the following steps to get the most benefit out of your master note set.

Step 1: Recite what you know.   As you approach exam time, use the terms in your bare-bones notes as cues for reciting what you know about a topic. Try reciting out loud during study sessions, writing your responses on paper, making flash cards, or working with a partner. Active reciting like this will help you move beyond passive understanding (able to repeat information) to a deeper understanding (able to answer in-depth questions on an exam or apply concepts to problems).

Step 2: Use critical thinking.   Reflect on ideas as you review your combined notes:

- Generate examples from other sources that illustrate central ideas. Write down new ideas or questions that come up as you review.

- Think of ideas from your readings or from class that support or clarify your notes.

- Consider what in your class notes differed from your reading notes and why.

- Apply concepts to problems at the ends of text chapters to problems posed during class or to real-world situations.

Step 3: Create study sheets.   This step puts your master notes in their shortest, most manageable (and portable) form. Whether on paper, a notecard, a Google doc, or a Notes document, a study sheet is a one-page synthesis of all key points on one theme, topic, or process. Use critical thinking skills to organize information into themes or topics that you will need to know on an exam.

> **Master note set**
> a complete, integrated note set that contains material from both class notes and text readings.

Different Views of Freedom and Equality in the American Democracy

I.   U.S. democracy based on 5 core values: freedom and equality, order and stability, majority rule, protection of minority rights, and participation.

     A. U.S. would be a "perfect democracy" if it always upheld these values.

     B. U.S. is less than perfect, so it is called an "approaching democracy."

II.   Freedom and Equality

     A. Historian Isaiah Berlin defines freedom as either positive or negative.

       1. Positive freedoms allow us to exercise rights under the Constitution, including right to vote.

       2. Negative freedoms safeguard us from government actions that restrict certain rights, such as the right to assemble. The 1st Amendment restricts government action by declaring that "Congress shall make no law . . ."

     B. The value of equality suggests that all people be treated equally, regardless of circumstance. Different views on what equality means and the implications for society.

      1. Equality of opportunity implies that everyone has the same chance to develop inborn talents.

        a. But life's circumstances—affected by factors like race and income—differ. This means that people start at different points and have different results. E.g., a poor, inner-city student will be less prepared for college than an affluent, suburban student.

        b. It is impossible to equalize opportunity for all Americans.

      2. Equality of result seeks to eliminate all forms of inequality, including economic differences, through wealth redistribution.

     C. Freedom and equality are in conflict, say text authors Berman and Murphy: "If your view of freedom is freedom from government intervention, then equality of any kind will be difficult to achieve. If government stays out of all citizen affairs, some people will become extremely wealthy, others will fall through the cracks, and economic inequality will multiply. On the other hand, if you wish to promote equality of result, then you will have to restrict some people's freedoms—the freedom to earn and retain an unlimited amount of money, for example."*

KEY TERM OUTLINE OF THE SAME MATERIAL

Different Views of Freedom and Equality in the American Democracy

I.   America's 5 core values: freedom and equality, order and stability, majority rule, protection of minority rights, and participation.

     A. "Perfect democracy"

     B. "Approaching democracy"

II.   Value #1—Freedom and equality

     A. Positive freedoms and negative freedoms

     B. Different views of equality: equality of opportunity versus equality of result

     C. Conflict between freedom and equality centers on differing views of government's role

Source: Larry Berman and Bruce Allen Murphy, *Approaching Democracy: Portfolio Edition,* Upper Saddle River, NJ: Prentice Hall, 2005, pp. 6–8.

Step 4: Review and review again. To deepen understanding and prepare for exams, review your condensed notes, study sheets, and critical thinking questions until you feel confident about the material. Vary your review methods, focusing on active involvement. Recite the material to yourself; have a Q and A session with a study partner; create and take a practice test. Another helpful technique is to summarize your notes in writing from memory after you review them. This will give you a fairly good indication of your ability to recall the information on a test.

A word of warning about comparing notes with study-group partners: Don't be surprised if each of you has a different take on what went on in class, especially if the material was difficult or the presentation confusing. When this happens, work together to reconstruct critical information and, if necessary, bring in other perspectives.

How Can You Take Notes Faster?
(won't things get left out if I move too fast?)

Personal **shorthand** is a practical intelligence strategy for writing faster. Because you are the only intended reader, you can misspell and abbreviate words in ways that only you understand.

Use these tips to create shorthand. You may already use some of them in your e-mails, texts, and instant messages. As useful as they are for note taking, make sure you do not use them in assignments that you turn in.

> **Shorthand**
> rapid handwriting that uses symbols, abbreviations, and shortened words.

1. Use standard abbreviations in place of complete words (examples include Q for question, w/o for without, b/c for because).

2. Remove vowels from the middle of words: prps = purpose, lwyr = lawyer, cmptr = computer.

3. Substitute word beginnings for entire words: info = information, subj = subject.

4. Form plurals by adding *s* to shortened words: prblms = problems.

5. Abbreviate proper nouns such as places, people, companies, scientific substances, and events: DC = Washington, D.C., H2O = water, Moz. = Wolfgang Amadeus Mozart.

6. If a word or phrase is repeated, write it out once, and then abbreviate it. For example, if you listen to a lecture on genetic links to breast cancer, start by writing "breast cancer gene 1," and then use BRCA1 as you continue.

© Konstantin Chagin/Shutterstock

In life, you never know where you may need to take notes—at the doctor's office, in a business meeting, or during a presentation. With active listening you will be able to hear information, and taking effective notes will help you evaluate what is important to remember, record it, understand it, and use it in the future.

HABIT IN ACTION WRAP-UP

© Courtesy of Johancharles Van Boers

What happened with Chuck?

As he worked to adjust to college and civilian life, Chuck realized that coming to terms with his combat injuries was his greatest challenge. From listening to and observing himself, he discovered his most effective daily coping strategy was maintaining a sense of humor. One day he woke up in a panic looking for his uniforms—then saw his textbooks and realized he was not in the Army, but in college. Thinking he was late, he got dressed and ran to class. As he sat in the back row wondering why he didn't recognize anyone, the professor said, "Why are you here? Your class doesn't meet until tomorrow." Luckily this understanding professor knew about his TBI issues. "Later on I reflected on what had happened and saw the humor," says Chuck. "By doing this I didn't dwell on my TBI, but instead learned to accept it for what it is."

Over time, Chuck has integrated the understanding he has from both military and civilian experiences into a full life as a teacher, leader, and mentor both in the Army and in the Lipan Apache community. He earned an Associates degree in Photography and a Bachelors of Science in Business Management and is working on a PhD in Ethnic Studies with an emphasis on Native American Indian Studies, and serves as the Lipan Apache War Chief. Though he still wakes confused, ready for combat instead of class, Chuck laughs his way through the confusion. He hopes that listening to his experiences will inspire Lipan Apache youth to persevere and succeed in the face of uncertainty. His goal is to help future generations understand that with education, character, and learning from life experiences, they can realize their enormous potential.

Connect this story to your life: Although the fast pace of modern life doesn't allow for much self-reflection, taking the time to listen to yourself and observe your thoughts builds the kind of understanding that allows you to grow. Find an opportunity—whether it is meditation, a walk, running or biking, a quiet moment with a cup of coffee or tea, or any other time to yourself—to build a greater understanding of what you need and what works for you. Use that understanding to move closer to the full expression of your value in the world.

Building Skills

Note the Important Points

Define switch-tasking, and identify whether it helps or hinders listening.

_____

Give three examples of verbal signposts that call your attention to important information.

1. _____

2. _____

3. _____

Name two actions you can take to prepare to take useful notes.

1. _____

2. _____

Describe the benefit of reviewing and revising notes after class time.

1. _____

2. _____

Identify three note-taking formats.

1. _____

2. _____

3. _____

Describe the three sections of the Cornell T-note format.

1. _____

2. _____

3. _____

List the steps you should take to study effectively using a master note set.

1. _____

2. _____

3. _____

Describe two ways to create shorthand that can help speed up note taking.

1. _____

2. _____

Critical Thinking

applying learning to life

Evaluate Listening and Note Taking

Choose a class meeting when you took notes in class, and contact a classmate who was also present. Exchange copies of your notes from that day. Read each other's notes while considering what, if anything, may have affected your listening skills during that class meeting.

Classmate's name: _____

Date of class notes: _____

Next rewrite your notes, on paper or in an electronic document, including useful ideas and supporting details from your classmate's notes.

Answer the following questions:

What, if anything, was missing from your notes that you gained from your classmate's notes?

_____

_____

What did you learn about the material from that day's class from reading your classmate's notes?

_____

_____

Name any listening barrier(s) that affected your note-taking ability on that day.

_____

Name any changes you plan to make in your note-taking strategy following this exercise.

_____

_____

If you found this helpful, consider meeting again with this classmate to review notes.

Team Building

collaborative solutions

Create a Note-Taking Team

In this course or another, join with two or three classmates to review one another's class notes. The goal is to strengthen note-taking techniques by learning from others.

1. Choose a day that all members of the group attended class. Before you connect, give the other group members a copy of your notes from that day (either a hard copy or a jpg or pdf file, depending on whether you will meet in person or virtually).

2. Carefully read over your own notes as well as the notes others give you, thinking back to what information from that class you found important enough to write down. List the strengths and weaknesses of each note set, noting where you think important material may be missing.

3. Come together in person or virtually to share your evaluations. Consider choice of note-taking format, effectiveness of shorthand, comprehensiveness of notes (material included and omitted), usefulness of the notes as a study tool, and so on. Discuss what techniques worked well for most or all of your group, and consider ways to use them.

4. With what you learned about your notes from the comments of group members and from their note-taking choices, describe how you will improve your note taking going forward, including specific strategies and changes.

listen

Combine Class and Text Notes

Build your critical thinking and summarizing skills by creating a master note set for material you need to study right now. Choose a class in which you have an upcoming test requiring preparation. Create a master note set geared toward the material you will be tested on.

1. Identify the day(s) of notes you will use.

_____

_____

2. Identify the textbook and chapter title you will use.

_____

_____

Use the instructions in the text to create your master note set.

Name one important piece of information in the text that was not in your notes.

_____

_____

Name one important piece of information in your notes that was not in the text.

_____

_____

You have created a valuable tool. Use it as you study for the test and, afterward, evaluate the effect it had on your performance as well as on how prepared you felt. Write your evaluation below.

_____

_____

9

memory and studying

retaining what you learn

JAIRO ALCANTARA, *student,*
Baruch College

Although most of his family lives in the Dominican Republic, Jairo Alcantara was born in the United States and grew up in Queens, New York, with his mother, sister, and brother. From an early age Jairo knew that he identified as gay. His family never discussed sexual orientation, and in the absence of information, he perceived his feelings as normal.

However, as he grew older and encountered negative perceptions about homosexuality in the school system, he became more guarded. In middle school Jairo was outed by classmates and was even jumped by a group of boys because of his sexual orientation. The burden of coping with gay bashing continued at the local public high school, until a day when he was the only attendee at a job counseling group meeting. The teacher who ran the group set her agenda aside and asked him how he was doing. He revealed his struggles to her, and she told him about Harvey Milk, a small high school designed to support LGTB students. She helped him apply, and he spent his junior and senior years there, in a nurturing environment where he was able to be a "regular person" and learn.

When Jairo gained entrance to college and began his coursework, the environment was radically different from the protective "bubble" of Harvey Milk. Shellshocked, he began to draw inward to protect himself. One day in Human Services class, in a discussion about marginalized communities, a student spoke out against people who identified as LGBT. Jairo could not bring himself to address her comments, but later he was upset that he stayed silent. He wondered: How could he shift his mentality so that he could thrive as a student as well as build awareness on behalf of his community?

(to be continued . . .)

What you and others perceive affects what you do and how you learn. Inaccurate perceptions can be an opportunity to build awareness. You'll learn more about Jairo's experience at the end of the chapter.

Working through this chapter will help you to:

■ Understand how memory works. p. 224

■ Build your ability to retain and recall information. p. 227

■ Build studying effectiveness with targeted strategies. p. 229

■ Identify and use mnemonic devices and other memory techniques. p. 238

Text and photo used by permission from Jairo Alcantara

perceive Note—and then look beyond—what you see and hear. Open your sensory pathways up to all kinds of information. *Build awareness* so that you can lock information into long-term memory in a meaningful way.

How Does Memory Work?
(does it matter when computers and smartphones are everywhere?)

All learning and performance depends on memory because the information you remember—concepts, facts, processes, formulas, and more—is the raw material with which you think, write, create, build, and perform your day-to-day actions in school and out. Memorization also forms a foundation for higher-level thinking, because you need to recall and understand information before you can apply, analyze, synthesize, or evaluate it.

Why do you need a strong memory when you can look up information on a computer or smartphone nearly anytime? One reason is that the reservoir of facts in your long-term memory powers your intellectual potential. When you continually add new information to your reservoir, you are more able to generate new ideas and potential solutions to problems. Furthermore, the workplace often demands that you act on what you know. A nurse, for example, can't stop to look up information every time he draws blood or sets up an IV.

Through the effort of studying and a positive attitude, you build a memory that can help you move toward your goals. This chapter provides memory-improvement techniques that you can make your own. First, explore how memory works.

The Information Processing Model of Memory

Memory refers to the way the brain stores and recalls information or experiences that are acquired through the five senses. While you take in thousands of pieces of information every second—everything from the color of your chair to how your history text describes Abraham Lincoln's presidency—you remember little of it. Unconsciously, your brain sorts through stimuli and stores only what it considers important.

Learning and memories occur through chemical and structural changes in brain cells (neurons). Refer to Key 9.1 as you read how the brain forms lasting memories:

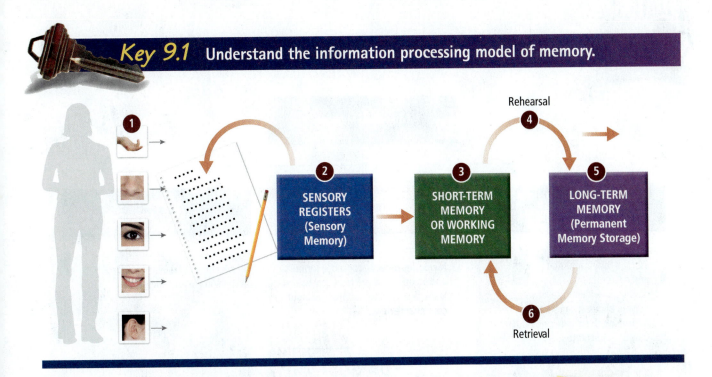

Key 9.1 Understand the information processing model of memory.

Rehearsal

1

2 **SENSORY REGISTERS** (Sensory Memory)

3 **SHORT-TERM MEMORY OR WORKING MEMORY**

4

5 **LONG-TERM MEMORY** (Permanent Memory Storage)

6 Retrieval

1. Raw information, gathered through the five senses, reaches the brain.

2. This information enters **sensory registers**, where it stays for only seconds.

3. You then pay attention to the information that seems most important to you. This moves it into **short-term memory**, also known as working memory, which contains what you are thinking at any moment and makes information available for further processing. Short-term memory lasts no more than about 30 seconds and has limited storage. You can temporarily keep information in short-term memory through *rote rehearsal*—the process of repeating information to yourself or even out loud (you use rote rehearsal, for example, when dialing a phone number you just learned).

4. Focused, active rehearsal of information, repeated over time, builds the awareness you need to move information to . . .

5. . . . **long-term memory**. To create these memories, neurons build or strengthen connections to one another.[1] Long-term memory is the storage house for everything you know, from Civil War battle dates to the location of your grade school. Most people retain memories of personal experiences and procedures longer than concepts, facts, formulas, and dates.

   Long-term memory has three separate storage locations, as shown in Key 9.2.

6. When you need a piece of information from long-term memory, the brain retrieves it and places it in short-term memory. On test day, this enables you to choose the right answer on a multiple-choice question or lay out a fact-based argument for an essay question.

Sensory registers
brain filters through which sensory information enters the brain and is sent to short-term memory.

Short-term memory
the brain's temporary information storehouse in which information remains for a few seconds.

Long-term memory
the brain's permanent information storehouse from which information can be retrieved.

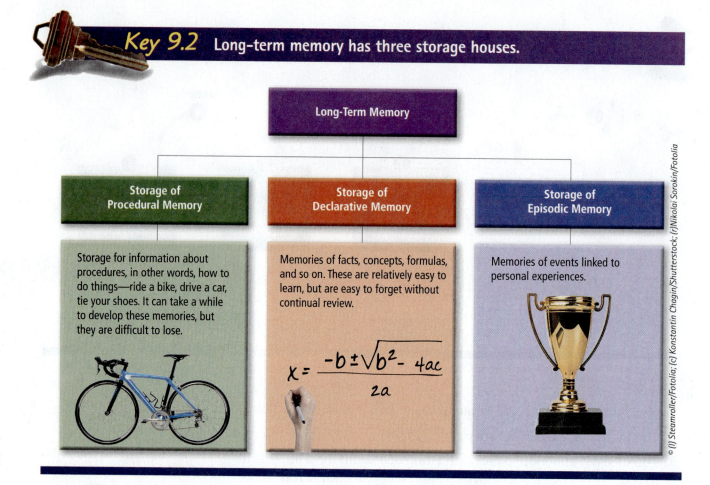

Long-Term Memory

Storage of Procedural Memory

Storage for information about procedures, in other words, how to do things—ride a bike, drive a car, tie your shoes. It can take a while to develop these memories, but they are difficult to lose.

Storage of Declarative Memory

Memories of facts, concepts, formulas, and so on. These are relatively easy to learn, but are easy to forget without continual review.

$$x = \frac{-b \pm \sqrt{b^2 - 4ac}}{2a}$$

Storage of Episodic Memory

Memories of events linked to personal experiences.

© (l) Steamroller/Fotolia; (c) Konstantin Chagin/Shutterstock; (r)Nikolai Sorokin/Fotolia

Why You Forget

Issues with health, nutrition, and stress can cause memory problems. Research shows that even short-term stress can interfere with cell communication in the learning and memory regions of the brain.[2] However, the most common reason that information fails to stay in long-term memory is ineffective studying—not enough effort is made to move from initial perception to building lasting awareness.

Retaining information requires continual review. If you review the material over time—after 24 hours, a week, a month, 6 months, and more—you will most likely retain it. If you do not review, the neural connections will weaken, and eventually you will forget. Neuroscientist Karim Nader's research has shown that once a memory is solidified in the brain, it is to some extent rebuilt each time it is remembered and can be altered by environment or circumstances when it is rebuilt.[3] For your purposes as a college student, this emphasizes the importance of both regular repetition and studying in as consistent an environment as you can manage.

Now that you know more about how memory works, get down to the business of how to retain the information you think is important and access that information when you need it.

How Can You Remember
What You Study?
(for more than just test day?)

Whatever you study—textbooks, course materials, notes, primary sources—your goal is to anchor important information in long-term memory so that you can *use it*, for both short-term goals like tests and long-term goals like a career as an information technology consultant. Try a variety of strategies to see which helps you retain the most information. One great way to do this is to use *journalists' questions*—six questions journalists tend to ask as a writing aid:

1. **When**, **where**, and **who**: Determine the times, places, and company (or none) that suit you.

2. **What** and **why**: Choose what is important to study, and set the rest aside.

3. **How**: Find the specific tips and techniques that work best for you.

When, Where, and Who: Choosing Your Best Setting

The when, where, and who of studying is all about self-knowledge and self-management—perceive how you study, build awareness of what works for you, and put it to work.

When

The first part of *when* is *how much*. Having the right amount of time for the job is crucial. One formula for success is this: For every hour you spend in class each week, spend at least 2 to 3 hours preparing for the class. For example, if you are carrying a course load of 12 credit hours, you should spend at least 24 hours a week studying outside of class.

The second part of *when* is *what time*. If two students go over their biology notes from 8 to 9 A.M., but one is a morning person and the other is a night owl, you can guess who has more of a chance of remembering the information. First, determine what time is available to you in between classes, work, and other commitments. Then, thinking about when you function best, choose your study times carefully, prioritizing peak energy times as much as you can.

The third part of *when* is *how close to original learning*. Because most forgetting occurs right after learning, the most effective review happens close to when you first learn the material. Try to review notes the same day you took them or summarize a text chapter shortly after you read it.

The final part of *when* is *when to stop*. When your brain is no longer responding, take a break or get some sleep.

© Blend Images/Shutterstock

The study location that works for you depends on individual needs and preferences. These students have found that they can concentrate effectively at individual desks in the library.

Where

Where you study matters. As with time, consider your restrictions first—what locations are available to you, close by, and open when you have time free.

Many students like to study in a library. Both college and municipal libraries may have a variety of study locations available such as quiet rooms that don't allow talking, social areas where study groups can discuss materials, rooms where computer terminals are available for research, and so on. Living spaces (rooms or common areas), public spaces such as coffee shops, and outdoor areas can be useful study spots. On-campus students may want to try studying in an empty classroom. Wherever you study, analyze how well you are able to focus. If you become aware that a particular location holds too many distractions for you, try someplace different.

Who

Some students prefer to study alone, and others work in pairs or groups. Many mix it up, doing some kinds of studying (such as first reading) alone, and others (such as problem sets) with one or more people. Some find that they prefer to study certain subjects alone and others with a group.

Group study enhances your ability to remember information because it encourages repeating information aloud (in person) or in writing (for online groups); exposes you to other ideas and approaches; and increases the chance that information will be covered comprehensively.[4] Try to exchange phone numbers or e-mails early in the term, so that you can put online or in-person study groups together before exam crunch time.

One final part of *who* is perceiving *who might be distracting*. You may have friends who want you to go out. You may have young children or other family members who need you. Tell your friends and family members why studying is important to you, and do your best to separate study time from time with family and friends.

What and Why: Evaluating Study Materials

It is impossible, inefficient, and unnecessary to study every word and bit of information. Before you study, think critically: Build awareness of *what* is important to study by examining *why* you need to know it. Here's how:

Choose materials to study.   Put away materials or notes you know you do not need to review. Looking at the notes, textbooks, and other materials left, determine what chapters or sections are important to know for your immediate goal (for example, studying for a test) and why. Thinking about the "why" can increase your focus.

Prioritize materials.   Determine what you need the most work on. Put those challenging materials first, and dedicate more time to them than you do to easier materials.

Set specific goals. Look at what you need to cover and the time available, and decide what to accomplish—for example, you will read pages of a certain textbook chapter, review three sets of class notes, and create a study sheet from both the book and your notes. Check things off as you go.

Within the sections you study, separate main points from unimportant details. Ask yourself, "What is the most important information?" Highlight only the key points in your texts, and write notes in the margins about main ideas.

How: Using Study Strategies

Now that you have figured out the *when, where, who, what,* and *why* of studying, focus on the *how*—the strategies that will anchor information in your brain. You may already use several. Try as many as you can, and keep what you perceive works. Key 9.3 shows the strategies that follow.

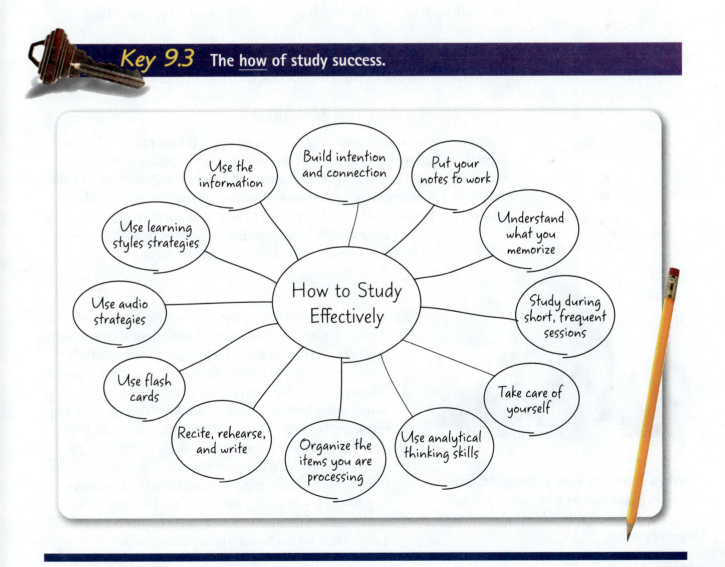

Key 9.3   The how of study success.

Use the information

Build intention and connection

Put your notes to work

Use learning styles strategies

Understand what you memorize

Use audio strategies

How to Study Effectively

Study during short, frequent sessions

Use flash cards

Take care of yourself

Recite, rehearse, and write

Organize the items you are processing

Use analytical thinking skills

Have Purpose, Intention, and Emotional Connection

Often, when you can remember the lyrics to dozens of popular songs but not the functions of the pancreas, emotion (usually positive) is involved. When you care about something, your brain responds differently, and you learn and remember more easily.

Try to create a purpose and will to remember academic materials by generating an emotional connection. For example, an accounting student might think of a friend who is running a small business and consider how effective accounting helps that friend to pay bills on time, record income, and make tax payments.

Put Your Notes to Work

Even the most comprehensive, brilliant notes won't help you if you don't review them. Regularly reread your notes in batches (for example, every 1 or 2 weeks) to build your recall of information. As you reread, do the following:

- Fill in any gaps or get help with trouble spots.
- Mark up your notes by highlighting main ideas and key supporting points.
- Add recall or practice test questions in the margins.
- Add relevant points from homework, text, and labwork into your notes.

Understand What You Memorize

It sounds obvious, but something that has meaning is easier to recall than something that makes little sense. This basic principle applies to everything you study. Figure out logical connections, and use these connections to help you learn. For example, in a plant biology course, memorize plants in family groups; in a history course, link events in a cause-and-effect chain. When you have trouble remembering something new, think about how the new idea fits into what you already know.

Study During Short, Frequent Sessions

You can improve your chances of remembering material if you learn it more than once. A pattern of short sessions, say three 20-minute study sessions followed by brief periods of rest, is more effective than continual studying with little or no rest. Try studying on your own or with a classmate during breaks in your schedule. Although studying between classes isn't for everyone, many students perceive it helps them remember more.

In addition, scheduling regular, frequent review sessions over time will help you retain information more effectively. If you have 2 weeks before a test, set up study sessions three times per week instead of putting the final 2 days aside for hours-long study marathons.[5]

© Hemera Technologies/AbleStock.com/Getty Images

When you study with a classmate, you can help each other understand difficult concepts as well as fill in the holes in each other's notes.

Take Care of Yourself

Even though busy students often get less sleep than they need, research indicates that shortchanging your sleep during the week impairs your ability to remember and learn, even if you try to make up for it by sleeping all weekend.[6] Sleep improves your ability to remember what you studied before you went to bed. So does having a good breakfast. Even if you're running late, grab something quick so that you aren't going to class on an empty stomach.

Exercise is another key component. The latest research shows that regular exercise followed by food and rest can significantly improve the functioning of the parts of the brain most involved in memory.[7]

Use Critical Thinking Skills

Critical thinking encourages you to associate new information with what you already know. Imagine you have to remember information about the signing of the Treaty of Versailles, which ended World War I. How can critical thinking help?

- Recall everything that you know about the topic.
- Think about how this event is similar to other events in history.
- Consider what is different and unique about this treaty in comparison to other treaties.
- Explore the causes that led up to this event, and look at the event's effects.
- Evaluate how successful you think the treaty was.

This critical exploration makes it easier to remember the material you are studying.

Organize the Items You Are Processing

There are a few ways to do this:

- **Divide material into manageable sections.** Master each section, put all the sections together, and then test your memory of all the material.

- **Use the chunking strategy. Chunking** increases short-term and long-term memory capacity. For example, while it is hard to remember these 10 digits—4808371557—it is easier to remember them in three chunks—480 837 1557. Try to limit groups to 10 items or fewer. The 8-day study plan in Key 9.4 relies on chunking.

- **Use organizational tools.** Put your note-taking knowledge to work using an outline, a think link, or another tool to record material and make connections among the elements.

- **Be careful when studying more than one subject.** Avoid studying two similar subjects back-to-back. Your memory may be more accurate when you study history after biology rather than chemistry after biology.

Chunking

placing disconnected information into smaller units that are easier to remember.

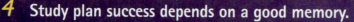

Key 9.4 Study plan success depends on a good memory.

DAY 8 (IN EIGHT DAYS, YOU'LL BE TAKING A TEST)

PLANNING DAY

- List everything that may be on the exam. (Check your syllabus and class notes; talk with your instructor.)
- Divide the material into four learning chunks.
- Decide on a study schedule for the next 7 days—when you will study, with whom you will study, the materials you need, and so on.

DAY 7 (COUNTDOWN: 7 DAYS TO GO)

- Use your preferred study techniques to study chunk A.
- Memorize key concepts, facts, formulas, and so on that may be on the test.
- Take an active approach to learning: take practice tests, summarize what you read in your own words, use critical thinking to connect ideas.

DAY 6 (COUNTDOWN: 6 DAYS TO GO)

- Use the same techniques to study chunk B.

DAY 5 (COUNTDOWN: 5 DAYS TO GO)

- Use the same techniques to study chunk C.

DAY 4 (COUNTDOWN: 4 DAYS TO GO)

- Use the same techniques to study chunk D.

DAY 3 (COUNTDOWN: 3 DAYS TO GO)

- Combine and review chunks A and B.

DAY 2 (COUNTDOWN: 2 DAYS TO GO)

- Combine and review chunks C and D.

DAY 1 (COUNTDOWN: 1 DAY TO GO)

PUT IT ALL TOGETHER: REVIEW CHUNKS A, B, C, AND D

- Take an active approach to review all four chunks.
- Make sure you have committed every concept, fact, formula, process, and so on to memory.
- Take a timed practice test. Write out complete answers so that concepts and words stick in your memory.
- Create a sheet with important information to memorize (again) for test day.

TEST DAY—DO YOUR BEST WORK

- Look at your last-minute study sheet right before you enter the test room so that difficult information sticks.
- As soon as you get your test, write down critical facts on scrap paper.

Source: Adapted from the University of Arizona. "The Eight-Day Study Plan." From http://ulc.arizona.edu/documents/8day_074.pdf

Recite, Rehearse, and Write

Rereading is not enough on its own; you can reread without learning or remembering. However, the more you can repeat, and the more ways you can repeat, the more likely you are to remember. When you *recite* material, you repeat key concepts aloud, in your own words. *Rehearsing* is silent repetition. *Writing* is repetition on paper. Try this plan:

- As you read, focus on *main ideas*, which are usually found in the topic sentences of paragraphs. Then recite, rehearse, or write the ideas down.

- Convert each main idea into a key word, phrase, or visual image. Write each on an index card and put its related main idea on the back.

- One by one, look at the cues on your cards and recite, rehearse, or write all the associated information you can recall. Check your recall against the original material.

Use Flash Cards

Flash cards give you short, repeated review sessions that provide immediate feedback. Use the front of a 3-by-5-inch index card to write a word, idea, or phrase you want to remember, and on the back write a definition, explanation, example, and other key facts. You can also create electronic flash cards, on sites like Cram.com, which you can study on a device or easily share with other students. Key 9.5 shows two flash cards used to study for a psychology exam.

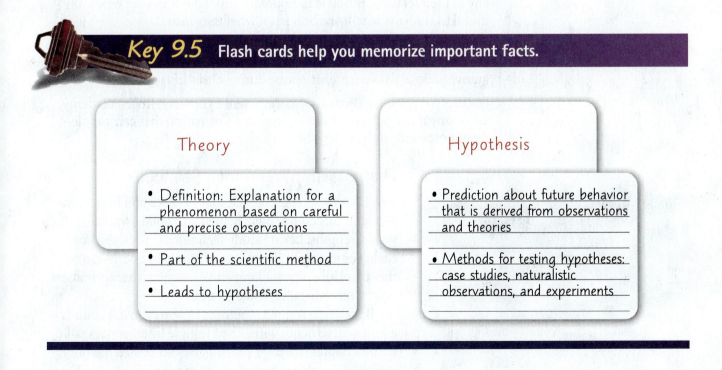

Key 9.5 Flash cards help you memorize important facts.

Theory
- Definition: Explanation for a phenomenon based on careful and precise observations
- Part of the scientific method
- Leads to hypotheses

Hypothesis
- Prediction about future behavior that is derived from observations and theories
- Methods for testing hypotheses: case studies, naturalistic observations, and experiments

Here are some suggestions for making the most of your flash cards:

- *Use the cards as a self-test.* As you go through them, divide them into two piles—the material you know and the material you are learning.

- *Carry the cards with you and review them frequently.* You'll learn the most if you start using cards early in the course, well ahead of exam time.

- *Shuffle the cards and learn the information in various orders.* This will help you avoid putting too much focus on some items and not enough on others.

- *Test yourself in both directions.* First, look at the terms and provide the definitions or explanations. Then turn the cards over and reverse the process.

- *Reduce the stack as you learn.* Eliminate cards when you know them well. As the pile shrinks, your motivation may grow. Do a final review of all the cards before the test.

Use Technology and Apps

Although an app is not necessarily better than a set of index cards, modern technology has greatly expanded your study options. Try out different tools to perceive what works for you.

- *Store study documents on a cloud server.* A server like Dropbox or Box keeps your materials on the cloud where you can access them from any device—your smartphone, a computer at home, a computer at school, your son's iPad, and so on.

- *Listen to podcasts.* An increasing amount of information is presented in podcasts—audio segments that are downloadable to your computer, smartphone, or MP3 player. Ask your instructors if they intend to make any of their lectures available in podcast format. Podcasts are especially useful to students who learn best from what they hear.

- *Manage study time electronically.* Self-management apps, such as Studious, can remind you of study sessions, tests, and due dates. You can even program Studious to silence your phone during class time.

- *Use electronic resources.* Dictionary.com, Science Glossary, Khan Academy, and many more online resources provide information that can supplement notes and study materials.

© LifeBound, LLC

Use Learning Preference Strategies

Any learning preference self-assessments you have completed in this course have helped you build awareness of your strengths. Locate study techniques applicable for each. For example, if you scored highly in bodily-kinesthetic learning, try walking while listening to information you've recorded on a voice memo.

Be open to trying something new—even if it sounds a little odd to begin with. The Multiple Intelligences table in this chapter (see page 236) suggests MI-related memory strategies. Try those that relate to your strengths—or, if you want to develop in areas that are more challenging for you, try strategies that relate to those intelligences.

Use the Information

In the days after you learn something new, try to use the information in every way you can. Apply it to new situations and link it to problems. Explain the material to a classmate. Test your knowledge to make sure the material is in long-term memory. "Don't confuse recognizing information with being able to recall it," says learning expert Adam Robinson. "Be sure you can recall the information without looking at your notes for clues. And don't move on until you have created some sort of sense-memory hook for calling it back up when you need it."[8] As you will see next, mnemonic devices create sense-memory hooks that are difficult to forget.

Inside Tips from Carol, Career Coach

What is your typical response to a task? Do you try to get away with a bare minimum of effort . . . or seek to accomplish exactly what is requested . . . or attempt to go as far beyond expectations as you can? As an employee, meeting and going beyond expectations increases your value. So no matter how easy a task like looking things up electronically may be, you will get noticed if you retain essential information in memory and save your time and energy for problem solving and idea generation.

Ask yourself now: In what way am I willing to go beyond expectations today, either in my academic work or on the job? Consider how you want to be perceived as an employee, and determine what actions you can take to make that an accurate perception.

ALL ABOUT YOU

Describe how you perceive your ability to remember and study right now. Include a rating from 1 to 10 (1 being low ability, and 10 being high).

_____

_____

Build your awareness: What factors make remembering a challenge for you?

_____

Finally, check the three strategies you believe will most help you improve your memory.

Have purpose and emotional connection	Put notes to work	Understand what you memorize
Study during short and frequent sessions	Take care of yourself (sleep, food, exercise)	Use critical thinking skills
Divide material into sections	Use the chunking strategy	Use organizational tools
Recite, rehearse, and write	Use flash cards (hard copy, audio, electronic)	Use technology and apps
Pay attention to learning preferences	Use information (apply, explain, link to problems)	Make a strategic study schedule

MULTIPLE INTELLIGENCE
STRATEGIES FOR MEMORY

Name a set of information that you have to know for a particular course: _____.
In the right-hand column, record specific ideas for how MI strategies can help you retain that information.

Intelligence	Use MI Strategies to Remember More Effectively	Identify MI Strategies that Can Help You Retain Information
Verbal-Linguistic	▪ Develop a storyline for a mnemonic first; then work on the visual images. ▪ Write out answers to practice essay questions.	
Logical-Mathematical	▪ Create logical groupings that help you memorize knowledge chunks. ▪ When you study material in the middle, link it to what comes before and after.	
Bodily-Kinesthetic	▪ Reenact concepts physically if you can to solidify them in memory. ▪ Record information onto a digital recorder and listen as you walk between classes.	
Visual-Spatial	▪ Focus on visual mnemonics such as mental walks. ▪ Use markers to add color to the images you use in your mnemonics.	
Interpersonal	▪ Do flash card drills with a study partner. ▪ Recite important material to a study partner.	
Intrapersonal	▪ Listen to an audio podcast that reviews test material. ▪ Create mnemonic devices and test yourself on the material.	
Musical	▪ Play music while you brainstorm ideas. ▪ Create a mnemonic in the form of a musical rhyme.	
Naturalistic	▪ Organize what you have to learn so you see how everything fits together. ▪ Sit outside and go through your flash cards.	

TAKE ACTION
Answer Your Journalist's Questions

Think about a study session you've had in the past that you believe did not prepare you well for a test, and recall what strategies you used—if any. Now, plan a study session that will take place within the next 7 days—one that will help you learn something important to know for one of your current courses. Answer the questions below to create your session:

1. *When* will you study, and for how long?

   _____

2. *Where* will you study?

   _____

3. *Who* will you study with, if anyone?

   _____

4. *What* will you study?

   _____

5. *Why* is this material important to know?

   _____

6. *How* will you study it—what strategy (or strategies) do you plan to use?

   _____

7. Thinking about the journalists' questions, and this structure, how would you have improved your previous study session?

   _____

8. Final step—put this plan to work. Name the date you will use it. _____

Evaluate your experience: What worked? What didn't? Would you make the same choices next time or different ones?

_____

_____

How Can Mnemonics Boost Recall?

(they seem like so much work, do they help?)

Mnemonic devices

memory techniques that use vivid associations and acronyms to link new information to what you already know.

Memory techniques known as **mnemonic devices** (pronounced neh-MAHN-ick) can help you learn and recall information. Mnemonics make information unforgettable through unusual mental associations and visual pictures. Instead of learning new facts by *rote* (repetitive practice), associations give you a "hook" on which to hang these facts and retrieve them later.

Because mnemonics take effort to create and motivation to remember, use them only when necessary—for instance, to distinguish confusing concepts that consistently trip you up. Also, know that no matter how clever they are and how easy they are to remember, mnemonics have nothing to do with understanding. Their sole objective is to help you memorize.

Mnemonics all involve some combination of *imagination* (coming up with vivid and meaningful images), *association* (connecting information you need to know with information you already know), and *location* ("locating" pieces of information in familiar places). Here are some common types to try.

Visual Images and Associations

Turning information into mental pictures helps improve memory, especially for visual learners. To remember that the Spanish artist Picasso painted *The Three Women,* you might imagine the women dancing to a Spanish song with a pig and a donkey (pig-asso). The most effective images involve bright colors, three dimensions, action scenes, and humor.

Here is another example: Say you are trying to learn some Spanish vocabulary, including the words *carta, libro,* and *dinero.* Instead of relying on rote learning, you might come up with mental images such as those in Key 9.6.

The Method of Loci

This technique involves imagining storing new ideas in familiar locations. Say, for example, that on your next biology test you have to remember the

Key 9.6   Visual images aid recall.

SPANISH WORD	DEFINITION	MENTAL IMAGE
carta	letter	A person pushing a shopping cart filled with letters into a post office.
dinero	money	A man eating lasagna at a diner. The lasagna is made of layers of money.
libro	book	A pile of books on a table at a library.

In the bedroom, you imagine eating a **tiny sub** sandwich (subatomic particle).

Looking at the mess in the closet, you think of how it seems that an **atom bomb** went off in there (atom).

In the hallway, you imagine a **mole crawling** through (molecule).

In the bathroom, you think of your **Argan oil** hair treatment (organelle).

At the counter in the kitchen, you notice the plugs for everyone's **cell** phones (cell).

In the living room, you like to keep a box of **tissues** (tissue).

At the front door, you visualize a delivery of **organic** food (organ).

In the outside hall, you imagine many delivery people with a **system** of passing the **organic** food box from hand to hand down to you (organ system).

And at the building entrance, you think of a group of people all talking on **multiple cell** phones (multicellular organism).

levels of organization of matter, up to the size of a multicellular organism. Think of a route through your living space, for this example, an apartment. You have a bedroom, closet, hallway, bathroom, kitchen, living room, front door, outside hall, and building entrance. At each spot along the way, you "place" a concept you want to learn. You then link the concept with a similar-sounding word or phrase that brings an image to mind (see Key 9.7 above).

Acronyms

Another helpful association method involves **acronyms**. In history class, you can remember the Allies during World War II—Britain, America, and Russia—with the acronym BAR. This is an example of a *word acronym* because the first letters of the items you want to remember spell a word. The word (or words) spelled don't necessarily have to be real words. See Key 9.8 for an acronym—the name Roy G. Biv—that will help you remember the colors of the spectrum.

Other acronyms take the form of an entire sentence, in which the first letter of each word in each sentence stands for the first letter of the memorized term. This is called a *list order acronym*. When astronomy students want to remember the list of planets in order of their distance from the sun (Mercury, Venus, Earth, Mars, Jupiter, Saturn, Uranus, and Neptune), they might learn this sentence: My very elegant mother just served us nectarines.

Suppose you want to remember the names of the first six U.S. presidents. You notice that the first letters of their last names—Washington, Adams, Jefferson, Madison, Monroe, and Adams—together read W A J M M A. To remember them, first you might insert an e after the J and create a short

Acronym
a word formed from the first letters of a series of words created to help you remember the series.

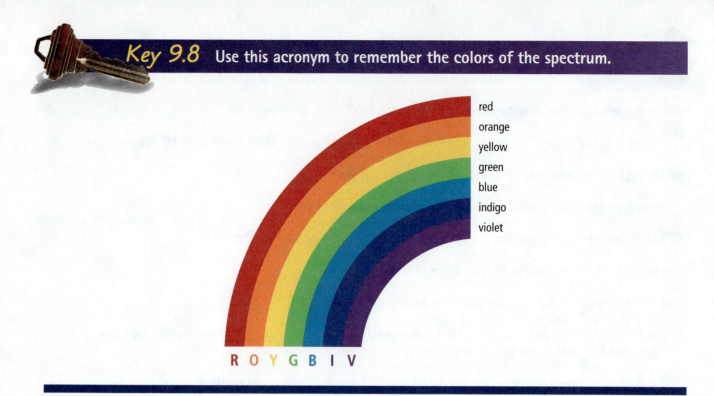

red
orange
yellow
green
blue
indigo
violet

R O Y G B I V

nonsense word: *wajemma*. Then, to make sure you don't forget the nonsense word, visualize the six presidents sitting in a row and wearing pajamas.

Songs and Rhymes

Some classic mnemonic devices are rhyming poems that stick in your mind. One you may have heard is the rule about the order of "i" and "e" in spelling:

I before E, except after C, or when sounded like A as in "neighbor" and "weigh." Four exceptions if you please: either, neither, seizure, seize.

Music can be an exceptional memory tool. For example, many people who grew up in the 1970s know the Preamble to the Constitution because of the Schoolhouse Rock Preamble Song (look it up on YouTube and see if it doesn't stick in your head). Make up your own poems or songs, linking familiar tunes or rhymes with information you want to remember.

For example, thinking back to the "wajemma" mnemonic, imagine that you want to remember the presidents' first names as well. You might set those first names—George, John, Thomas, James, James, and John—to the tune of "Happy Birthday." Or, to extend the history theme, you might use the first musical phrase of the National Anthem.

Improving your memory requires energy, time, and work. It also helps to master the SQ3R (Survey, Question, Read, Recite, Review) textbook study technique. By going through the steps in SQ3R and using the specific memory techniques described in this chapter, you will be able to learn more in less time, remember what you learn long after exams are over, and build memory skills that will serve you well in the workplace.

STUDENT TO STUDENT

Dr. Linus Pauling made a major scientific discovery—one that would win him the Nobel Prize for Chemistry—while doodling during a long train ride. Combined with the awareness he had built ahead of time, the train environment generated an "aha" moment that would change modern medicine.[9] Pair up with a fellow student. Take turns asking each other:

What environment seems to best help you generate ideas? How does being engaged in social media or electronic communication affect your brainpower and perception? What specific actions are you willing to take to maximize your awareness and thinking skills?

 perceive

HABIT IN ACTION WRAP-UP

© Courtesy of Jairo Alcantara

What happened with Jairo?

That moment in class opened the door to a new assertiveness for Jairo. He became determined to stand up for the LGBT community whenever the opportunity arose. In an anthropology class not long after, during a discussion of the film *Paris Is Burning* and the ethnic and gay communities involved in ball culture, a student asked a question that the professor, as a Caucasian heterosexual, was not able to answer. Jairo spoke up about his own experiences going to balls while at Harvey Milk, bringing clearer perception to both his fellow students and the appreciative professor.

In another class on women's culture and society, a conversation about the perception of homosexuality among particular African tribes led to a discussion of how people know they are gay and when they should come out. Jairo grabbed the chance to share his experience. He emphasized to the class that people must go at their own pace and that for a parent to dictate the timeline of discovery, or to approach it negatively, can create animosity and fray family ties. "It's my body and my life," he says. "I am the one who has to deal with how society treats me, so I need to be in charge of how I present myself and interact with others." With his growing assertiveness and determination, Jairo will continue to build awareness through college and beyond, to the benefit of both the LGBT community and the larger human community.

Connect this story to your life: What do you wish people perceived about you more accurately? Whether it's something as identity-defining as Jairo's or a less personally significant aspect of yourself, you may benefit from helping those you care about to know you better. Consider ways to build awareness of that aspect of yourself. Consider, too, how to build awareness of the important people in your life so that you perceive them more comprehensively as well.

Building Skills

Note the Important Points

Identify what each of the following does in the information processing model of memory:

sensory registers _____

short-term memory _____

long-term memory _____

Name the six journalists' questions and describe how they help you study effectively.

_____

_____

_____

_____

_____

_____

Name the three aspects of mnemonic devices that help you remember material.

_____

_____

_____

Describe two different types of mnemonics.

1. _____

2. _____

Critical Thinking

applying learning to life

Evaluate Study Choices

Describe a set of information that you have to know well for a course you are taking this term.

_____

Identify two strategies from the chapter that you are willing to use as you work to remember this information.

1. _____

2. _____

Use both during your next study session. Afterward, describe how each worked. Was it helpful? Would you use it again?

_____

_____

Identify two opportunities you will use to study this information, naming time and location for each.

1. _____

2. _____

After you have tried both, identify which worked better for you, and why.

_____

_____

Team Building

Individual and Collective Memory

Gather as a class. You'll need a timer or a stopwatch. (If your class meets online, your instructor will need to provide two collections of 15 images each for you to use with this exercise.)

- Students take turns placing one item on a table (if possible, avoid duplicate items). When 15 items are laid out, allow 2 minutes for everyone to look at them.

- Cover the items. Each person should list as many items as possible.

- Compare the lists to the actual items to see how you did.

- Talk as a group about the results, what you didn't remember and why, and what helped you remember.

Now repeat the exercise working in groups of 3–4. First create a new group of items. Allow 2 minutes to look at them as before, but groups are permitted to talk and create a plan for how to remember everything—they can assign items to people, come up with a mnemonic, and so on. Then cover the items and each group makes a list together.

Compare and contrast the individual experience and the group experience. What worked better for you? What was more difficult? How will you choose to study for your next test—alone, with a group, or a combination of both?

perceive

Improve Your Memory for Test Success

Name the course you are taking right now that presents the toughest memory challenge for you. Describe the material you have to remember.

_____

_____

Identify the date of your next test and how long you have to study for it:

_____

_____

Describe two strategies from the chapter that you believe will help you get better test results. Check each of these off after you try them.

1. _____

_____

2. _____

_____

After your test, evaluate the results: How much did these techniques improve test performance?

_____

_____

_____

_____

10

test taking I

test preparation and objective tests

ALBERT GONZALES, *Senior Manager Corporate Relations, National Society of Hispanic MBAs*

Albert Gonzales grew up in California in the 1960s. He lived with his family in a poor migrant Mexican community segregated from the white areas, a neighborhood where he risked being threatened or getting in a fight just walking to the store to buy bread. His alcoholic father was frequently violent, sometimes resulting in the family having to leave in the middle of the night to seek safety at a friend's house.

By chance, Albert was one of five children from the local Mexican school who were pulled out and bussed across town to a white school in an early integration effort. He felt resentment from other students, their parents, even the teaching staff, and he hated school. When he was 15, his father threw the family out of the house, and Albert dropped out of school and started working full time. He got involved with local gangs and drug dealing—despite the violent lifestyle, the gang members imposed rules and boundaries that made him feel secure and accepted.

In the midst of this troubled time, he wound up with a girlfriend who became pregnant. He felt his life was in a tailspin and thought he would end up in prison for the rest of his life because he killed someone or perhaps someone would kill him. He continued using drugs, figuring that he would make the most of his time while it lasted. One late night when he was 19 years old he found himself alone, high on PCP, and realized that he could not continue living this way. He was on his knees and out of hope. How could he turn his life around from this point?

(to be continued . . .)

Life brings risks, and if you can see in a risk an opportunity to extend yourself in a new direction, positive change can result. You'll learn more about Albert's experience at the end of the chapter.

Working through this chapter will help you to:

- Create a test preparation plan. p. 248
- Study effectively for tests. p. 252
- Manage text anxiety. p. 254
- Identify and address different types of objective questions. p. 261
- Learn from test mistakes. p. 265

Text and photo used by permission from Albert Gonzales

risk Taking calculated risks allows you to test your limits and take action that moves you ahead. With the risk of every test comes the opportunity to *extend* your knowledge and skill.

How Can Preparation Improve Test Performance? *(is there anything that will make it easier?)*

The goal of a test is to see what you know. If you are doing the day-to-day work of learning—attending class, staying on top of assignments, completing readings and projects, and participating in class discussions—you are preparing to succeed in testing situations.

What makes a testing situation more challenging than demonstrating knowledge on your own terms is being required to show what you know during a preset period of time, in a certain setting, and with—or without—particular tools. You are generally not in charge of the circumstances, as will be the case with many of the tests that come over the course of your life. Coping with that is a crucial life skill. The following strategies prepare you for the challenge of test taking.

Gather Information

Before you begin studying, find out as much as you can about the test.

What Type of Test?

Investigate the following.

- **Types of questions.** Will the questions be objective (multiple choice with only one correct answer, multiple choice with more than one correct answer, true–false, sentence completion), subjective (essay), or a combination?

- **Test logistics.** What are the date, time, and location of the test? Is it an in-class or a take-home exam? Will you complete it in person or online?

- **Supplemental information and tools.** Is the test open-book (meaning you can use your class text), open note (meaning you can use any notes you've taken), both, or neither? Can you use a graphing calculator or any other tool?

- **Value of the test.** Some test grades may be a higher percentage of your final grade than others. Plan and prioritize your study efforts according to the value of the quiz or test.

Although students may perceive online tests and open-book tests as easier than traditional tests, they can actually be tougher. The fact that you have access to resources often leads instructors to create challenging questions that require more critical thinking. For the best chance at a successful result, prepare for an online or open-book exam as you would any other test.

Instructor-led review sessions can provide opportunities to strengthen learning and ask questions. Try to attend review sessions if you can.

What Are You Expected to Know?

Read your syllabus and talk to your instructor to get a clear idea of the following.

- **Topics that will be covered.** Will the test cover everything since the term began, or will it be more limited?

- **Material you will be tested on.** Will the test cover only what you learned in class and in the text, or will it also include outside readings?

  What else can you do to predict what will be on a test?

- **Use your textbook.** Check features such as summaries, vocabulary terms, and study questions for clues about what's important to remember.

- **Take advantage of review sessions.** Many instructors offer in-person or online review sessions before midterms and finals. Ask questions at these sessions and note the questions others ask.

- **Communicate with your instructor.** Discussing the test one-on-one, in person or virtually, may clarify misunderstandings and help you focus on what to study.

- **Get information from people who already took the course.** Try to get a sense of test difficulty, what materials are usually covered, and the types of questions asked.

- **Examine old tests,** if the instructor makes them available. You may find old tests on reserve in the library or online. Old tests will help you answer questions like:

  - Do tests focus on examples and details, general ideas and themes, or a combination?

  - Are the questions straightforward or confusing and sometimes tricky?

  - Will you be asked to apply principles to new situations and problems?

Experience is a great teacher when it comes to test taking. After taking the first exam in a course, you will have a better idea of what to expect from that instructor over the rest of the term.

What Materials Should You Study?

With your understanding of what you need to know for the test, you can decide what to study.

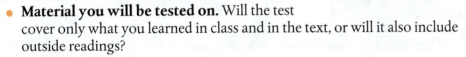

- **Sort through materials.** Go through your notes, texts, related primary sources, and handouts. Choose what you need to study, and set aside materials you don't need.
- **Prioritize materials.** Arrange your chosen materials in order of priority so that you focus the bulk of your time on the information you most need to understand.

Use Time-Management Strategies to Schedule Study Time

Want to be as ready as possible for a test? Don't wait until the night before to study for it, and don't assume that paying attention during class time is enough. The most effective studying takes place in several sessions over a period ranging from a few days to a few weeks (depending on how much material you need to learn). Use time-management skills to lay out a study schedule.

- **Consider relevant factors.** Note the number of days until the test, when in your days you have time available, and how much material you have to cover.
- **Schedule a series of study sessions.** If you need to, define what materials you will focus on for each session.
- **Enter study sessions in your planner.** Do this ahead of time, just as you would for a class or work appointment. Set alarms on your smartphone to signal start and stop times for your study sessions, if it helps.

Finally, stick to your commitment. Risk the time, extend your effort, and it will pay off.

Use Goal-Setting Strategies to Complete Your Plan

Getting ready for a test can be a SMART goal. Make your preparation plan:

- **Specific.** Get clear on what you will be tested on and what you need to study.
- **Measurable.** Acknowledge what you accomplish each study session.
- **Achievable.** Stay up-to-date with coursework so that you can feel confident on test day.
- **Realistic.** Give yourself enough time and resources to get the job done.
- **Time Bound.** Anchor each step toward the test in your schedule.

A comprehensive study plan will help you work SMART. Consider your study materials, the number of days until the test, your ongoing responsibilities, and the time you can study each day. Use a checklist to slot specific tasks into each study session, but be flexible to accommodate last-minute schedule changes. The Take Action exercise will help you organize.

Complete this checklist for your next exam to define your study goals, get organized, and stay on track. Make extra copies to use with other important exams, and start filling them out as soon as exams are announced.

Course: _____ *Instructor:* _____

Date, time, and place of test: _____

Type of test (is it a midterm, a test, a minor quiz?): _____

Information from instructor (types of questions, test length, effect on final grade, etc.): _____

_____

Topics to be covered, in order of importance:

1. _____

2. _____

3. _____

4. _____

_____

Study schedule, including study materials (texts, class notes, homework problems, and so on) and the dates and times you plan to complete each:

MATERIAL   STUDY DATE AND TIME

1. _____   _____

2. _____   _____

3. _____   _____

4. _____   _____

5. _____   _____

Materials to bring to the test (textbook, sourcebook, calculator, computer):

_____

_____

Special study arrangements (study-group meetings, instructor conference, tutoring), including scheduled times:

_____

_____

Study-routine adjustments to maximize your strongest intelligences (for example, interpersonal learners could study with others, musical learners could create learning tunes, bodily-kinesthetic learners could listen to lectures on an MP3 player while walking to class):

_____

_____

Life-management issues (such as rearranging work hours to study with a classmate):

_____

_____

Source: Adapted from Ron Fry, *"Ace" Any Test*, 3rd ed., Franklin Lakes, NJ: Career Press, 1996, pp. 123–124.

Review Using Study Strategies

Put your plan and schedule to work. Use what you have learned about learning, thinking, reading, memory, and studying during this course to understand and remember material.

- **Think critically.** College exams often ask you to analyze and apply material. For example, a history test may have you discuss a primary source in historical context. Ask yourself critical thinking questions using the higher levels of Bloom's taxonomy.

- **Use SQ3R.** This reading method provides an excellent structure for reviewing your reading materials.

- **Consider your learning preferences.** Use study strategies that engage your strengths. When necessary, incorporate strategies that boost your areas of challenge.

- **Remember your best settings.** Use the locations, times, and company that suit you best.

- **Employ specific study strategies.** Consider your favorites. Use a flash card app, audio strategies, chunking—anything that suits you and the material.

- **Create mnemonic devices.** These work exceptionally well for remembering lists or groups of items. Use mnemonics that make what you review stick.

- **Actively review your combined class and text notes.** Summaries and master sets of combined text and class notes provide comprehensive study tools.

- **Make and take a pretest.** Use end-of-chapter text questions to create a pretest. If your course doesn't have a text, develop questions from notes, assigned readings, and old homework problems. Some texts provide a website with online activities and pretests to help you review. Answer questions under test-like conditions—in a quiet place, with no books or notes (unless the exam is open book), and with a clock to tell you when to quit.

© Pressmaster/Fotolia

Prepare Physically

To work at your best under pressure, get as much sleep as you can the night before the exam. Sleep improves your ability to remember what you studied before you went to bed. By contrast, research has shown that sleep deprivation, which is rampant among college students, results in lower levels of recall and a decrease in cognitive performance.[1] Eat a light, well-balanced meal with plenty of protein. When time is short, don't skip breakfast—grab a quick meal such as a few spoonfuls of peanut butter, a banana, or a high-protein energy bar.

Part of successful test preparation is knowing when to stop. Take breaks during long study sessions, and get the sleep you need before test day.

Make the Most of Last-Minute Cramming

Cramming often results in information going into your head and popping right back out when the exam is over. If learning is your goal, cramming will not help you reach it. The reality, however, is that you are likely to cram for tests, especially midterms and finals, from time to time in your college career. Use these hints to make the most of your time:

> **Cramming**
> studying intensively and around the clock right before an exam.

- **Focus on crucial concepts.** Summarize the most important points and try to resist reviewing notes or texts page by page.

- **Create a last-minute study sheet to review right before the test.** Write down key facts, definitions, and formulas on a single sheet of paper, index cards, or an electronic note app.

- **Arrive early.** Review your study aids until you are asked to clear your desk.

After your exam, step back and evaluate your performance. Did cramming help, or did it load your mind with disconnected details? Did it increase or decrease test anxiety? If you find that in a few days you remember very little, know that this will work against you in advanced courses and careers that build on this knowledge. Plan to extend yourself more next time, and start studying earlier.

Prepare for Final Exams

Studying for final exams, which usually take place the last week of the term, is a major commitment that requires careful time management. Your college may schedule study days (also called a "reading period"), lasting from a day or two to a couple of weeks, between the end of classes and the beginning of finals. Take advantage of this time to prepare for exams and finish papers. With classes no longer in your calendar, you have more time to work and prepare.

Plan out your reading period at least a week before it starts. Note when each final takes place, and plan several study sessions in the days before each final exam time, setting aside blocks of time assigned to specific subject areas. If you have family responsibilities, let children and other family members know how your schedule will change during reading period and finals, and try to arrange for extra childcare or other support ahead of time.

How Can You Work Through Test Anxiety? *(and what causes it?)*

Test anxiety
debilitating physical and psychological symptoms that interfere with doing your best work before and during a test.

A moderate amount of stress can have a positive effect, making sure you are alert, ready to act, and geared up to do your best. Some students, however, experience incapacitating stress before and during exams, especially midterms and finals. **Test anxiety** can cause sweating, nausea, dizziness, headaches, and fatigue. It can reduce concentration and cause you to forget everything you learned. Sufferers may get lower grades because their performance does not reflect what they know or because their fear has affected their ability to prepare effectively.

Two Sources of Test Anxiety

Test anxiety has two different sources, and students may experience one or both:[2]

- **Lack of preparation:** Not having put in the work to build knowledge of the material
- **Dislike of testing situations:** Being nervous about a test because of its very nature

For anxiety that stems from being unprepared, the answer is straightforward: Get prepared. All of the information in this chapter about creating and implementing a study plan and schedule is designed to give you the best possible chance of doing well on the test. If you are able to stay calm when you feel ready for a test, effective preparation is your key test anxiety strategy.

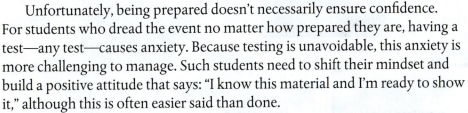

STUDENT TO STUDENT

Consider how you react to tests. Pair up with a fellow student and ask each other:

When do you feel test anxiety? Is it for certain types of tests or certain subjects more than others? If test anxiety isn't a problem, what do you think contributes to your pretest calm? Once you identify any specific fears, generate ideas together about how to overcome them.

risk

Unfortunately, being prepared doesn't necessarily ensure confidence. For students who dread the event no matter how prepared they are, having a test—any test—causes anxiety. Because testing is unavoidable, this anxiety is more challenging to manage. Such students need to shift their mindset and build a positive attitude that says: "I know this material and I'm ready to show it," although this is often easier said than done.

Anxiety is defined as an emotional disturbance, meaning that it tends to be based on an imagined risk rather than an actual one, and often leads you away from your goals rather than toward them.[3] If you experience test anxiety, work toward a more realistic view of your abilities:

- **Reconceive the failure you think you are facing.** Downplay the negative by considering the possibility that you may be more prepared than you realize, or that the test is not as important as it seems, or not as difficult as you believe it to be.

- **Cut the task down to size.** Define your specific goal for this test. Identify what issues may affect your ability to reach that goal, and target those issues specifically.

- **Build a realistic, positive, and productive attitude** that says, "I know this material and I'm ready to show it." Key 10.1 provides several ways to do this.

Test Time Strategies to Address Anxiety

It's test time. You've arrived at the testing location or have set yourself up at a computer to take an online test. How can you be calm and focused? These strategies may help.

© wavebreakmedia/Shutterstock

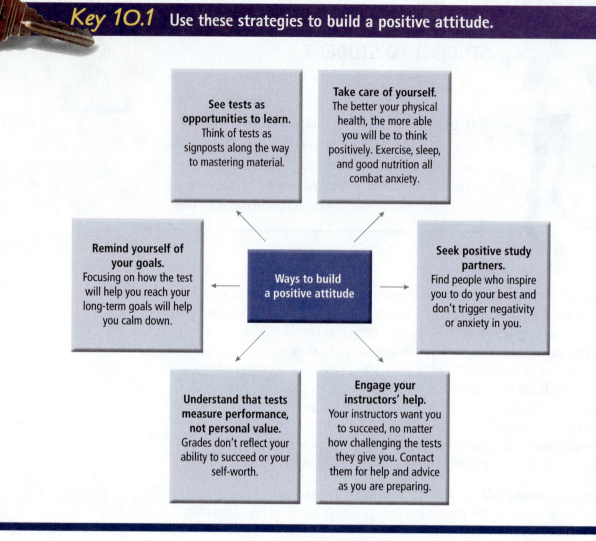

See tests as opportunities to learn. Think of tests as signposts along the way to mastering material.

Take care of yourself. The better your physical health, the more able you will be to think positively. Exercise, sleep, and good nutrition all combat anxiety.

Remind yourself of your goals. Focusing on how the test will help you reach your long-term goals will help you calm down.

Ways to build a positive attitude

Seek positive study partners. Find people who inspire you to do your best and don't trigger negativity or anxiety in you.

Understand that tests measure performance, not personal value. Grades don't reflect your ability to succeed or your self-worth.

Engage your instructors' help. Your instructors want you to succeed, no matter how challenging the tests they give you. Contact them for help and advice as you are preparing.

Manage your environment.   Sit where you will be most calm. If it helps, listen to music on an MP3 player while you wait for the test to begin.

Reassure yourself with positive self-talk.   Tell yourself that you can do well and that it is normal to feel anxious, particularly before an important exam.

Write down your feelings.   Researchers have found that if students take a few minutes before an exam to put their feelings in writing, they post higher grades and have less anxiety. Without worrying about writing quality, express your fears and anxieties about the test on a piece of paper, computer, or smartphone. "It's almost as if you empty the fears out of your mind," says researcher and psychology professor Sian Beilock.[4]

Practice relaxation. Close your eyes, breathe deeply and slowly, and visualize positive images like finishing the test with confidence. Or try a more physical tensing-and-relaxing method:5

1. Put your feet flat on the floor.

2. With your hands, grab underneath the chair.

3. Push down with your feet and pull up on your chair at the same time for about 5 seconds.

4. Relax for 5 to 10 seconds.

5. Repeat the procedure two or three times.

6. Relax all your muscles except the ones that are actually used to take the test.

Some of these strategies may seem odd or embarrassing. However, they might also improve your test performance. Consider whether a little embarrassment might be worth it.

Test Anxiety and the Returning Student

If you're returning to school after years away, you may wonder how well you will handle exams. To deal with these feelings, focus on what you have learned through life experience, including the ability to handle work and family pressures. Without even thinking about it, you may have developed time-management, planning, organizational, and communication skills needed for test success and college success in general. You may also know yourself well, which will help you choose strategies that work for you.

Furthermore, your life experiences can give real meaning to abstract classroom ideas. For example, workplace relationships may help you understand social psychology concepts, and refinancing your home mortgage may help you grasp a key concept in economics—how the actions of the Federal Reserve Bank influence interest rate swings.

Inside Tips from Sarah, Academic Coach

Children aren't the only ones who are calmed and motivated by special objects. Ask yourself: What small item helps you feel supported and calm? One or more objects may hold special meaning for you—a photograph, a stone or crystal, a wristband, a piece of jewelry, a hat or other clothing item. Consider bringing or wearing a special object, and use it to get focused and calm yourself either before or during a test. Afterward, evaluate whether it helped to comfort and motivate you. Decide on what you will do in the future based on this experience.

What General Strategies Promote Test Success? (if the subject matter is really hard, will any strategy help?)

The following strategies will help you do your best on any test.

Test Day Strategies

Choose the right seat.   If your test is in-person and not online, find a seat that will help you maximize focus and minimize distractions. You may want to avoid sitting near friends.

Write down key facts.   Before you look at the test, write down key information, including formulas and definitions, that you don't want to forget. (If your test is a hard-copy question sheet, write on the back so your instructor knows you made these notes after the test began.)

Start with the big picture.   Scan the questions—how many in each section, types, difficulty, point values—and use what you learn to schedule your time. For example, if for a 90-minute test you think the writing section will take you more time than the short-answer section, you can budget an hour for the essays and 30 minutes for the short-answer questions.

Directions count, so read them.   Reading test directions carefully can save you trouble. For example, you may be required to answer only one of three essay questions; you may also be told that you will be penalized for incorrect responses to short-answer questions.

Mark up the questions.   Mark up instructions and keywords to avoid careless errors. Circle **qualifiers** such as *always, never, all, none, sometimes,* and *every;* verbs that communicate specific instructions; and concepts that are tricky or need special attention.

Be precise when taking an online or machine-scored test.   Use the right pencil (usually a #2) on machine-scored tests, and mark your answer in the correct space, filling it completely. Periodically, check the answer number against the question number to make sure they match. For online tests that require you to select answers with the cursor, be careful to click on the one you want. Before you start, find out whether the test allows you to go back and change answers.

Work from easy to hard.   Begin with the easiest questions. Being able to answer them fairly quickly will boost your confidence and leave more time for harder questions. Mark tough questions as you reach them, and return to them after answering the questions you know.

Qualifiers
words and phrases that can alter the meaning of a test question and that require careful attention.

Watch the clock. If you are worried about time, you may rush through the test and have time left over. When this happens, check over your work instead of finishing early. If, on the other hand, you are falling behind, be flexible about the best use of the remaining time.

Take a strategic approach to questions you cannot answer. Even if you are well prepared, you may face questions you do not understand. Key 10.2 has ideas for how you can extend your efforts instead of leaving questions unanswered.

Use special techniques for math tests. In addition to these general test-taking strategies, the techniques in Key 10.3 can help you achieve better results on math exams.

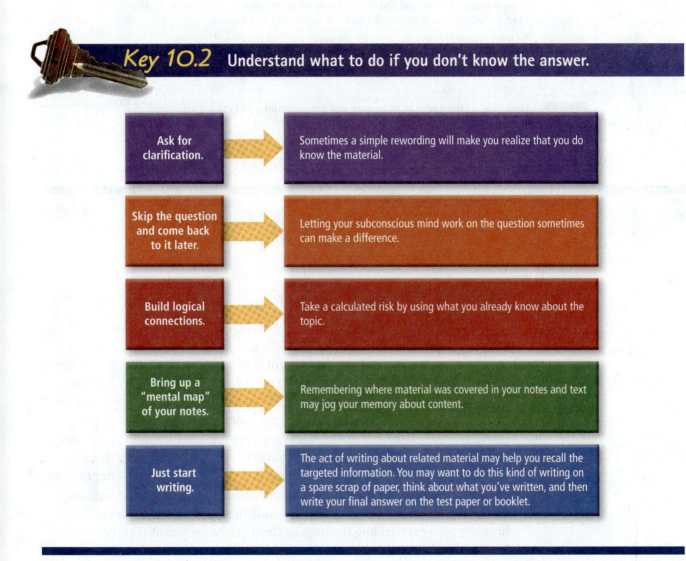

Key 10.2 Understand what to do if you don't know the answer.

Ask for clarification.	→	Sometimes a simple rewording will make you realize that you do know the material.
Skip the question and come back to it later.	→	Letting your subconscious mind work on the question sometimes can make a difference.
Build logical connections.	→	Take a calculated risk by using what you already know about the topic.
Bring up a "mental map" of your notes.	→	Remembering where material was covered in your notes and text may jog your memory about content.
Just start writing.	→	The act of writing about related material may help you recall the targeted information. You may want to do this kind of writing on a spare scrap of paper, think about what you've written, and then write your final answer on the test paper or booklet.

Read through the exam first. When you receive an exam, read through every problem quickly and make notes on how you might attempt to solve the problems.

Analyze problems carefully. Categorize problems according to type. Take the "givens" into account, and write down any formulas, theorems, or definitions that apply. Focus on what you want to find or prove.

Estimate to come up with a "ballpark" solution. Then work the problem and check the solution against your estimate. The two answers should be close. If they're not, recheck your calculations.

Break the calculation into the smallest possible pieces. Go step-by-step and don't move on to the next step until you are clear about what you've done so far.

Recall how you solved similar problems. Past experience can provide valuable clues.

Draw a picture to help you see the problem. Visual images such as a diagram, chart, probability tree, or geometric figure may help clarify your thinking.

Be neat. Sloppy numbers can mean the difference between a right and a wrong answer. A 4 that looks like a 9 will be marked wrong.

Use the opposite operation to check your work. Work backward from your answer to see if you are right.

Look back at the question to be sure you did everything. Did you answer every part of the question? Did you show all required work?

Maintain Academic Integrity

Cheating as a strategy to pass a test or get a better grade robs you of the opportunity to learn, which, ultimately, is your loss. Cheating also jeopardizes your future if you are caught. You may be reprimanded—or even expelled—if you violate your school's code of academic integrity. Furthermore, cheating that goes on your record can damage your ability to get a job.

Cheating has gone high-tech in recent years, with students using their cell phones, MP3 players, graphing calculators, and Internet-connected laptops to share information with other test-takers or search the Internet.[6] Because high-tech cheating can be hard to detect in large rooms, some instructors ban electronic devices. Leave at home or turn off what instructors don't allow.

The pressure to succeed can drive students to thoughts of academic dishonesty. However, feeling the urge to cheat generally means you haven't learned the material. Ask yourself: Am I in college to learn information I can use? Or to cheat my way to a decent GPA and sigh with relief when I'm done?

Retention of knowledge is necessary both to complete future coursework and to thrive in the workplace. Your choices will have a lasting impact on your future and your life; if you choose to risk time and extend effort, it is likely to pay off.

How Can You Master Objective Test Questions? *(are there better and worse ways to handle those?)*

Every type of test question has a different way of finding out how much you know. For **objective questions**, you choose or write a short answer, often making a selection from a limited number of choices. Multiple-choice, fill-in-the-blank, matching, and true/false questions fall into this category.

As you review the sample questions in the following section, look also at the Multiple Intelligence Strategies for Test Taking. Harness the strategies that fit your learning strengths to prepare for exams. Note that some suggestions are repeated in the following sections, in order to reinforce the importance of these suggestions and their application to different types of test questions.

Objective questions

test questions that ask you to select the correct answer from a limited number of choices or write in a word or phrase.

ALL ABOUT YOU

Following are six situations that provide cheating *opportunities*. On a scale of 1 to 5, 1 being the least likely and 5 being the most likely, assess whether you would cheat in each situation. There's no need to write your responses. Just think of what you would do in each case. Be honest with yourself.

1. You can see the answers of the person sitting next to you, who is a good student.
2. Your instructor doesn't want the class to look at any of his previous tests, but a friend offers you a copy of the test from the same class last term.
3. Your instructor doesn't have a clue about technology, so it would be easy to tweet or send Snapchat messages during the test for help with tough questions.
4. Your instructor allows you to answer essay questions on your laptop. You have a Wi-Fi connection, so you can search the Internet for information.
5. A friend shows you how to write test facts on the inside of a water bottle label and then re-glue the label back on the bottle.
6. You hear about some YouTube videos that demonstrate cheating methods that are virtually detection-proof.

What did you learn from your answers? If you believe that you are likely to cheat, think about what could happen if you are found out and how your choice will affect what you learn. Finally, think about what cheating may mean for your future.

MULTIPLE INTELLIGENCE STRATEGIES

For Objective Test Questions

Describe an upcoming objective exam (date, course, exam type): _____.
In the right-hand column, record specific ideas for how MI strategies can help you prepare for it.

Intelligence	Use MI Strategies to Improve Objective Question Performance	Identify MI Strategies that Can Help You
Verbal-Linguistic	▪ Read carefully to understand every word of every question. ▪ Do language-oriented questions first, saving extra time for questions involving visual or quantitative elements.	
Logical-Mathematical	▪ Focus on quantitative and/or objective questions first, saving extra time for more subjective work such as essays. ▪ Use logic to narrow choices in multiple-choice and matching questions.	
Bodily-Kinesthetic	▪ Select a test-taking location where you feel comfortable. ▪ Take brief physical breaks—stretch your muscles at your seat, or if you are taking a test online, stand up and walk around.	
Visual-Spatial	▪ Focus on the length and number of the blanks in fill-in-the-blank questions. ▪ Create mind maps to connect ideas and analyze different possibilities.	
Interpersonal	▪ Replay study-group conversations in your mind to remember facts. ▪ Think through an answer by imagining you are explaining it to someone.	
Intrapersonal	▪ If you hit a difficult question, take a deep breath and focus on what you know about the topic. ▪ Visualize answering every question correctly.	
Musical	▪ Remember any rhymes or tunes you created to help you learn. Recite them silently to yourself to recall an answer. ▪ If you are taking an online test, play music that helps you focus.	
Naturalistic	▪ If your instructor permits, or if you are taking an online test on a portable computer, work outdoors (weather permitting). ▪ If your test has different types of questions, complete one category of question at a time.	

Multiple-Choice Questions

Multiple-choice questions are the most popular type of question on standardized tests. The following analytical and practical strategies will help you answer them:

- **Read the directions carefully and try to think of the answer before looking at the choices.** Then read the choices and make your selection.

- **Underline key words and phrases.** If the question is complicated, try to break it down into small sections that are easy to understand.

- **Make sure you read every word of every answer.** Focus especially on qualifying words such as *always, never, tend to, most, often,* and *frequently.* Look also for negatives in a question ("Which of the following is *not* …").

- **When questions are linked to a reading passage, read the questions first.** This will help you focus on the information you need to answer the questions.

The following examples show the kinds of multiple-choice questions you might encounter in an introductory psychology course (the correct answer follows each question):

1. Although you know that alcohol is a central nervous system depressant, your friend says it is actually a stimulant because he does things that he wouldn't otherwise do after having a couple of drinks. He also feels less inhibited, more spontaneous, and more entertaining. The reason your friend experiences alcohol as a stimulant is that
   a. Alcohol has the same effect on the nervous system as amphetamines.
   b. Alcohol has a strong placebo effect.
   c. The effects of alcohol depend almost entirely on the expectations of the user.
   d. Alcohol depresses areas in the brain responsible for critical judgment and impulsiveness. **(answer: d)**

2. John drinks five or six cups of strong coffee each day. Which of the following symptoms is he most likely to report?
   a. nausea, loss of appetite, cold hands, and chills
   b. feelings of euphoria and well-being
   c. anxiety, headaches, insomnia, and diarrhea
   d. time distortion and reduced emotional sensitivity **(answer: c)**

Source: Charles G. Morris and Albert A. Maisto, *Understanding Psychology,* 10th ed., p. 145. © 2013 Pearson Education, Inc. Reprinted by permission of Pearson Education, Inc., Upper Saddle River, NJ.

True-or-False Questions

Read true-or-false questions carefully to evaluate what they are asking. Look for absolute qualifiers (such as *all, only,* and *always* that often make an otherwise true statement false) and conservative qualifiers (*generally, often, usually,* and *sometimes* that often make an otherwise false statement true). For example,

© Marek/Fotolia

"The grammar rule 'I before E except after C' is *always* true" is false, whereas "The grammar rule 'I before E except after C' is *usually* true" is true.

Be sure to read *every* word of a true-or-false-question to avoid jumping to an incorrect conclusion. Common problems in reading too quickly include missing negatives (*not, no*) that would change your response, and deciding on an answer before reading the complete statement.

The following examples show the kinds of true–false questions you might encounter in an introductory psychology course (the correct answer follows each question):

Indicate whether the following statements are true (T) or false (F):

1. Alcohol is implicated in more than two-thirds of all automobile accidents.   (true)
2. Caffeine is not addictive.   (false)
3. Recurring hallucinations are common among users of hallucinogens.   (true)
4. Marijuana interferes with short-term memory.   (true)

Source: Charles G. Morris and Albert A. Maisto, *Understanding Psychology*, 10th ed., p. 145. © 2013 Pearson Education, Inc. Reprinted by permission of Pearson Education, Inc., Upper Saddle River, NJ.

Matching Questions

Matching questions ask you to match the terms in one list with the terms in another list. For example, the directions may tell you to match a communicable disease with the microorganism that usually causes it. The following strategies will help you handle these questions.

- **Make sure you understand the directions.** The directions tell you whether each answer can be used only once (common practice) or more than once.

- **Work from the column with the longest entries.** The column on the left usually contains terms to be defined or questions to be answered, while the column on the right has definitions or answers. As a result, entries on the right are usually longer than those on the left. Reading those items only once will save time.

- **Start with the matches you know.** On your first run-through, pencil in these matches.

- **Finally, tackle the matches of which you're not sure.** Think back to your class lectures, text notes, and study sessions as you try to visualize the correct response. If one or more phrases seem to have no correct answer and you can use answers only once, consider the possibility that one of your sure-thing answers is wrong.

Fill-in-the-Blank Questions

Fill-in-the-blank questions, also known as sentence completion questions, ask you to supply one or more words or phrases. These strategies will help you make successful choices.

- **Be logical.** Insert your answer, then reread the sentence from beginning to end to be sure it makes sense and is factually and grammatically correct.

- **Note the length and number of the blanks.** If two blanks appear right after one another, the instructor is probably looking for a two-word answer. If a blank is longer than usual, the correct response may require additional space.

- **If there is more than one blank and the blanks are widely separated, treat each one separately.** Answering each as if it is a separate sentence-completion question increases the likelihood that you will get at least one answer correct.

- **If you are uncertain, guess.** Have faith that after hours of studying, the correct answer is somewhere in your subconscious mind and that your guess is not completely random.

The following examples show fill-in-the-blank questions you might encounter in an introductory psychology course (correct answers follow questions):

1. Our awareness of the mental processes of everyday life is called _____. (consciousness)

2. The major characteristic of waking consciousness is _____. (selective attention)

3. In humans, sleeping and waking follow a _____ cycle. (circadian)

4. Most vivid dreaming takes place during the _____ stage of sleep. (REM)

Source: Charles G. Morris and Albert A. Maisto, *Understanding Psychology*, 10th ed., p. 130. © 2013 Pearson Education, Inc. Reprinted by permission of Pearson Education, Inc., Upper Saddle River, NJ.

The purpose of a test is to see how much you know, not merely to get a grade. Embrace this attitude to learn from your mistakes.

How Can You Learn from Test Mistakes?
(can't I just throw a test out when I get my grade?)

Congratulations! You've finished the exam and gone on to a well-deserved night of sleep. At the next class meeting you feel rejuvenated and ready to accept a high score. As you receive your corrected test, you look wide-eyed at your grade. *How could that be?*

© Courtesy of Sarah Lyman Kravits

No one aces every test or understands every piece of material perfectly. Making mistakes on tests and learning from them is an essential part of the academic experience. Instead of throwing a test out after getting a bad grade, risk the effort to extend your learning by examining what you didn't do well. When you identify what you can improve, you can make better study choices and anticipate an improved performance on your next exam. Here are some helpful actions to take:

Ask yourself global questions that may help you identify correctable patterns. Honest answers can help you change the way you study for the next exam.

- What were your biggest problems? Did you get nervous, misread questions, not study enough or effectively, leave out important study materials, not apply knowledge enough?

- Did your instructor's comments clarify where you slipped up? Did your answer lack specificity? Did you fail to support your thesis well? Was your analysis weak?

- Were you surprised by the questions? For example, did you expect them all to be from the lecture notes and text instead of from your notes and text and supplemental readings?

- Did you make careless errors? Did you misread the question or directions, blacken the wrong box on the answer sheet, skip a question, write illegibly?

- Did you make conceptual or factual errors? Did you misunderstand a concept? Did you fail to master facts or concepts?

Rework the questions you got wrong. Based on instructor feedback, try to rewrite an essay, recalculate a math problem from the original question, or redo questions following a reading selection. If you discover a pattern of careless errors, redouble your efforts to be more careful, and save time to double-check your work.

After reviewing your mistakes, fill in your knowledge gaps. If you made mistakes because you didn't understand important concepts, develop a plan to learn the material.

Talk to your instructor. Focus on specific mistakes on objective questions or a weak essay. The fact that you care enough to review your errors will make a good impression. If you are not sure why you were marked down on an essay, ask what you could have done better. If you feel that an essay was unfairly graded, ask for a rereading. When you use your emotional intelligence and approach your instructor in a nondefensive way, you are likely to receive help.

Rethink the way you studied. Make changes to avoid repeating your errors. Use varied techniques to study more effectively so that you can show yourself and your instructors what you are capable of doing. The earlier in the term you make positive adjustments the better, so make a special effort to analyze and learn from early test mistakes.

If you fail a test, don't throw it away. Use it to review troublesome material, especially if you will be tested on it again. You might also want to keep it as a reminder that you can improve. When you compare a failure to later successes, you'll see how far you've come.

Tests are a fact of life in college. How you handle them has a major impact on your sense of accomplishment and happiness. Risk doing your best to prepare for and take tests so that you will know how to extend yourself as you face tests in the workplace and in life.

© Courtesy of Albert Gonzales

HABIT IN ACTION WRAP-UP

What happened with Albert?

That night Albert asked God, "If you are still there and can prove it, I will do whatever it takes to live well." At that moment a newfound clarity came to him. The next morning he woke up with no residual effects from the drug. He decided then to risk radical change. He put away the gang lifestyle, stopped using drugs, and began reading the Bible, with a dictionary nearby to help him understand complex words and concepts. He worked on the relationship with his girlfriend who gave birth to a daughter, and later another daughter, and they married. He took college classes and began working as a Salvation Army youth center director.

Feeling compelled to extend himself to help others, he and a friend developed a dropout prevention program called SERVE—helping students find balance in Social, Emotional, Recreation, Vocation, and Education areas—in conjunction with the Placentia-Yorba Linda Unified school district. Their work to help students find balance, move away from victimization, and move toward goals was exceptionally successful in increasing graduation and college attendance rates, and he worked there for 16 years.

Albert extended his range further in recent years, first working in development for the American Red Cross and now running the sales team for the National Society of Hispanic MBAs. He continues to risk energy and time helping people set aside the trashcan of excuses and get committed to something. "I took away from society in my early years, and I feel a mandate to give back," he says. "You don't get less if you give to others, you actually expand the pie of resources by helping people." Albert's goal is to help struggling people turn their lives around like he did, so that his story becomes just one of many inspiring tales of success.

Connect this story to your life: It is human, and common, to hang back in a "comfort zone" and avoid taking risks. However, productive risk-taking can extend your knowledge, your reach, and your skills in a way that increases your ability to achieve your most valued goals. Identify one risk you are in a position to take. How might this risk extend you in a way that benefits you— and maybe others around you? Plan out how you would take this risk. Give it a try to see what happens.

Building Skills
for successful learning

Note the Important Points

List three specific test preparation strategies.

1. _____

2. _____

3. _____

Define "cramming" and describe how to use it when study time is short.

_____

_____

Identify the two sources of test anxiety.

1. _____

2. _____

List three test-day success strategies.

1. _____

2. _____

3. _____

Define each question type.

Multiple-choice questions _____

_____

True/false questions _____

_____

Matching questions _____

_____

Fill-in-the-blank questions _____

_____

How can it benefit you to review tests and correct mistakes?

_____

_____

_____

Critical Thinking

Analyze How You Perform on Objective Tests

First, look at the common issues listed here. Circle any that tend to affect your performance on tests. Use the blank spaces to add issues you have that are not listed.

Incomplete preparation

Fatigue

Poor time management

Weak understanding of concepts

Ineffective guessing techniques

Confusion about directions

Test anxiety

External distractions (hunger, worries)

_____

_____

Analyze your most recent objective exam experience by answering the following questions.

1. Identify the types of questions that you answered most successfully.

_____

2. Identify the types of questions that gave you the most difficulty.

_____

3. Analyze your errors. Did you misread instructions? Misunderstand qualifiers? Need more study time?

_____

_____

Thinking about how you've answered the questions above, name two strategies from this chapter that you intend to use, and describe how you will use them.

Strategy 1: _____

_____

Strategy 2: _____

_____

Benchmark to Improve Your Test—Preparation Habits

Benchmarking is a business practice in which companies evaluate their own performance, compare it to how other companies perform, figure out where they need work, and take any necessary action to improve. You can use benchmarking right now to learn how others prepare for exams and to adopt the best practices that will work for you:

Step1: Join with two or three others who are taking a course with you that has a test coming up. Ask each group member to keep a running list of everything he or she does to prepare for this test. Among the items on the lists may be:

- Making a study checklist and posting it on my bulletin board

- Spending 2 hours a day studying at the library in the week before the exam

- Using apps to make mind maps and note summaries

- Getting a partner to drill me on multiple-choice questions from old tests

- Using SQ3R to review material

- Recording information on Voice Memo and listening to it between classes

- Having a pretest breakfast with a study group

- Getting to sleep by midnight the night before the exam

Step 2: After the exam, share your lists in person or online. Compare and contrast preparation routines. What do you have in common? What is different? What worked, and didn't, for each of you?

Step 3: On separate paper or in a computer file, write down what you learned from the habits of others, and how you will extend that learning to your preparation for upcoming exams.

risk

Place Responsible Risk Taking at the Center of Your Education

Getting the most out of your college involves risk—putting yourself on the line in challenging courses. List two courses you plan to take in the next year that are difficult but necessary for your success. (Consult the course catalog for specific course titles.)

Course 1: _____

Course 2: _____

Now list three steps you will take to reduce the fear you are likely to have before big exams in these courses. As you think, consider the words of neuroscientist Dr. Gregory Berns: "*Fear prompts retreat. . . . It makes it impossible to concentrate on anything but saving your skin . . .*"[7]

Action 1: _____

_____

Action 2: _____

_____

Action 3: _____

_____

11

test taking II

essay tests and graded projects

MICHELE WESLANDER QUAID, *co-founder and chief executive officer of Global Nexus Alliance, and founder and chief executive officer of Sunesis Nexus LLC*

Michele Weslander Quaid's childhood circumstances were not what most people would consider a springboard to success. Raised below the poverty line by a hardworking single mother, she developed the creativity to adjust to circumstances that were out of her control. Michele's mother lived by values that instilled in her daughter the determination to work through and solve tough problems, paired with an enthusiastic willingness to take on challenging subjects. A strong sense of purpose gave Michele a desire to go where she could make a positive difference for others.

Through hard work and determination, Michele graduated as the valedictorian of her high school class and was honored with the school science award. As a first-generation college student from a blue-collar family, she did not have guidance from family members regarding technical studies or college pursuits, but she had the drive and persistence to imagine a different future. Wanting to pioneer new capabilities in space to benefit the U.S. and the world, she optimized her experience at Seattle Pacific University, focusing on the applied sciences and earning a B.S. in Physics and Engineering Science with honors, after which she earned an M.S. in Optics from the University of Rochester.

Though she had always envisioned NASA as the logical next step, Michele spent the next few years working as an image scientist and systems engineer in industry supporting the government, where she successfully delivered new and innovative operational capabilities. However, she had not yet realized her vision for creating positive change for others around the world, and wondered where she would be called to make the most difference.

(to be continued . . .)

Every moment in today's world brings updated technology and new information – benefiting from these things demands the ability to adjust to change and optimize for maximum benefit. You'll learn more about Michele's experience at the end of the chapter.

Working through this chapter will help you to:

■ Construct answers to essay (subjective) questions. p. 276

■ Create and deliver an effective presentation. p. 285

Text and photo used by permission from Michele Weslander Quaid

adjust Be ready and able to adjust your actions to fit changing situations. When the unexpected happens, success depends on your ability to *optimize* the situation.

How Can You Do Your Best Work on Essay Tests?
(even when writing is not your strength?)

All essay questions are subjective. **Subjective questions** require you to plan, organize, draft, and refine a response. Essay questions ask you to express your knowledge and views in a less structured way than short-answer questions. With freedom of thought and expression comes the challenge to organize your ideas and write well under time pressure. To improve your performance, focus on three areas:

> **Subjective questions** require you to plan, organize, draft, and refine a response.

- **Detail management.** As eager as you may be to get started and avoid running out of time, focus first on test directions and questions.

- **Time management.** Your time-management skills will help you parcel out your work in the limited time you have and perform effectively under pressure.

- **Writing skill.** Even though you are operating in a shorter time frame, you still need to work through a basic writing process.

Read the Directions and Questions Carefully

Pay attention to test directions. Your essay may need to be a certain length, for example, or use a specified format (for example, you may have to write a business letter). Most often you will handwrite your essay, although in some instances you will type it into a field on a computer. The directions will also tell you whether you need to answer all or some of the questions and, if only some, how many.

Next, read each question carefully, using critical thinking to identify exactly what the question is asking. As you read, focus on *action verbs*, which tell you how your instructor wants you to answer (see Key 11.1). Underline these verbs and use them as a guide. Finally, decide which question or questions to tackle (if there's a choice).

Answering essay questions effectively depends on understanding action verbs, said Kim Flachmann, professor of English at California State University at Bakersfield. "It may help to copy these words in the margin. Between the performance words are the content words—what you're being asked about."[1]

ACTION VERB	DEFINITION	EXAMPLES FROM DIFFERENT DISCIPLINES
Analyze	Break into parts and discuss each part separately.	Analyze how children were viewed in such Romantic novels as *Jane Eyre* and *Wuthering Heights*.
Compare	Explain similarities and differences.	Compare the public perception and treatment of Vietnam War veterans with the perception and treatment of veterans who fought in Iraq or Afghanistan.
Contrast	Distinguish between items being compared by focusing on differences.	Contrast how the body reacts to live versus killed vaccines.
Criticize	Evaluate the issue, focusing on its problems or deficiencies.	Criticize how Freud's theory of human nature viewed women.
Define	State the essential quality or meaning.	Define posttraumatic stress disorder (PTSD).
Describe	Paint a picture; provide the details of a story or the main characteristics of a situation.	Describe three basic beliefs shared by the Jewish, Christian, and Islamic religions.
Diagram	Present a drawing, chart or other visual.	Diagram the forces that affect the speed of an automobile on the open road.
Discuss	Examine completely, using evidence and often presenting both sides of an issue.	Discuss how the American family has changed in the past decade.
Enumerate/ list/identify	Specify items in the form of a list.	Identify the stages in development of a human embryo.
Evaluate	Give your opinion about the value or worth of something, usually by weighing positive and negative effects, and justify your conclusion.	Evaluate the effect of the death penalty as a deterrent to crime.
Elaborate on	Start with information presented in the question, and then add new material.	Elaborate on the view that human development continues throughout the life span.
Explain	Make the meaning of something clear, often by discussing causes and consequences.	Explain how wind energy is converted to electricity.
Illustrate	Supply examples.	Illustrate three different approaches to handling discipline problems in an elementary school classroom.
Interpret	Explain your personal views and judgments.	Interpret the results of the latest scientific studies on the effects of statin drugs on the incidence of heart attacks.
Justify	Discuss the reasons for your conclusions or for the question's premise.	Justify the economic bailout of financial institutions in 2008 and 2009.

(continued)

ACTION VERB	DEFINITION	EXAMPLES FROM DIFFERENT DISCIPLINES
Outline	Organize and present main and subordinate points.	Outline two basic approaches to writing a business e-mail.
Prove	Use evidence and logic to show that something is true.	Prove that economic struggle was a primary cause of World War II.
Refute	Use evidence and logic to show that something is not true or how you disagree with it.	Refute this statement: Left to themselves, free markets will correct problems that threaten their stability and growth.
Relate	Connect items mentioned in the question, showing, for example, how one item influenced the other.	Relate the rise in Jewish immigration to the United States in the early 20th century to the persecution of Jews in Russia and Poland.
Review	Provide an overview of ideas and establish their merits and features.	Review three trends that are currently influencing fashion design.
State	Explain clearly, simply, and concisely.	State the history of lunar exploration.
Summarize	Give the important ideas in brief, without comments.	Summarize three popular Internet marketing strategies.
Trace	Present a history of the way something developed, often by showing cause and effect.	Trace the history of the civil rights movement from Martin Luther King to Barack Obama.

Inside Tips from Carol, Career Coach

As you show what you know on tests and presentations for different courses, you broaden your knowledge and become more comfortable with a wide variety of subjects. This prepares you for the workplace, where many companies—especially small startups, of which there are more every day—will require you to function effectively in different areas. For example, in addition to being a skilled writer, an editor at a small publishing house needs to understand budgeting, design, marketing, and human resource management.

When you have to learn material or skills that don't seem relevant to your career goals, ask yourself: How am I building my value as an employee? Consider ways in which what you are learning might make you even more employable. You might find yourself more motivated to perform at the top of your abilities.

Map Out Your Time

Use time-management strategies to make the most of your allotted time.

- Look at how much time you have, how many essays you need to write, and how hard the questions seem.

- Decide how much time to devote to each. You may want to note your time frames—on scrap paper, the corner of your test page, or an exam booklet—to keep track. Consider breaking time down into smaller segments for each part of the process; for example, if you have 20 minutes to answer a question, use 5 to plan, 10 to draft, and 5 to review and finalize.

- Remember that things don't always go as planned. If your work on an essay takes longer than expected, adjust by reducing the time you use to answer other essays. If you are writing on a computer, check with your instructor ahead of time about what to do if you experience technological issues. Optimize your time in each moment as the test unfolds.

Use a Shortened Version of the Writing Process

The basic process of writing has four steps: planning, drafting, revising, and editing. Following is a version of the writing process specifically tailored to essay writing in a testing situation.

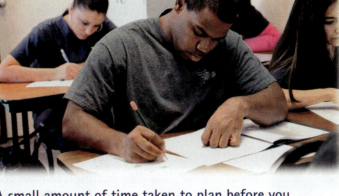

Plan

The biggest advantage you can give yourself is planning time. Take a minute or two to think through and organize your answer before you begin. Instead of scrambling for ideas as you write, you will be carrying out an organized plan, resulting in a better essay and reduced stress.

A small amount of time taken to plan before you write will save you a lot of time you might have spent reworking an unplanned essay test response.

Think carefully about what the question is asking and what you know, and define your goal—what you intend to say in your answer. On scrap paper, outline or map your ideas and supporting evidence.

Then come up with a **thesis statement** that outlines the goal you've set, illustrating both content and, if applicable, your point of view. If necessary—and if you have the time—reorganize your outline or think link into an exact writing roadmap.

When you are asked to apply concepts to new ideas and situations, take a deep breath and try to link what you know with what you are being asked. You might also go a step further, says Professor Flachmann. "I always tell students to try to find a unique way into the question that not everybody is going to use. For example, if you are asked the causes of World War II, you may want to state and compare them to the causes of World War I. That's the way to get a higher grade and use your best critical thinking skills."[2]

To answer the third essay question in the box on the next page, one student created the planning outline shown in Key 11.2. Notice how abbreviations and shorthand help the student write quickly. Writing "Role of BL in IC" is much faster than "Role of Body Language in Interpersonal Communication."

Thesis statement
a statement that is the central core of your essay around which arguments are based.

© Courtesy of Sarah Lyman Kravits

Here are some examples of essay questions you might encounter in a communication course. In each case, notice the action verbs from Key 11.1.

1. Summarize the role of the self-concept as a key to interpersonal relationships and communication.
2. Explain how internal and external noise affects the ability to listen effectively.
3. Describe three ways that body language affects interpersonal communication.

Draft

Your first draft on an exam is usually the one you hand in, because there is rarely any time for revision. If you take time in the planning stage, you will have enough material for a complete answer. Use the following guidelines:

- Remind yourself of test directions (how long your essay should be or whether it needs to take a particular format) and use this knowledge to guide your work.

- State your thesis, getting to the point quickly. Then move to the evidence that backs it up. Spend the bulk of your time developing your thesis, supporting evidence, and logic.

- Pay attention to how you organize your ideas and how you support them with evidence. Try to structure your essay so that each paragraph presents an idea that supports the thesis. Key 11.3 identifies commonly used organizational methods.

- Use clear language and tight logic to link ideas to your thesis and to create transitions between paragraphs.

Key 11.2   Create an informal outline during essay tests.

Essay question: Describe three ways in which body language affects interpersonal communication.

Roles of BL in IC

   1. To contradict or reinforce words
     —e.g., friend says, "I'm fine"
   2. To add shades of meaning
     —saying the same sentence in 3 diff. ways
   3. To make lasting 1st impression
     —impact of nv cues and voice tone greater than words
     —we assume things abt person based on posture, eye contact, etc.

ORGANIZATIONAL STRUCTURE	WHAT TO DO	EXAMPLE
Arrange ideas by time.	Describe events in order or reverse order.	In chronological order, describe the events that led to the declaration of war in Europe in 1939.
Arrange ideas according to importance.	Start with the idea that carries the most weight and move to less important ideas. Or move from the least to the most important ideas.	In order of importance, describe five factors that led to Hitler's rise in Germany after World War I.
Arrange ideas by problem and solution.	Start with a problem and then discuss solutions.	Describe the failed plot, at the highest level of the German military command, to kill Hitler.
Arrange ideas to present an argument.	Present one or both sides of an issue.	Present reasons why President Roosevelt decided against bombing the railroad tracks that led to the concentration camps and what his critics said about the decision.
Arrange ideas in list form.	Group a series of items.	List the Allied military leaders from the United States, Great Britain, and France and their roles in the war effort.
Arrange ideas according to cause and effect.	Show how events, situations, or ideas cause subsequent events, situations, or ideas.	Show the relationship between the U.S. involvement in World War II and the end of the economic depression.
Arrange ideas through the use of comparisons.	Compare and contrast the characteristics of events, people, situations, or ideas.	Compare the leadership styles of President Roosevelt and English Prime Minister Winston Churchill.
Arrange by process.	Go through the steps in a process: a "how-to" approach.	Describe the process by which U.S. manufacturing facilities began producing armaments for war.
Arrange by category.	Divide topics into categories and analyze each in order.	Discuss the success of the air and sea assaults on Europe.

- Look back at your outline periodically, and adjust if you have forgotten anything you meant to cover.
- Wrap it up with a short, to-the-point conclusion.

Drafting an essay in a test setting does not always go smoothly, even when you are fully prepared. Any student can hit a wall during an essay test and have trouble continuing, or even starting, an essay. If it happens to you, make choices that help you optimize the situation. One useful choice is to

© wavebreakmedia/Shutterstock

just start writing, even if you are unsure of what you want to say. You don't want to be sitting in front of an empty page when time is called. Consider beginning to write the body of your essay on the second page of your test booklet, leaving the first page blank so that you can go back and create an introduction once you have a clearer idea of what to say.[3]

Revise

Although you may not have the time or opportunity to rewrite your entire answer, you can certainly adjust and improve it with minor deletions or additions (in the margin if you are writing by hand). If you find a hole in your work—an idea without support, for example, or some unnecessary information—add the new material and take out what you don't need. When adding material on a handwritten essay, you can use an editing mark like a caret to insert it (neatly so it remains legible) or note that inserts can be found on separate pages. If you have more than one insert, label each to avoid confusion (Insert #1, Insert #2, etc.).

As you check over your essay, ask yourself these questions:

- Have I answered the question?
- Does my essay begin with a clear thesis statement, and does each paragraph start with a strong topic sentence that supports the thesis?
- Have I provided strong support in the form of examples, statistics, and other relevant facts to prove my argument?
- Is my logic sound and convincing? Does every sentence communicate my point?
- Have I covered all the points in my original outline or map?
- Is my conclusion an effective wrap-up?

Edit

Check for mistakes in grammar, spelling, punctuation, and usage. The correct use of language leaves a good impression and reduces problems that may lower your grade.

Key 11.4 shows the student's completed response to the essay on body language including the word changes and inserts she made while revising the draft.

Neatness is crucial. No matter how good your ideas are, if your instructor can't read them, your grade will suffer. If your handwriting is a problem, try printing or skipping every other line, and be sure to write on only one side of the page. Students with illegible handwriting might ask to take the test on a computer. Students taking essay tests on computers will not have handwriting issues but should still pay close attention to punctuation, grammar, spelling, and clarity.

QUESTION: Describe three ways that body language affects interpersonal communication.

Body language plays an important role in interpersonal communication and helps shape the impression you make. *, especially when you meet someone for the first time* Two of the most important functions of body language are to contradict and reinforce verbal statements. When body language contradicts verbal language, the message ~~conveyed~~ *delivered* by the body is dominant. For example, if a friend tells you that she is feeling "fine," but her posture is slumped, *her eye contact minimal,* and her facial expression troubled, you have every reason to wonder whether she is telling the truth. If the same friend tells you that she is feeling fine and is smiling, walking with a bounce in her step, and has direct eye contact, her body language is ~~telling the truth.~~ *accurately reflecting and reinforcing her words.*

The nonverbal cues that make up body language also have the power to add shades of meaning. Consider this statement: "This is the best idea I've heard all day." If you were to say this three different ways—in a loud voice while standing up; quietly while sitting with arms and legs crossed and looking away; and while ~~maintening~~ *maintaining* eye contact and taking the receiver's hand—you might send three different messages.

Finally, the impact of nonverbal cues can be greatest when you meet someone for the first time. *Although first impressions emerge from a combination of nonverbal cues, tone of voice, and ~~choice of words,~~ nonverbal elements (cues and tone) usually come across first and strongest.* When you meet someone, you tend to make assumptions based on nonverbal behavior such as posture, eye contact, gestures, and speed and style of movement.

In summary, nonverbal communication plays a ~~crusial~~ *crucial* role in interpersonal relationships. It has the power to send an accurate message that may ~~destroy~~ *belie* the speaker's words, offer shades of meaning, and set the tone of a first meeting.

TAKE ACTION
Write to the Verb

This exercise will help you focus on action verbs as you answer essay questions. Before you begin, choose three action verbs from Key 11.1 that you have seen in essay questions.

- Start by choosing a topic you have studied in this course—for example, the brain's memory storage systems, or learning preferences. Write your topic here:

_____

- Put yourself in the role of instructor. Write an essay question on this topic, using one of the action verbs you chose to frame the question. For example, "*Analyze* the role of rehearsal in keeping information in long-term memory."

_____

_____

- Now rewrite your original question twice more, using the other two action verbs you chose and adjusting the question to the verb each time.

1. _____

_____

2. _____

_____

Finally, analyze how each new verb changes the focus of the essay. Describe the goal of each essay question. Notice how they differ.

1. _____

_____

2. _____

_____

How Can You Deliver an Effective Team Presentation?

(doesn't it depend completely on the quality of the team?)

With the importance of collaboration in school and in the workplace, many instructors assign team presentations that are delivered to the class. These presentations require planning, research, thought about individual and group content, and focus on delivery. Because team presentations are often graded, learning the basics is important to your academic success.

Team projects, also called group projects, reflect the wisdom of this Japanese proverb: "*None of us is as smart as all of us.*" The ability to collaborate is one of the most important skills you will learn in college. Being part of a group has significant benefits as well as a few drawbacks:

© Endostock/Fotolia

- **Benefits.** Teams tap into the varied academic, creative, and practical strengths and skills, as well as intelligences, of different people. A well-functioning group pools these human assets in order to deliver an excellent product on schedule. The product would not have been possible had one person worked alone.

- **Drawbacks.** When you work in a team, you are no longer in total control of project quality and timing. This is a problem if one or more team members slack off. You may also encounter people who are difficult (or impossible) to work with, as well as logistical problems like getting everyone together at the same time.

Instructors often assign projects to student groups. Members share the work, support each other in the learning process, and receive individual grades for their efforts. Knowing what to expect will help you adjust to whatever the experience brings and will optimize your work.

Elements of a Team Project

Although every team project is different, it usually involves the following elements:

Instructor assigns the project.   Group presentations are usually described in the class syllabus and can be a significant portion of your course grade. The syllabus may indicate the project theme but leave specific topic choice to each group. Your instructor will spell out what is expected, so be sure to listen carefully and ask questions.

MULTIPLE INTELLIGENCE STRATEGIES

For Team Projects

If you have a team project you will have to work on this term, identify it here _____.
In the right-hand column, record specific ideas for how MI strategies can help you prepare for it.

Intelligence	Use MI Strategies to Prepare for a Team Project	Identify MI Strategies to Use with Your Project
Verbal–Linguistic	▪ During your first meeting, focus on the action verbs to define the project's focus. ▪ To capture ideas, take extensive notes during team meetings.	
Logical–Mathematical	▪ Take notes on 3 by 5 cards, and organize them by topic. ▪ Create a sequential outline of the project preparation process.	
Bodily–Kinesthetic	▪ Visit places that offer needed resources or that are related to your topic—companies, libraries, etc. ▪ After a meeting, take a physical activity break to think about your top ideas and see what new thoughts come up.	
Visual–Spatial	▪ Incorporate colorful visual aids into your presentation. ▪ Whenever the group meets, use a think link to map out concepts and support.	
Interpersonal	▪ Between group meetings, bounce ideas off other group members via group text or e-mail. ▪ Be a peer editor to other group members; read one another's drafts, and give constructive feedback.	
Intrapersonal	▪ Think about the feelings the project raises in you, and if need be, come up with ways to cope and adapt. ▪ Schedule enough time for research and analysis on your own so you can make suggestions on what the team creates.	
Musical	▪ Play relaxing music while you plan your first draft. ▪ If appropriate to do so, write and perform a song as part of your presentation.	
Naturalistic	▪ Have one meeting outside to inspire ideas. ▪ Look for relationships among ideas that, on the surface, appear different.	

adjust

STUDENT TO STUDENT

The success of a team project often depends on the ability of group members to work together. Define what you are willing to do to promote team success. Pair up with a fellow student and ask each other:

What does it cost you and your team if you do less than your team expects of you? What does it cost you and your team if you do extra work when someone else doesn't fulfill responsibilities? What actions are you willing to take if team members are not sharing the load effectively?

Create teams.   Often, instructors may divide the class into groups using a random or structured method, wanting students to work with others they don't know as well. Sometimes instructors may allow students to create teams on their own. If you are in the position to pick your own team, choose classmates for their ability, their conscientiousness, and their easy personality, not because they are your friends or are popular. Your whole experience in the group will be affected by this decision.

Have your first team meeting.   The goal is to talk about the assignment as a whole and outline the project parts, making sure that everyone is on the same page and there are no misunderstandings of the goal or responsibilities. At this meeting you should identify:

© Goodluz/Shutterstock

- **Your audience.** Giving a presentation to other people, whether online or in person, requires knowing who they are and why they would be interested in what you have to say. Understanding their motivation will help you choose your topic, words, and tone.

- **Your goal.** Get clear on the outcome you hope to achieve. Do you want your audience to do something? Do you want to change the way they think about something? Do you want to solve a problem? This goal becomes the purpose of the presentation and drives its content.

- **Your format.** Will you be presenting in person? Will you be creating a presentation that will be shown virtually to students in an online course? Know your parameters so that you can design your presentation accordingly.

- **Team communication points.** To achieve your goal, what points do you need to make? Certain information will be necessary to inform, educate, or persuade your audience.

- **Each team member's roles and responsibilities.** The clearer and more specific you can be in defining what each person will do, the greater the chance that everyone will do what they say they will do.

- **Team preparation schedule.** Lay out dates and times for meetings, research sessions, and work sessions as well as interim and final deadlines.

Whether or not there is an "official" team leader, it is likely that at least one person will take on this role. The team leader has organizational and scheduling responsibility and depends on group support.

Start individual work. You complete your part of the project on your own, but the role your work plays in the end result should always be on your mind. If the group is presenting the project in front of the class, think also of the presentation.

- **Plan.** Brainstorm your topic, determine your thesis, write an outline, do research, and adjust your thesis and outline, if necessary.

- **Draft your contribution.** Dive into the details. Your main challenges are to organize your material, integrate your research into your work, use logic to connect evidence to main ideas, and choose the right words and/ or visuals to express your thoughts.

Gather for a second meeting (or more if necessary). When you and other group members are finished with your drafts, share your work. If possible, send your drafts via e-mail before the meeting, so people will have time to read them and offer comments and ideas. Then fit the presentation pieces together according to the outline created at the first meeting. Expect that your work—and everyone else's—will need adjustment, so don't be discouraged by the need for more work. You are not working alone, so this give and take is part of the process.

As you improve and combine materials, work to:

- **Integrate visual aids.** Images, charts, maps, or other visuals draw people's attention, explain complicated concepts, and help people remember important information. You can use a flip chart or a white board to draw or write as you go, or use prepared PowerPoint slides, videos, Prezi, animation—anything that enhances your audience's understanding of the topics in the presentation. If you import graphics from websites into your presentation, be sure to cite your sources.

- **Keep text to a minimum.** If you use slides or Prezi or any other visual that includes text, do *not* put down every word you plan to say. Simply note important points you want people to remember and then elaborate on them with your own words. For helpful advice, check out www.presentationzen.com.

- **Tell a story.** If you really want people to remember what you say, weave in stories throughout your presentation. People remember stories better than they remember individual facts. Give real examples. Share personal experiences. Break up your presentation with humorous anecdotes. Your presentation will stick with people when you tell stories.

Have a final group meeting.   At this final stage, focus on:

- Polishing the writing
- Finalizing the presentation
- Planning your delivery (if your team is required to present the project to the class)

Practice Your Performance

Up until now, your team has worked together to create the project material. If your project is final when written, your work ends here. However, if you have to make a class presentation, these suggestions will help:

- **Know everyone's role as well as your own.** Generally, one person will spearhead the presentation while others play supporting roles, although for some presentations team members have fairly equal project segments. Make sure you know what you are supposed to do and when. The success of the project depends on everyone working together.

- **Know the parameters.** How long does each team or team member have? If you are presenting virtually, how long should the presentation be? If you are presenting in person, be aware of where your classmates will be and what props are available (for example, a podium, table, whiteboard, "smart classroom" setup with a computer linked to a projector). If you are using electronic equipment, test it before the presentation.

- **Focus on your nonverbal behavior.** If you are presenting in person or in a virtual format that will show an image of you speaking, your body position, voice, and clothing contribute to the impression you and other group members make. The goal is to look and sound good and to appear relaxed. Try to make eye contact with classmates, and walk around if you are comfortable doing so.

- **Practice ahead of time.** In your last meeting prior to the presentation, do a test run. If possible, practice in the room where you will speak. Gather some friends to act as your audience. Make an audio or video recording and evaluate your performance.

- **Give your team members support.** Give them your full attention and try to help if they need your expertise or seem flustered. You are in this together. Plan ahead how you will adjust to last-minute issues that may crop up, including anyone being absent.

- **Envision your success.** Take deep breaths. Smile. Know that your audience wants you to succeed.

- **Be prepared for questions.** Your instructor or classmates may ask questions when the presentation is over. Your team leader may decide who should answer a question, so be prepared. Listen carefully to each question, think before you speak, and jot down ideas. Answer only part of a question if that's all you can do. Your goal is to emphasize what you know rather than what you do not know.

On a scale of 1 to 10, with 1 being the lowest and 10 being the highest, rate yourself on your ability in various aspects of team presentations. For any skills on which you give yourself a 7 or higher, write a job title or workplace task that uses that particular strength.

Team Presentation Skill	Rating	Job Title or Work Task
Speaking in front of others		
Online/library research		
Communication with others		
Writing ability		
Organizational ability		
Time management		
Leadership and motivating others		
Comfort with visuals and technology		
Flexibility		
Stress management		
Willingness to help others		
Being able to handle questions		

Working with a Virtual Team

If you are taking an online class, your may be working with group members whom you have never met face to face. Technology enables you to be part of **virtual teams** that may be as effective as face-to-face teams.

Your communication tools include e-mail, group text or group messaging on social media (Facebook, Instagram, and so on), chat rooms, groups set up on social networking sites, Wikis, document-sharing sites, Doodles or shared calendars for scheduling, and more. Use Google Docs or other document-sharing programs to give and receive feedback on written work. And, of course, call team members when real-time conversations are needed. Many phones have three-way call capability, so three people can gather on a "conference" call.

Whether you are working online or face to face, the success of any group project depends on clear, regular communication. The bonus of working so closely with a team is that your ties to one or more members are likely to extend beyond the project. Your teammates may become friends and people you can rely on for help throughout the course.

Virtual teams
teams in which members work together by using e-mail, social networking, instant messaging, and other technologies.

© Courtesy of Michele Weslander Quaid

HABIT IN ACTION WRAP-UP

What happened with Michele?

The tragic events of 9/11/2001 created an immediate need for change in the U.S. national security community. Per her reputation as an innovator and agent of change, Michele was recruited by the U.S. Government, becoming one of the youngest leaders ever sworn in as a senior executive (the civilian equivalent of a general). Working with government agencies and the military on sensitive projects around the world including in Iraq and Afghanistan, she created and spearheaded initiatives designed to optimize information sharing and collaboration among the United States and its allies, affecting organizational changes others had considered impossible. Her overarching goal of improving operations and protecting citizens drove her to risk speaking truth to power and leading with the courage of her convictions. Michele's unwavering commitment to support those in harm's way led her into combat zones, and her efforts positively impacted American and Coalition troops such that certain units within the special operations community gave her the callsign "Warrior Goddess."

Michele's decisive leadership, bias for action, and notable accomplishments in delivering innovative solutions led to Google recruiting her as the Chief Technology Officer for the Public Sector & Chief Innovation Evangelist in 2011. Given her purpose-driven quest to improve the lives of people, Michele thrived at Google, where passionate agents for change are welcomed and where sharing, innovation, intelligent risk taking, learning from failure, and the needs of the user take focus. Always wanting to maximize opportunities to do the most good, Michele is taking on new and exciting challenges as the founder and CEO of Sunesis Nexus LLC, an independent consulting company, and as co-founder and CEO of Global Nexus Alliance, a nonprofit humanitarian organization.

Connect this story to your life: Thinking about how Michele has adjusted several times in her life to optimize her ability to make a difference, consider your own life now. Which of your talents and abilities would you like to optimize? What adjustments can you make — in your work, your education, your habits, your mindset — that will encourage this? Describe your goal and the specific adjustments you will make to get there.

Building Skills

Note the Important Points

Identify, in sequence, the four writing process steps to use when answering essay test questions.

1. _____

2. _____

3. _____

4. _____

List and explain three different organizational plans for writing an essay.

1. _____

_____

2. _____

_____

3. _____

_____

List and describe at least three elements in the process of creating a team presentation.

1. _____

_____

2. _____

_____

3. _____

_____

Describe three strategies for practicing your team performance.

1. _____

2. _____

3. _____

Define *virtual team.* _____

_____

Critical Thinking

applying learning to life

Team Research

Join with three other classmates and decide on two narrow research topics that interest all of you and that you can investigate quickly. The first topic should be current and in the news—for example, building fuel-efficient cars, body piercing, or the changing U.S. family. The second topic should be more historical—for example, the polio epidemic in the 1950s, the Irish potato famine, or South Africa's apartheid.

Working alone, team members should use the college library and the Internet to research both topics. Set a research time limit of no more than 1 hour per topic. The goal should be to collect a list of sources for later investigation. When everyone is finished, the group should come together to discuss the research process. Among the questions group members should ask each other are:

- How did you "attack" and organize your research for each topic?

- What research tools did you use to investigate each topic?

- How did the nature of your research differ from topic to topic? Why do you think this was the case?

Finally, discuss what you learned that might improve the way you collaborate for a team presentation. Write your findings here:

_____

_____

_____

_____

_____

Team Building

collaborative solutions

Tap the Diversity of Your Presentation Team

Working successfully with others requires that you first be able to identify the talents and skills that are important to team success. Complete this exercise to pinpoint the different strengths people bring.

Step 1: Come together with three classmates to work in an in-person or virtual group. Together, go over the list of helpful team presentation skills found in the All About You exercise. Students should submit two items to the group:

- Their five strongest skills from the All About You exercise

- Any other team presentation skill not mentioned that they have and consider important

Step 2: Compare your lists. Think about the qualities that people had in common, the qualities you included that others did not, and the qualities others chose that are not strengths of yours. After your discussion, answer these questions together:

What skills do you, as a group, consider to be highest priority for the success of a team? Name a maximum of five.

_____

_____

_____

How balanced is your group—do you have team members who display strength in all areas you consider important? If not, what skill areas are you missing?

_____

_____

What skill area(s) not found in the text have you added to the list of essential team presentation success skills?

_____

_____

adjust

Practice, Practice, Practice

You have just studied strategies for taking essay tests. Consider three that will help improve your performance on upcoming tests. Write these strategies here:

1. _____

2. _____

3. _____

Examine your schedule to find an upcoming test that will include essay questions. Ask your instructor to provide several sample essay questions for you to use to practice, or create some yourself using your text or other materials. Write two here:

1. _____

2. _____

Now, create a pretend testing situation for yourself in a quiet setting with a timer. Using the strategies you named (and any others you like), create an answer to both of the essay questions you listed above, timing yourself each time and stopping when the timer goes off. Evaluate your work afterward and note what you could do better. Consider repeating this exercise again if you have identified ways in which you can improve.

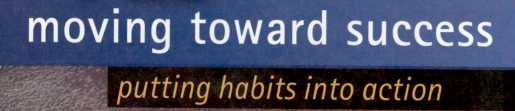

12

moving toward success

putting habits into action

If you're reading this, you've explored a comprehensive set of Habits for Success that will support your efforts now and in the future. The features and exercises throughout the text have encouraged you to use these habits in the context of different topics. This final chapter of *Keys to Effective Learning* gives you the opportunity to expand this use to different areas—both in and out of school—and to check in on your progress in making the habits a part of your life.

Working through this chapter will help you to:

- Continue to build the Habits for Success. p. 298
- Apply each habit in personal situations. p. 300
- Connect the habits to professionalism and employability. p. 312

© sritangphoto/Shutterstock

How Do You Continue to Build Habits for Success?
(will they eventually require less effort?)

As you have seen, the Habits for Success are an amazing collection of action-promoting strategies that fuel success. They encourage you to perform at your best by acting intelligently and appropriately in any situation. "As Aristotle said, 'We are what we repeatedly do. Excellence, then, is not an act but a habit,'" quotes Professor Art Costa, whose research led to the development of the habits. Professor Costa adds this: "Only by routinely practicing [the Habits for Success] can we assure ourselves that we are thinking clearly, confronting problems intelligently, and making wise decisions."[1]

Costa's research uncovered five characteristics common to people who are regular habit users:

1. **Inclination:** They tend to use and return to behavioral patterns that work.

2. **Value:** They value the behaviors that work rather than other, less useful ones.

3. **Sensitivity:** They notice when it is possible, and appropriate, to use certain behaviors.

4. **Capability:** They have the basic skills and ability to carry out the behaviors.

5. **Commitment:** They make a continual effort to evaluate how they did and to improve their performance.[2]

Activate these characteristics and they, in turn, will encourage you to rely on the habits even more. They will help you finish strong, imagine, inquire, contribute, and much more. (Key 12.1 recaps all 11 habits.) The nature of habits is that the more you put them into practice, the more natural they become and the less conscious effort and planning they require. Over time, if you use a Habit for Success often enough, you will find yourself using it without having to make a conscious decision to do so. The beauty of making the habits true habits is that you not only benefit from them consistently, but you free up brainpower to put toward skill building, creative growth, and even more developed critical thinking.

© Gabriel Blaj/Fotolia

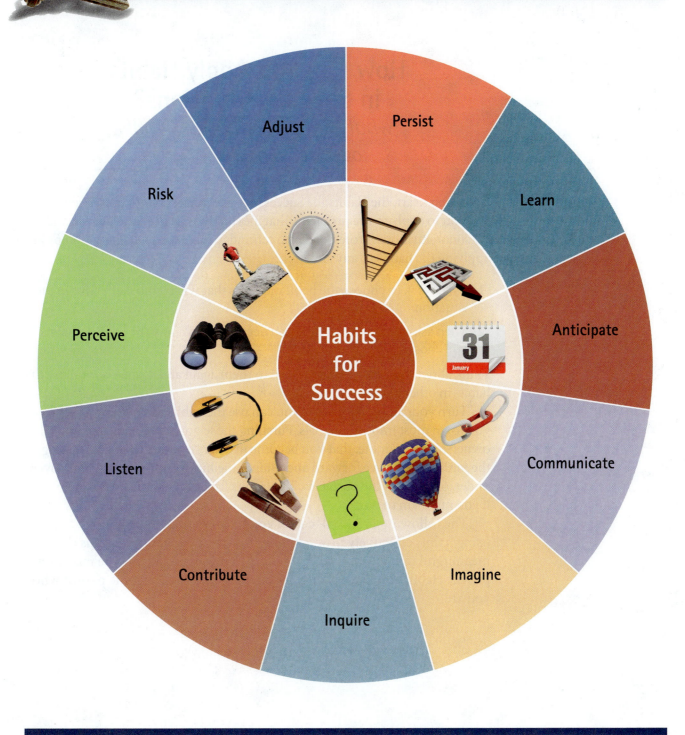

Through the features in each chapter you have gotten to know each habit. Take time now to expand your understanding of how you can use them in a wide variety of situations.

How Can You Apply Habits in Specific Situations?
(what difference can they make outside of this course?)

At their heart, the Habits for Success are problem-solving tools, ready for you to apply to the problems that inevitably arise in school, work, and personal situations. Professor Costa reminds problem solvers of two steps in applying the habits to any situation:

1. First, work to choose the habit or habits that will be most effective in the situation.

2. Then ask questions that help you decide *how* to apply the habit or habits you chose.

Think about these steps—and return to them again and again—as you use the habits in other contexts.

Turn your attention to how you can use the habits as you seek to achieve your own most important goals. Pursuing those goals demands that you take ownership of your life, that you become in essence your own leader, taking the initiative to move forward and finding the motivation to keep going over, under, or through the obstacles. The Habits for Success can and will help you if you put them to work.

The following grids will coach you to acknowledge where you are using habits effectively now, explore how to apply habits to goals that are meaningful to you, and connect habits to professionalism. The more you put the Habits for Success into action, the more they become part of who you are.

PERSIST. Stick to whatever you are doing until you complete it. Finish strong.

Original location: Chapter 1, "Getting Started"

Thinking about your life right now, answer the following:

Describe a goal toward which you are currently persisting successfully.	
What does your progress toward this goal say about you?	
Describe a situation in which you are struggling to persist.	
What is this challenge costing you?	
What are you willing to do to finish strong in this situation?	
Describe specifically how you will take this action.	
Name a person who will help you remain accountable to this action and finish strong.	
A potential employer asks you about how you persist. What evidence do you give?	

LEARN. Strive to know more.
Take initiative to learn throughout your life.
Self-direct.

Original location: Chapter 2, "Learning Preferences"

Thinking about your life right now, answer the following:

Describe something that you are taking the initiative to learn.	
What does this initiative say about you?	
Describe a situation in which you need to self-direct more effectively.	
What is this challenge costing you?	
What are you willing to do to take initiative in this situation?	
Describe specifically how you will take this action.	
Name a person who will help you remain accountable to your plan to self-direct.	
A potential employer asks you about your willingness to learn new things. What evidence do you give?	

ANTICIPATE. Manage impulsive behavior by defining your goals before beginning. Plan a set of actions that will lead you toward your goals.

Original location: Chapter 3, "Time and Money"

Thinking about your life right now, answer the following:

Describe a situation where you anticipated and planned ahead effectively.	
What does this successful planning say about you?	
Describe a situation in which you did not plan ahead.	
What is your lack of a plan costing you?	
What can you plan now to make the most of the situation?	
Describe specifically how you will take this action.	
Name a person who will help you remain accountable to this action and plan.	
A potential employer asks you about your ability to anticipate and plan. What evidence do you give?	

COMMUNICATE. Learn to ask for help and give help when you can. Connect with purpose to others and their ideas, especially when you are part of a team.

Original location: Chapter 4, "Setting and Reaching Goals"

Thinking about your life right now, answer the following:

Describe a situation in which you are communicating effectively.	
What does this purposeful connection say about you?	
Describe a situation in which you are struggling to communicate.	
What is this lack of connection costing you?	
What are you willing to do to connect with purpose in this situation?	
Describe specifically how you will take this action.	
Name a person who will help you remain accountable to this action and communicate.	
A potential employer asks you about how you communicate in team settings. What evidence do you give?	

IMAGINE. You have the power to imagine. Use it to <u>expand</u> your thinking and create new and clever ideas and solutions to problems.

Original location: Chapter 5, "Critical and Creative Thinking"

Thinking about your life right now, answer the following:

Describe a task or problem for which you have generated a useful new idea or solution.	
What does this use of your power to imagine say about you?	
Describe a situation for which you are not yet able to generate helpful ideas.	
What is this inability to expand your thinking costing you?	
What are you willing to do to generate creative ideas for this situation?	
Describe specifically how you will take this action.	
Name a person who will help you remain accountable to this action and expand your thinking.	
A potential employer asks you about your imagination and problem solving. What evidence do you give?	

INQUIRE. Questions help you see what you know and what you don't know. Use questions to <u>excavate</u> and anchor new knowledge.

Original Location: Chapter 6, "Active Reading"

Thinking about your life right now, answer the following:

Describe a goal you have achieved through your willingness to ask questions.	
What does this goal achievement say about you?	
Describe a situation in which you are struggling to inquire and excavate knowledge.	
What is this inability to question costing you?	
What are you willing to do to excavate knowledge in this situation?	
Describe specifically how you will take this action.	
Name a person who will help you remain accountable to this action and inquire.	
A potential employer asks you about how willing you are to inquire in work situations. What evidence do you give?	

CONTRIBUTE. Contribute what you already know to move toward individual or team goals. Your contribution will add value to any learning or problem solving process.

Original location: Chapter 7, "Reading and Information Literacy"

Thinking about your life right now, answer the following:

Describe a situation in which your contribution added value to a team's pursuit of a goal.	
What does this willingness to contribute say about you?	
Describe a situation in which you feel you are not adding value.	
What is this challenge costing you?	
What are you willing to do to contribute effectively in this situation?	
Describe specifically how you will take this action.	
Name a person who will help you remain accountable to this action and contribute.	
A potential employer asks you about how you add value to a team. What evidence do you give?	

LISTEN. Consider what others have to say as you work to <u>understand</u> perspectives that differ from yours. Listen for ideas that diverge from your own thinking.

Original location: Chapter 8, "Listening and Note Taking"

Thinking about your life right now, answer the following:

Describe a situation in which your listening has created useful understanding.	
What does this willingness to listen say about you?	
Describe a situation in which you are having trouble understanding another perspective.	
What is this difficulty costing you?	
What are you willing to do to listen and understand someone else's perspective in this situation?	
Describe specifically how you will take this action.	
Name a person who will help you remain accountable to this action and listen effectively.	
A potential employer asks you about how open you are to the perspectives of others. What evidence do you give?	

PERCEIVE. Note–and then look beyond–what you see and hear. Open your sensory pathways to all kinds of information. <u>Build awareness</u> in order to remember information and use it later.

Original location: Chapter 9, "Memory and Studying"

Thinking about your life right now, answer the following:

Describe a situation in which your ability to perceive has a positive effect.	
What does this awareness say about you?	
Describe a situation in which you lack perception and awareness.	
What is this challenge costing you?	
What are you willing to do to build awareness in this situation?	
Describe specifically how you will take this action.	
Name a person who will help you remain accountable to this action and build awareness.	
A potential employer asks you about your ability to be perceptive and aware in a team situation. What evidence do you give?	

RISK. Test your limits and move ahead through taking calculated risks. With risk comes the opportunity to <u>extend</u> your knowledge and skill.

Original location: Chapter 10, "Test Taking I"

Thinking about your life right now, answer the following:

Describe a situation where a calculated risk is leading you toward a goal effectively.	
What does this risk-taking action say about you?	
Describe a situation in which you are hesitant to risk.	
What is this unwillingness to risk costing you?	
What are you willing to do to take a calculated risk in this situation?	
Describe specifically how you will take this action.	
Name a person who will help you remain accountable to this action and extend yourself.	
A potential employer asks you about how you take risks to extend knowledge and skill. What evidence do you give?	

ADJUST. Be ready and able to adjust your actions to fit changing situations. When the unexpected happens, success depends on your ability to optimize a situation.

Original location: Chapter 11, "Test Taking II"

Thinking about your life right now, answer the following:

Describe a change that you handled effectively by adjusting and optimizing.	
What does this adjustment say about you?	
Describe a situation in which you are struggling to adjust to change.	
What is this struggle costing you?	
What are you willing to do to adjust to this situation and optimize?	
Describe specifically how you will take this action.	
Name a person who will help you remain accountable to this action and adjust effectively.	
A potential employer asks you about how able you are to adjust to change. What evidence do you give?	

How Can the Habits for Success Increase Professionalism and Employability?

(what about them will help a person get and keep a good job?)

In a fast-moving world, with college costs rising and academic work occupying a significant amount of time and energy, one particular question is on the minds of so many students (perhaps yours included): *What is this worth to me?* In other words, what are you getting from this experience that you can use to improve your life after college?

You may be thinking that you will never use some fact from your history class that showed up on a test, a particular mathematical formula, or the understanding of the political structure in Myanmar. This may be true, depending on your career pursuit. Here, however, is the bigger picture and a more important point for you to remember: **Every habit that promotes success in a college setting also makes you professional, more likely to be employed, and more able to thrive and move up in the workplace.**

When you value being on time to class meetings, you become more likely to be on time to work meetings. When you read and listen to other students' opinions receptively, you become more able to cooperate effectively in team settings. When you find a way to be open to learning new academic information, even (and especially) when it doesn't seem important to you, you build your willingness to learn things on the job—and some of what you learn at work will almost certainly seem more important to your supervisor than to you. A responsible, cooperative worker who is open to learning new things is someone with a strong chance of being hired, retained, and promoted.

As a matter of fact, the Habits for Success you have been developing correspond nearly one-to-one with what modern employers want to see, and hire, in employees. If you refer to reputable surveys like the National Association of Colleges and Employers (NACE) Job Outlook 2015, which you may have read about earlier in this text, the correlation is immediately evident. In Key 12.2 you can see how each habit connects with a quality that employers have stated they are looking for in their employees.

As you can see, your work this term is well worth your time and energy. You are taking the raw material that is you and molding it into a package that the workplace wants—building your employability without sacrificing your unique strengths and qualities. You are creating the best possible you to offer the workplace—and the workplace needs everything you can give.

© Courtesy of Sarah Lyman Kravits

Taking courses in an area of interest builds professionalism as well as knowledge. These students get hands-on experience in respiratory therapy as well as advice from an experienced instructor.

HABIT	EMPLOYERS WANT TO SEE ...	EMPLOYEES WITH THIS HABIT ...
PERSIST. Stick with it until you complete it. Finish strong.	*Strong work ethic*	Persist with tasks they are assigned, pushing to overcome obstacles, until they finish strong.
LEARN. Be a lifelong learner, always seeking to know more. Take initiative and be self-directed.	*Technical/computer skills*	Self-direct to learn whatever new technical and/or computer skills become necessary as companies respond to rapid and ongoing technological change.
ANTICIPATE. Design a plan of action and define specific goals before beginning.	*Initiative*	Anticipate what it will take to complete work tasks, and plan out effective schedules and assignments to accomplish those tasks.
COMMUNICATE. Ask for help and give help when you can. Connect with others with a purpose in mind.	*Communication skills*	Communicate up (to supervisors), down (to subordinates), and across (to peers) in constructive and productive ways.
IMAGINE. Expand your thinking to create new and useful ideas, solutions, and techniques.	*Analytical skills*	Generate ideas when a work problem arises, expanding possibilities to include the ideas of others.
PERCEIVE. Build awareness of the information that comes your way through sensory pathways.	*Detail-oriented*	Work to stay aware of details that must be managed, needs of others such as co-workers and customers, and the most emotionally intelligent way to handle situations.
INQUIRE. Use questions to build knowledge. Excavate problems so you can solve them before they grow out of control.	*Problem-solving skills*	Are willing to ask questions of anyone and about any problem, knowing that progress and solutions will come from the increased knowledge and understanding that inquiry brings.

(continued)

HABIT	EMPLOYERS WANT TO SEE . . .	EMPLOYEES WITH THIS HABIT . . .
CONTRIBUTE. Use your past knowledge and experiences to add value to problem solving.	*Ability to work in a team*	Are team players, willing to contribute their strengths but also always keeping the greater goal of the team in mind.
LISTEN. Consider what others have to say, and work to understand perspectives that differ from yours.	*Interpersonal skills*	Can balance sharing their own ideas with the ability to listen to, understand, and value the ideas of others.
RISK. Take productive risks. Extend your limits wisely.	*Leadership*	Take the lead when they see an opportunity to productively extend their own limits and the limits of the company.
ADJUST. Have the flexibility to shift your actions. Optimize how you react to a changing situation.	*Flexibility/adaptability*	Can be flexible, adjusting to changes small and large, optimizing any situation to gain whatever is possible.

Source: Employer information from NACE Research: Job Outlook 2015
(https://www.naceweb.org/s11122014/job-outlook-skills-qualities-employers-want.aspx)

© mangostock/Fotolia

You are only beginning your lifelong career as an accountable, cooperative, and creative contributor to the world. As long as you aim to do your best, whatever that means from day to day or situation to situation, you invite growth. As you continue to learn and work, you will strengthen your skills and set yourself up for success with people from all backgrounds, cultures, ages, and stages. The opportunity to make a difference for yourself and others has never been greater. As you use your habits to find intelligent approaches to problems, you will join people everywhere who aspire to change the world in ways both wide-ranging and tiny, improving life for themselves and for all.

ALL ABOUT YOU

Take a moment to think about how you currently use the habits. After you complete this self-assessment, compare it with the similar one you completed in Chapter 1 to evaluate changes and growth.

First, rate each based on how much you think you have and use that habit right now—from 1 (I don't have it at all) to 10 (I live this habit).

_____ Persist

_____ Learn

_____ Anticipate

_____ Communicate

_____ Imagine

_____ Perceive

_____ Inquire

_____ Contribute

_____ Listen

_____ Risk

_____ Adjust

Next, *underline* what you consider to be your three strongest habits. Then, **circle** what you consider the three habits that you need to develop most.

Questions to ponder:

- Are your strongest and weakest habits the same as they were in Chapter 1? Why or why not?

- What habit have you improved the most?

- What habit needs the most work?

- What other reflections do you have on your experience of building the Habits for Success?

Problem–Solving Strategies for Math and Science Courses

Because *word problems* are the most common way you will encounter quantitative thinking throughout your life, being able to solve them is crucial. Word problems can be tough, however, because they force you to translate between two languages—one expressed in words and one expressed in numbers and symbols. Although math is a precise language, English and other living languages tend to leave more room for interpretation. This difference in precision makes the process of translating difficult.

Steps to Solving Word Problems

Translating English or any other language into math takes a lot of practice. George Polya, in his 1945 classic *How to Solve It*, devised a four-step method for attacking word problems.[1] The basic steps reflect the general problem-solving process you may have explored in this text, and they will work for any word problem, whether in a math or science course.

1. **Understand the individual elements of the problem.** Read the problem carefully. Understand what it is asking. Know what information you have. Know what information is missing. Draw a picture, if possible. Translate the given information from words into mathematical language (e.g., numbers, symbols, formulas).
2. **Name and explore potential solution paths.** Think about similar problems that you understand and how those were solved. Consider whether this problem is an example of a mathematical idea that you know. In your head, try out different ways to solve the problem to see which may work best.
3. **Choose a solution path and solve the problem.** As you carry out your plan, check the precision of each of your steps.
4. **Review your result.** Check your answer for accuracy, if possible. Make sure you've answered the question the problem is asking. Does your result seem logical in the context of the problem? Are there other ways to do the problem?

Different problem-solving strategies will be useful to you when you are solving word problems. On a given problem, evaluate which strategy will work best and then apply it. The following section outlines several problem-solving strategies by working through word problem examples.[2]

Problem–Solving Strategies

The following sample problems are designed to give you an overview of problem types and to boost your ability to think critically through some basic math strategies.

Strategy 1. Look for a pattern.

G. H. Hardy (1877–1947), an eminent British mathematician, described mathematicians as makers of patterns and ideas. The search for patterns is one of the best strategies in problem solving. When you look for a pattern, you think inductively, observing a series of examples and determining the general idea that links the examples together.

Example: Find the next three entries in the following:

a. 1, 2, 4, _____ , _____ , _____

b. O, T, T, F, F, S, S, _____ , _____ , _____

Solutions to Example:

a. When identifying patterns, you may find a different pattern than someone else does. This doesn't mean yours is wrong. Example *a* actually has several possible answers. Here are two:

1. Each succeeding term of the sequence is twice the previous term. In that case, the next three values would be 8, 16, 32.

2. The second term is 1 more than the first term, and the third term is 2 more than the second. This might lead you to guess the fourth term is 3 more than the third term, the fifth term is 4 more than the fourth term, and so on. In that case, the next three terms are 7, 11, 16.

b. Example *b* is a famous pattern that often appears in puzzle magazines. The key to it is that "O" is the first letter of one, "T" is the first letter of two, and so on. Therefore, the next three terms would be E, N, and T for eight, nine, and ten.

Strategy 2. Make a table.

A table can help you organize and summarize information. This may enable you to see how examples form a pattern that leads you to an idea and a solution.

Example: How many ways can you make change for a half dollar using only quarters, dimes, nickels, and pennies?

Solutions to Example:
You might construct several tables and go through every possible case. You could start by seeing how many ways you can make change for a half dollar without using a quarter, which would produce the following tables:

Quarters	0	0	0	0	0	0	0	0	0	0	0	0	0	0	0	0	0	0
Dimes	0	0	0	0	0	0	0	0	0	0	0	1	1	1	1	1	1	1
Nickels	0	1	2	3	4	5	6	7	8	9	10	0	1	2	3	4	5	6
Pennies	50	45	40	35	30	25	20	15	10	5	0	40	35	30	25	20	15	10

Quarters	0	0	0	0	0	0	0	0	0	0	0	0	0	0	0	0	0	0
Dimes	1	1	2	2	2	2	2	2	2	3	3	3	3	3	4	4	4	5
Nickels	7	8	0	1	2	3	4	5	6	0	1	2	3	4	0	1	2	0
Pennies	5	0	30	25	20	15	10	5	0	20	15	10	5	0	10	5	0	0

There are 36 ways to make change for a half dollar without using a quarter. Using one quarter results in this table:

Quarters	1	1	1	1	1	1	1	1	1	1	1	1
Dimes	0	0	0	0	0	0	1	1	1	1	2	2
Nickels	0	1	2	3	4	5	0	1	2	3	0	1
Pennies	25	20	15	10	5	0	15	10	5	0	5	0

Using one quarter, you get 12 different ways to make change for a half dollar. Lastly, using two quarters, there's only one way to make change for a half dollar. Therefore, the solution to the problem is that there are $36 + 12 + 1 = 49$ ways to make change for a half dollar using only quarters, dimes, nickels, and pennies.

Strategy 3. Identify a subgoal.
Breaking the original problem into smaller and possibly easier problems may lead to a solution to the original problem. This is often the case in writing a computer program.

Example: Arrange the nine numbers 1, 2, 3, . . . , 9 into a square subdivided into nine sections in such a way that the sum of every row, column, and main diagonal is the same. This is called a *magic square.*

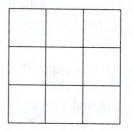

Solution to Example:
The sum of any individual row, column, or main diagonal has to be one-third the sum of all nine numbers (or else they wouldn't be the same). The sum of $1 + 2 + 3 + 4 + 5 + 6 + 7 + 8 + 9 = 45$. Therefore, each row, column, and main diagonal needs to sum to $45 \div 3 = 15$. Now, you need to see how many ways you can add three of the numbers from 1 to 9 and get 15. When you do this, you should get:

$9 + 1 + 5 = 15$ $8 + 3 + 4 = 15$
$9 + 2 + 4 = 15$ $7 + 2 + 6 = 15$
$8 + 1 + 6 = 15$ $7 + 3 + 5 = 15$
$8 + 2 + 5 = 15$ $6 + 4 + 5 = 15$

Now, looking at your magic square, notice that the center position will be part of four sums (a row, a column, and the two main diagonals). Looking back at your sums, you see that 5 appears in four different sums; therefore, 5 is in the center square:

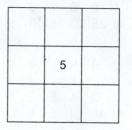

Now, in each corner, the number there appears in three sums (row, column, and a diagonal). Looking through your sums, you find that 2, 4, 6, and 8 each appear in three sums. Now you need to place them in the corners in such a way that your diagonals add up to 15:

2		6
	5	
4		8

Then, to finish, all you need to do is fill in the remaining squares so that 15 is the sum of each row, column, and main diagonal. The completed square is as follows:

2	7	6
9	5	1
4	3	8

Strategy 4. Examine a similar problem.   Sometimes a problem you are working on has similarities to a problem you've already read about or solved. In that case, it is often possible to use a similar approach to solve the new problem.

Example: Find a magic square using the numbers 3, 5, 7, 9, 11, 13, 15, 17, and 19.

Solution to Example:
This problem is very similar to the example for Strategy 3. Approaching it in the same fashion, you find that the row, column, and main diagonal sum is 33. Writing down all the possible sums of three numbers to get 33, you find that 11 is the number that appears four times, so it is in the center:

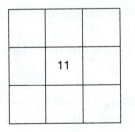

The numbers that appear three times in the sums and will go in the corners are 5, 9, 13, and 17. This now gives you:

13		17
	11	
5		9

Problem Solving Strategies for Math and Science Courses

Finally, completing the magic square gives you:

13	3	17
15	11	7
5	19	9

Strategy 5. Work backward.   With some problems, you may find it easier to start with the perceived final result and work backwards.

>*Example:* In the game of "Life," Carol had to pay $1,500 when she was married. Then, she lost half the money she had left. Next, she paid half the money she had for a house. Then, the game was stopped, and she had $3,000 left. With how much money did she start?

Solution to Example:
Carol ended up with $3,000. Right before that, she paid half her money to buy a house. Because her $3,000 was half of what she had before her purchase, she had 2 × $3,000 = $6,000 before buying the house. Prior to buying the house, Carol lost half her money. This means that the $6,000 is the half she didn't lose. So, before losing half her money, Carol had 2 × $6,000 = $12,000. Prior to losing half her money, Carol had to pay $1,500 to get married. This means she had $12,000 + $1,500 = $13,500 before getting married. Because this was the start of the game, Carol began with $13,500.

Strategy 6. Draw a diagram.   Drawing a picture is often an aid to solving problems, especially for visual learners. Although pictures are especially useful for geometrical problems, they can be helpful for other types of problems as well.

>*Example:* There were 20 women at a round table for dinner. Each woman shook hands with the woman to her immediate right and left. At the end of the dinner, each woman got up and shook hands with everybody except those who sat on her immediate right and left. How many handshakes took place after dinner?

Solution to Example:
To solve this example with a diagram, it might be a good idea to examine several simpler cases to see if you can determine a pattern of any kind that might help. Starting with two or three people, you can see there are no handshakes after dinner because everyone is adjacent to everyone else.

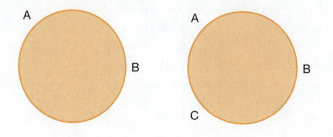

Now, in the case of four people, we get the following diagram, connecting those people who shake hands after dinner:

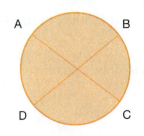

In this situation, you see there are two handshakes after dinner, AC and BD. In the case of five people, you get this picture:

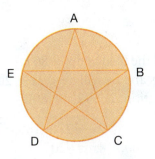

In this case, you have five after-dinner handshakes: AC, AD, BD, BE, and CE. Six people seated around a circle gives the following diagram:

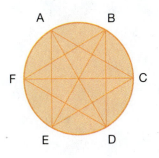

In this diagram, there are now a total of nine after-dinner handshakes: AC, AD, AE, BD, BE, BF, CE, CF, and DF. By studying the diagrams, you realize that if there are N people, each person would shake N − 3 people's hands after dinner. (They don't shake their own hands or the hands of the two people adjacent to them.) Because there are N people, that would lead to N(N − 3) after-dinner handshakes. However, this would double-count every handshake because AD would also be counted as DA. Therefore, there are only half as many actual handshakes. So, the correct number of handshakes is [N(N − 3)] ÷ 2. Finally, then, if there are 20 women, there would be 20(17) ÷ 2 = 170 after-dinner handshakes.

Strategy 7. Translate words into an equation. This strategy is often used in algebra.

Example: A farmer needs to fence a rectangular piece of land. He wants the length of the field to be 80 feet longer than the width. If he has 1,080 feet of fencing available, what should the length and width of the field be?

Solution to Example:

The best way to start this problem is to draw a picture of the situation and label the sides:

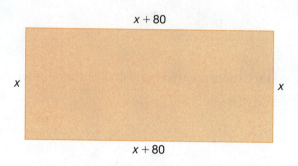

Let x represent the width of the field and $x + 80$ represent the length of the field. The farmer has 1,080 feet of fencing, and he will need $2x + 2(x + 80)$ feet of fencing to fence his field. This gives you the equation: $2x + 2(x + 80) = 1080$

Multiplying out:	$2x + 2x + 160 = 1080$
Simplifying and subtracting 160:	$4x = 920$
Dividing by 4:	$x = 230$
Therefore,	$x + 80 = 310$
As a check, you find that	$2(230) + 2(310) = 1080$

Chapter 1

1. "Attitudes and Characteristics of Freshmen at 4-year Colleges, Fall 2007," *The Chronicle of Higher Education: 2008–9 Almanac*, Volume 55, Issue 1, p. 18. Data from: "The American Freshman: National Norms for Fall 2007," University of California at Los Angeles Higher Education Research Institute.
2. Franklin & Marshall College, "Why Is Counseling Services Important on Campus," 2009 (http://www .fandm.edu/counselingservices).
3. Janet Rae-Dupree, "Can You Become a Creature of New Habits?" *The New York Times*, May 4, 2008 (http://www.nytimes.com/2008/05/04/business /04unbox.html?ex=1210651200&en=e84617ddb814d 475&ei=5070).
4. Scott Young, "Tips for Breaking Bad Habits and Developing Good Habits," October 16, 2007 (http:// www.pickthebrain.com/blog/strategies-for-breaking -bad-habits-and-cultivating-good-ones).
5. Information for these strategies from Scott Young website and also from http://www.shapefit.com /habits.html.

Chapter 2

1. Howard Gardner, *Multiple Intelligences: New Horizons*. New York: Basic Books, 2006, p. 180.
2. Howard Gardner, *Multiple Intelligences: The Theory in Practice*, New York: HarperCollins, 1993, pp. 5–49.
3. Gardner, *Multiple Intelligences*, p. 7.
4. Candace Corielle and Sheldon H. Horowitz, *The State of Learning Disabilities: Facts, Trends, and Emerging Issues*. New York: National Center for Learning Disabilities, 2014, p. 3 (http://www.ncld.org/wp-content /uploads/2014/11/2014-State-of-LD.pdf).
5. Ibid, p. 5.
6. LD Advocates Guide, n.d., National Center for Learning Disabilities (www.ncld.org/index.php?option =content&task=view&id=291).
7. Office of Disability Employment Policy, Department of Labor, "The Why, When, What, and How of Disclosure in a Postsecondary Academic Setting (2007)," United States Department of Labor (http://www.dol.gov /odep/pubs/fact/wwwh.htm).

Chapter 3

1. Jim Hanson, "Your Money Personality: It's All in Your Head," University Credit Union, December 25, 2006 (http://hffo.cuna.org/012433/article/1440/html).

2. Jane B. Burka and Lenora M. Yuen, *Procrastination: Why You Do It, What to Do about It*, Reading, MA: Perseus Books, 1983, pp. 21–22.
3. Richard Sheridan and Lisamarie Babik, "Breaking Down Walls, Building Bridges, and Taking Out the Trash," *InfoQ*, December 22, 2010 (http://www.infoq .com/articles/agile-team-spaces).
4. Tony Schwarz, "Four Destructive Myths Most Companies Still Live By," *Harvard Business Review*, November 1, 2011 (http://blogs.hbr.org/schwartz/2011/11/four-destructive- myths-most-co.html).
5. "Takeaways and Quotes from Dr. John Medina's Brain Rules," Slideshare presentation, Slide 79 (http://www .presentationzen.com/presentationzen/2008/05 /brain-rules-for.html).
6. Schwartz, "Four Destructive Myths Most Companies Still Live By."
7. Hanson, "Your Money Personality."
8. "Fast Facts," National Center for Education Statistics, 2009 (http://nces.ed.gov/FastFacts/display.asp?id=31).
9. Beckie Supiano, "Many Community College Students Miss Out on Aid—Because They Don't Apply," *The Chronicle of Higher Education*, October 7, 2008 (http:// chronicle.com/daily/2008/10/4905n.htm).
10. College Board Advocacy and Policy Center, *Trends in Student Aid 2011*, The College Board, 2011, p. 3.
11. Robert Tomsho, "The Best Ways to Get Loans for College Now," *The Wall Street Journal*, August 13, 2008, p. D1.
12. Ben Woolsey and Matt Schulz, "Credit Card Statistics, Industry Facts, Debt Statistics," CreditCards.com, January 15, 2010 (http://www.creditcards.com /credit-card-news/credit-card-industry-facts -personal-debt-statistics-1276.php#youngadults).

Chapter 4

1. Information in this section is based on materials from Dr. Marlene Schwartz of the Rudd Center for Food Policy and Obesity at the University of Connecticut.
2. CBS News, "Help for Sleep-Deprived Students," April 19, 2004 (www.cbsnews.com/stories/2004/04/19 /health/main612476.shtml).
3. Herbert Benson, Eileen M. Stuart, et al., *The Wellness Book*, New York: Simon & Schuster, 1992, p. 292; and Gregg Jacobs, "Life Style Practices That Can Improve Sleep (Parts 1 and 2)," *Talk about Sleep*, 2004 (http://www .talkaboutsleep.com/sleep-disorders/archives /insomnia_drjacobs_lifestyle_part1.htm and http:// www.talkaboutsleep.com/sleep-disorders/archives /insomnia_drjacobs_lifestyle_practices_part2.htm).

4. Meeri Kim, "Blue light from electronics disturbs sleep, especially for teenagers," washingtonpost.com, September 1, 2014 (https://www.washingtonpost.com/national/health-science/blue-light-from-electronics -disturbs-sleep-especially-for-teenagers/2014/08/29 /3edd2726-27a7-11e4-958c-268a320a60ce_story.html).

5. Joel Seguine, "Students Report Negative Consequences of Binge Drinking in New Survey," The University Record, University of Michigan, October 25, 1999 (www.umich.edu/~urecord/9900/Oct25_99/7.htm).

6. Mike Briddon, "Struggling with Sadness: Depression among College Students Is on the Rise," Stressedoutnurses.com, April 22, 2008 (http:// www.stressedoutnurses.com/2008/04/struggling -with-sadness-depression-among-college-students -is-on-the-rise).

7. John D. Mayer, Peter Salovey, and David R. Caruso, "Emotional Intelligence: New Ability or Eclectic Traits?" September 2008, *American Psychologist*, 63 (6): 503.

8. Mayer, Salovey, and Caruso, "Emotional Intelligence," pp. 510–512.

9. Information in the sections on the five stages of building competency is based on Mark A. King, Anthony Sims, and David Osher, "How Is Cultural Competence Integrated in Education?" Cultural Competence (www.air.org/cecp/cultural/Q_integrated.htm#def).

10. Louis E. Boone, David L. Kurtz, and Judy R. Block, *Contemporary Business Communication*, Upper Saddle River, NJ: Prentice Hall, 1994, pp. 489–499.

Chapter 5

1. Vincent Ruggiero, The Art of Thinking, 2001, quoted in "Critical Thinking," accessed July 2006 from the website of Oregon State University, Academic Success Center (http://success.oregonstate.edu/criticalthinking.html).

2. Richard Paul, "The Role of Questions in Thinking, Teaching, and Learning," 1995, accessed April 2004 from the website of the Center for Thinking and Learning (http://www.criticalthinking.org/resources/articles /the-role-of-questions.shtml).

3. Charles Cave, "Definitions of Creativity," August 1999 (http://members.optusnet.com.au/~charles57/Creative /Basics/definitions.htm).

4. Robert Sternberg, *Successful Intelligence: How Practical and Creative Intelligence Determine Success in Life*, New York: Plume, 1997, p. 189.

5. Roger von Oech, *A Kick in the Seat of the Pants*, New York: Harper & Row, 1986, pp. 5–21.

6. Adapted from T. Z. Tardif and R. J. Sternberg, "What Do We Know about Creativity?" in *The Nature of Creativity*, R. J. Sternberg, ed., London: Cambridge University Press, 1988.

7. Susan Cain, "The Rise of the New Groupthink," *The New York Times*, January 13, 2012 (http://
www.nytimes.com/2012/01/15/opinion /sunday/the-rise-of-the-new-groupthink .html?pagewanted=1&_r=1&smid=fb-nytimes).

8. Michael Michalko, "Twelve Things You Were Not Taught in School about Creative Thinking," *Psychology Today*, December 2, 2011. (http://www .psychologytoday.com/blog/creative-thinkering /201112/twelve-things-you-were-not-taught-in -school-about-creative-thinking).

9. Michalko.

10. Dennis Coon, *Introduction to Psychology: Exploration and Application*, 6th ed., St. Paul, MN: West, 1992, p. 295.

11. Roger von Oech, *A Whack on the Side of the Head*, New York: Warner Books, 1990, pp. 11–168.

12. Sternberg, p. 236.

Chapter 6

1. Francis P. Robinson, *Effective Behavior*, New York: Harper & Row, 1941.

2. John Mack Faragher, Mari Jo Buhle, Daniel Czitrom, and Susan H. Armitage, *Out of Many: A History of the American People*, 5th ed., Upper Saddle River, NJ: Prentice Hall, 2005, p. xxxvii.

3. Benjamin S. Bloom, *Taxonomy of Educational Objectives, Handbook I: The Cognitive Domain*, New York: McKay, 1956.

4. Sarah Kessler, "38% of College Students Can't Go 10 Minutes Without Tech," May 31, 2011, Mashable.com (http://mashable.com/2011/05/31/college-tech -device-stats).

5. Jeremiah Owyang, "What Companies Should Know about Digital Natives," May 14, 2009, web-strategist .com (www.web-strategist.com/blog/2009/05/14 /what-companies-should-know-about-digital-natives).

6. Mark Bauerlein, "Online Literacy Is a Lesser Kind," September 19, 2008, The Chronicle of Higher Education (http://chronicle.com/article /Online-Literacy-Is-a-Lesser/28307).

7. Bauerlein.

8. Nicholas Carr, "Is Google Making Us Stupid?" *The Atlantic*, July/August 2008 (http://www.theatlantic. com/doc/200807/google).

9. Mary Beth Hertz, "The Right Technology May Be a Pencil," November 29, 2011, Edutopia.com (http:// www.edutopia.org/blog/technology-integration- classroom-mary-beth-hertz?utm_source=facebook &utm_medium=post&utm_content=blog&utm _campaign=techisapencil).

Chapter 7

1. "10 Points" from the National Council for the Social Studies. Used by permission of the National Council for the Social Studies.

2. Lori Leibovich, "Choosing Quick Hits over the Card Catalog," *The New York Times*, August 10, 2001, p. 1.
3. Adam Robinson, *What Smart Students Know*, New York: Three Rivers Press, 1993, p. 82.

Chapter 8

1. Alina Tugend, "Multitasking Can Make You Lose . . . Um . . . Focus," *The New York Times*, October 25, 2008.
2. System developed by Cornell professor Walter Pauk. See Walter Pauk, *How to Study in College*, 10th ed., Boston: Houghton Mifflin, 2011, pp. 236–241.
3. Ezra Klein, "Better Note-taking Through Technology," *The Washington Post*, May 16, 2011 (http://www.washingtonpost.com/blogs/ezra-klein/post/better-note-taking-through-technology/2011/05/09/AFMs8z4G_blog.html)

Chapter 9

1. Richard C. Mohs, "How Human Memory Works," howstuffworks.com, 2012 (http://science.howstuffworks.com/environmental/life/human-biology/human-memory1.htm).
2. University of California—Irvine (2008, March 13). "Short-Term Stress Can Affect Learning And Memory," *ScienceDaily*. (http://www.sciencedaily.com/releases/2008/03/080311182434.htm).
3. Greg Miller, "How Our Brains Make Memories," *Smithsonian Magazine*, May 2010 (http://www.smithsonianmag.com/science-nature/How-Our-Brains-Make-Memories.html?c=y&page=2).
4. Bulletpoints from Kenneth C. Petress, "The Benefits of Group Study," *Education*, 124, 2004 (http://www.questia.com/googleScholar.qst;jsessionid=L4TDXZJvQmb4whQFL7v1mjGfBgp4YGzjJyg0mL3g1SJKyjvXK4hN!-747430471!743789914?docId=5006987606).
5. Academic Skills Center "How to Avoid Cramming for Tests," Dartmouth College, 2001 (http://www.dartmouth.edu/~acskills/handouts.html).
6. "Study Shows How Sleep Improves Memory," *Science Daily*, June 29, 2005 (http://www.sciencedaily.com/releases/2005/06/050629070337.htm).
7. Gretchen Reynolds, "How Exercise Fuels the Brain," *New York Times*, February 12, 2012 (http://well.blogs.nytimes.com/2012/02/22/how-exercise-fuels-the-brain).
8. Adam Robinson, *What Smart Students Know: Maximum Grades, Optimum Learning, Minimum Time*, New York: Three Rivers Press, 1993, p. 118.
9. Jeanne McDowell, "Create Your Own Aha Moment," www.purpleclover.com, November 24, 2015 (http://www.purpleclover.com/lifestyle/2425-create-your-own-aha-moment/).

Chapter 10

1. "The Role of Sleep in Memory," Mempowered, January, 2012 (http://www.memory-key.com/improving/lifestyle/activity/sleep).
2. Barbara J. Speidel, "Overcoming Test Anxiety," Academic Success Center of Southwestern College (http://www.swccd.edu/~asc/lrnglinks/test_anxiety.html).
3. "Anxiety Management," Michigan Technological University (http://www.counseling.mtu.edu/anxiety_management.html).
4. Peter Gwynne, "The Write Way to Reduce Test Anxiety," Inside Science News Service, January 14, 2011 (http://www.usnews.com/science/articles/2011/01/14/the-write-way-to-reduce-test-anxiety).
5. From Paul D. Nolting, PhD, Math Study Skills Workbook, *Your Guide to Reducing Test Anxiety and Improving Study Strategies,* 2000 by Houghton Mifflin Company. Cited in "Test Anxiety," West Virginia University at Parkersburg (http://www.wvup.edu/Academics/more_test_anxiety_tips.htm).
6. Jill Duffy, "How Students Use Technology to Cheat and How Their Teachers Catch Them," PCMag.com, March 25, 2011 (http://www.pcmag.com/slideshow/story/262232/how-students-use-technology-to-cheat).
7. Gregory Berns, "When Fear Takes Over Our Brains," *The New York Times*, December 7, 2008, Business, p. 2.

Chapter 11

1. Dir. Mary Jane Bradbury, *Keys to Lifelong Learning Telecourse*, Videocassette. Intrepid Films, 2000.
2. Bradbury.
3. Ingolf Vogeler, "How to Prepare for an Essay Exam," Center for Teaching Excellence at the University of Wisconsin at Eau Claire, 2008 (http://www.uwec.edu/geography/ivogeler/essay.htm).

Chapter 12

1. Arthur L. Costa, "Habits for Success," in *Developing Minds: A Resource Book for Teaching Thinking*, Arthur L. Costa, ed., Alexandria, VA: Association for Supervision and Curriculum Development, 2001, p. 85.
2. Costa, p. 80.

Appendix

1. George Polya, *How to Solve It*, London: Penguin Books, 1990.
2. Rick Billstein, Shlomo Libeskind, and Johnny W. Lott, *A Problem Solving Approach to Mathematics for Elementary School Teachers*, pp. 5–22, 24–26, 28–36. Copyright 2004 Pearson Education, Inc. Reproduced by permission of Pearson Education, Inc. All Rights Reserved.

Index

- *Habits:* Labirinto: M.Gove/Fotolia; Ladder: SM Web/Fotolia; Calendar: Yganko /Fotolia; White chain with a red link: Viperagp/Fotolia; Hot air balloon: Vladyslav Danilin/Fotolia; Binoculars: VERSUSstudio/Fotolia; Post-it with ?: Priceless Photos /Fotolia; Construction: Rob Hyrons/Fotolia; Headphones: Anterovium/Fotolia; Rock climber: Granitepeaker/Fotolia; Electronic knob: Taras Livyy/Fotolia.

- *Multiple Intelligences:* Handshake: /Fotolia; Woman in lotus position: Aleksandrbagri /Fotolia; Maracas: Boggy/Fotolia; Butterfly: Pixelrobot/Fotolia; Closed notebook and pen: DmyTo/Fotolia; Basketball player: Vadymvdrobot/Fotolia; Calculator: Cginspiration/Fotolia; Camera: Andras Nagy/Fotolia. *Design Icons:* Take Action, Running men and women: Msanca/Fotolia; Powerful Questions, Male with sign: Natasa Tatarin/Fotolia; Building Skills Woman lecturing: Msanca/Fotolia; Multiple Pathways, group: Keko-ka/Fotolia; Critical Thinking, man in chair: Keko-ka/Fotolia.

- *InsideTips:* Courtesy of Sarah Lyman Kravits; Courtesy of Carol Carter.